Southeast Asian Education in Modern History

How particular has Southeast Asia's experience of educational development been, and has this led to an identifiably distinct Southeast Asian approach to the provision of education? Inquiry into these questions has significant consequences for our understanding of the current state of education in Southeast Asia and the challenges it has inherited.

This book contributes to a better understanding of the experience of educational development in Southeast Asia by presenting a collection of micro-historical studies on the subject of education policy and practice in the region from the emergence of modern education to the end of the twentieth century. The chapters fathom the extent to which contest has dominated over educational content in schools and establish the socio-cultural, political and economic bases upon which these contestations have taken place and the ways in which those forces have played out in the classroom. In doing so, the book conveys a sense of the extent to which modern forms of education have been both facilitated and shaped by the region's specific configurations; its unique demographic, religious, social, environmental, economic and political context. Conversely, they also provide examples of the sorts of obstacles that have prevented education from making as full an impact on the region's recent 'modern' transformation as might have been hoped or expected.

This book will be of interest to academics in the fields of Southeast Asian Studies, Asian Studies, education, nationalism, and history.

Pia Maria Jolliffe is a Research Fellow at Blackfriars Hall, University of Oxford, United Kingdom, an Old Member and Continuing Member at Linacre College, and a Teaching and Research Associate at the Nissan Institute of Japanese Studies, all at the University of Oxford. Her research interests include education, migration and the life course in the context of Japanese and Southeast Asian Studies.

Thomas Richard Bruce is Lecturer in Thai Studies at the Pridi Banomyong International College, Thammasat University. His research interests include Southeast Asian 'proto-industrialisation' and technology transfer. His doctoral thesis is on 'The Emergence and Development of Thailand's Shoe Industry, 1855–1997.'

Routledge Studies in the Modern History of Asia

Korean National Identity under Japanese Colonial Rule
Yi Gwangsu and the March First Movement of 1919
Michael D. Shin

English Language Teaching during Japan's Post-war Occupation
Politics and Pedagogy
Mayumi Ohara and John Buchanan

China and Southeast Asia
Historical Interactions
Edited by Geoff Wade and James K. Chin

Southeast Asian Education in Modern History
Schools, Manipulation, and Contest
Edited by Pia Maria Jolliffe and Thomas Richard Bruce

The Colonisation and Settlement of Taiwan, 1684–1945
Land Tenure, Law and Qing and Japanese Polices
Ruiping Ye

Newspapers and the Journalistic Public in Republican China
1917 as a Significant Year of Journalism
Qiliang He

The United States and Southeast Asian Regionalism
Collective Security and Economic Development, 1945–75
Sue Thompson

Japan's 'New Deal' for China
Propaganda Aimed at Americans before Pearl Harbor
June Grasso

Voices of the Korean Minority in Postwar Japan
Histories Against the Grain
Erik Ropers

For a full list of available titles please visit: https://www.routledge.com/Routledge-Studies-in-the-Modern-History-of-Asia/book-series/MODHISTASIA

Southeast Asian Education in Modern History
Schools, Manipulation, and Contest

**Edited by
Pia Maria Jolliffe and
Thomas Richard Bruce**

LONDON AND NEW YORK

First published 2019
by Routledge
2 Park Square, Milton Park, Abingdon, Oxon OX14 4RN

and by Routledge
711 Third Avenue, New York, NY 10017

Routledge is an imprint of the Taylor & Francis Group, an informa business

© 2019 selection and editorial matter, Pia Maria Jolliffe and Thomas Richard Bruce; individual chapters, the contributors

The right of Pia Maria Jolliffe and Thomas Richard Bruce to be identified as the authors of the editorial material, and of the authors for their individual chapters, has been asserted in accordance with sections 77 and 78 of the Copyright, Designs and Patents Act 1988.

All rights reserved. No part of this book may be reprinted or reproduced or utilised in any form or by any electronic, mechanical, or other means, now known or hereafter invented, including photocopying and recording, or in any information storage or retrieval system, without permission in writing from the publishers.

Trademark notice: Product or corporate names may be trademarks or registered trademarks, and are used only for identification and explanation without intent to infringe.

British Library Cataloguing in Publication Data
A catalogue record for this book is available from the British Library

Library of Congress Cataloging-in-Publication Data
Names: Jolliffe, Pia, editor. | Bruce, Thomas Richard, editor.
Title: Southeast Asian education in modern history : schools, manipulation, and contest / edited by Pia Jolliffe and Thomas Richard Bruce.
Description: Abingdon, Oxon ; New York, NY : Routledge, 2019. |
Series: Routledge studies in the modern history of Asia ; 133 |
Includes bibliographical references and index.
Identifiers: LCCN 2018019535| ISBN 9781138063181 (hbk) |
ISBN 9781315161211 (ebk)
Subjects: LCSH: Education–Southeast Asia–History. | Educational change–Southeast Asia–History. | Education–Social aspects–Southeast Asia.
Classification: LCC LA1144.5 .S68 2019 | DDC 370.954–dc23
LC record available at https://lccn.loc.gov/2018019535

ISBN: 978-1-138-06318-1 (hbk)
ISBN: 978-1-315-16121-1 (ebk)

Typeset in Times New Roman
by Taylor & Francis Books

Contents

List of illustrations   vii
List of contributors   viii

Introduction   1
PIA MARIA JOLLIFFE AND THOMAS RICHARD BRUCE

1 Myanma identity and the shifting value of the classical past: A case study of King Kyansittha in Burmese history textbooks, 1829–2017   12
ROSALIE METRO

2 The legend of the 'lost book' and the value of education among the Karen people in Myanmar and Thailand   30
PIA MARIA JOLLIFFE

3 The Modernisation of Female Education and the Emergence of Class Conflict Between Literate Groups of Women in Siam 1870–1910   39
NATANAREE POSRITHONG

4 Thailand's Early Adult Education in Textbooks: Inclusion, Exclusion and Literacy, 1940–1944   54
WASITTHEE CHAIYAKAN

5 Contesting 'Chinese' Education: Schooling in the Kuomintang Chinese Diaspora in Northern Thailand, 1975–2015   69
ARANYA SIRIPHON AND SUNANTA YAMTHAP

6 Vocational Education, Shoemaking, and the Emergence of a 'National' Economy in Thailand 1895–1973   83
THOMAS RICHARD BRUCE

7 Vần quốc ngữ: Teaching Modernity through Classics: Women's Education in Colonial Vietnam 103
MARTA LOPATKOVA

8 Tinkering your way to prosperity: Technical education, auto-mechanics and entrepreneurship in late-colonial Vietnam 122
ERICH DEWALD

9 Despite Education: Malaysian Nationhood and Economic Development 1874–1970 139
ELSA LAFAYE DE MICHEAUX

10 Full colour illustrations: Presentations of race in Singapore's history textbooks, 1965–2000 158
THEOPHILUS KWEK

11 State and Islamic Education Growing into Each Other in Indonesia 178
KEVIN W. FOGG

12 American Education in the Philippines and Filipino Values 194
JEREMIAH A. LASQUETY-REYES

Index 210

Illustrations

Figures

9.1 Average number of years of study for males who entered into the Malaysian educational system between 1910 and 1950   147
9.2 Average number of years of study for females who entered into the Malaysian educational system between 1910 and 1950   147

Tables

8.1 Enrolment and graduates of the Ecoles Pratiques 1897–1943   126
8.2 Registered automobiles in Indochina   131

Contributors

Thomas Richard Bruce is Lecturer in Thai Studies at Pridi Banomyong International College, Thammasat University. He received his PhD in History from SOAS, University of London.

Wasitthee Chaiyakan received her PhD in History from SOAS, University of London. She is a lecturer in the Faculty of Liberal Arts, Thammasat University.

Erich DeWald is a Lecturer in History at Leeds Beckett University. He received his PhD in history from SOAS and is currently finishing a manuscript on the social and cultural history of technology in modern Vietnam.

Kevin W. Fogg is the Albukhary Foundation Fellow in the History of Islam in Southeast Asia at the Oxford Centre for Islamic Studies and Islamic Centre Lecturer in the Faculty of History, University of Oxford. He is broadly interested in post-colonial Indonesia, ranging from his study of Islam in the Indonesian revolution to his current project about mass Islamic organizations outside of Java.

Pia Maria Jolliffe is a Research Fellow at Blackfriars Hall, University of Oxford, and Research Associate at the Nissan Institute of Japanese Studies, also at the University of Oxford.

Theophilus Kwek has recently completed an MSc in Refugee and Forced Migration Studies at the University of Oxford, and is now based in Singapore as a writer and researcher. He previously served as Publications Director at OxPolicy and Convener of Conversations in Singapore History, and helped to organize the Oxford Forum for International Development in 2014 and the Southeast Asian Studies Symposium in 2015. He has written for *The Diplomat* and the *South China Morning Post* as well as the *Singapore Policy Journal*, and reviewed for the *Singapore Review of Books* and *Asian Review of Books*. The research in this chapter has previously been presented at seminars at the University of Cambridge and The AGORA in Singapore.

List of contributors ix

Elsa Lafaye de Micheaux is Associate Professor in Development Studies and New Political Economy at Rennes 2 University in France. She is a member of the Centre of Southeast Asia Studies, Paris. As IRASEC (Institut de Recherche sur l'Asie du Sud-Est Contemporaine—Research Institute on Contemporary Southeast Asia) Research Fellow and University of Malaya Associate Researcher (2014–2016), she analysed the current transformation of Malaysian capitalism from a comparative perspective, focusing on the fast- evolving Malaysia-China relations. The findings of these years of research have been published in French (*IRASEC Occasional Paper*, 2017, 272p.). She has just released *The Development of Malaysian Capitalism, From British Rule to the Present Day* (446p.), SIRD, Petaling Jaya, 2017. She is currently co-director, together with David Delfolie, of the Institut Pondok Perancis (Kuala Lumpur) and leads an ASEAN-China-Norms research network.

Jeremiah A. Lasquety-Reyes obtained his MPhil in Philosophy, MA in Medieval and Renaissance Studies, and PhD in Philosophy at the Katholieke Universiteit Leuven, Belgium, as well as his BA and MA in Philosophy at the University of the Philippines Diliman. He has taught philosophy at both universities. He is currently doing research at the Universität Hamburg, Germany.

Marta Lopatková is a doctoral candidate and lecturer at the Institute of East Asian Studies at Charles University in Prague, Czech Republic. In her research she focuses on history, colonialism, intellectual and social life in French Indochina with an emphasis on gender studies and colonial modernity. She also studies gender, identity and equality issues among members of the Vietnamese community in the Czech Republic. In 2009 she graduated in Vietnamese Studies at Charles University and continued her Masters programme in Ethnology at the same university. She received her Masters degree in 2012. During the course of her Bachelor, Masters and PhD programmes she repeatedly received extended scholarships at Vietnam National University in Hanoi.

Rosalie Metro is an Assistant Teaching Professor in the College of Education at the University of Missouri-Columbia. She has been conducting research about Burma/Myanmar since 2000.

Natanaree Posrithong received her PhD in history from the School of Culture, History, and Language at the Australian National University, Canberra, in 2015. Her dissertation focused on the active roles of elite Siamese women during Siam's political and social transitions between 1870 and 1942. She is currently teaching at the Social Science Division of Mahidol University International College, Thailand. Her research interests include the roles of women during colonialism, the history of gender and sexualities, Modern Girl in Asia, nineteenth-century print media, and the history of women's health and reproductive rights.

Aranya Siriphon is currently an Assistant Professor in the Department of Sociology and Anthropology, Faculty of Social Sciences, Chiang Mai University, Thailand. She obtained her bachelor's degree in Journalism and Communication from Thammasat University and received her MA and PhD degrees in Social Science at Chiang Mai University. Her primary research interests are border and trans-border studies, media and journalism studies, and the recent Chinese mobility in the Mekong region.

Sunanta Yamthap is a lecturer at the Faculty of Mass Communication, Chiang Mai University, Thailand. She gained her bachelor's degree in Journalism and Mass Communication from Thammasat University, Thailand and her MA in Area Studies from University of Tsukuba, Japan. Her research interests are focused on journalism, health and tourism communication as well as international and intercultural communication.

Introduction

Pia Maria Jolliffe and Thomas Richard Bruce

How particular has Southeast Asia's historical experience of educational development been, and has this led to an identifiably distinct Southeast Asian approach to the provision of education? Enquiry into these questions has significant consequences for our understanding of the current state of education in Southeast Asia and the challenges it has inherited. This book hopes to contribute a better understanding of that experience with a collection of micro-historical studies on the subject of education policy and practice from the emergence of modern education in the nineteenth century to the end of the twentieth century.

Grouping the experiences of eleven different countries[1] – with their own, often unrelated languages (Myanmar/Burmese, Thai, Lao, Khmer, Vietnamese, Bahasa Indonesia/Malaysia, Tagalog) with a plethora of non-national languages and dialects – which happen to be in geographical proximity may be a little problematic for some; indeed Southeast Asianists have been arguing among themselves over the whole concept of a region for half a century, since the term's invention (Emerson, 1984; Halib and Huxley, 1996). The geography appears too fragmented. The division between events and culture on the mainland and in maritime Southeast Asia has often seemed too great. It often seems a region by default, the space between South and East Asia. But these countries do share some crucial commonalities; they are all 'developing' tropical states; they are dominated by Austronesian (maritime), Austroasiatic, Tai and Sino-Tibetan (mainland) peoples; they have had intimate contact with, and held their own with, Chinese, Indians and Europeans for at least a millennium; and all have undergone directly – or in Thailand's case rather indirectly – the stamp of the colonial presence; they have almost all been touched by the 'new' mass migrations of the nineteenth and twentieth centuries from both India and China. No other region in the world can boast the deep-rooted, substantial and often state-sponsored presence of all the world's great religions: Hinduism (today concentrated in Bali but historically throughout the region), Buddhism, Theravada in Myanmar, Thailand, Cambodia and Laos, and Mahayana in Vietnam; Islam in Indonesia, Malaysia, and Brunei (in the latter two of which it is the state religion), and

Christianity, of the Roman Catholic variety, in the Philippines and East Timor (Timor-Leste)[2].

But if the aim is to discover different outcomes following the application of a common input in order to throw light on the power and influence of institutions peculiar to each of those societies, then comparisons between nation-states with little in common are useful (see for example the more ambitious regional grouping study of John J. Cogan, Paul Morris and Murray Print (eds.), *Civic Education in The Asia-Pacific Region: Case Studies Across Six Societies*, New York: Routledge Falmer, 2002). Southeast Asia is therefore doubly a suitable unit for such comparative studies.

Previous attempts to examine education from a Southeast Asian regional standpoint are few, are concerned with contemporary development issues, and do not take an explicitly historical approach (Muhammad Shamsul Huq, *Education, Manpower, and Development in South and Southeast Asia*, Praeger, 1975; Ravi Kapoor, *Education and Social Stratification in Southeast Asia*, Delhi: Idarah-i Adabiyat-i Delli, 1985; M. Ramesh and Mukul G. Asher, *Welfare Capitalism in Southeast Asia: Social Security, Health and Education Policies*, London: Macmillan, 2000). The edited volume, *Reshaping Local Worlds: Formal Education and Cultural Change in Rural Southeast Asia* (Keyes, 1991), comprising eight contributions, critically examined state education as a motor of international development, but also suggested that the modern school produces neither 'modern men' nor merely a passive subordinate class (as some Marxist theorists have argued). Instead, each of the contributions viewed the transformations of rural communities in Southeast Asia as a consequence of the introduction of modern schooling, as the interplay of local or religious cultures and national culture mediated through the state school. The contributions in this volume also emphasised the aspect of continuity and mutual shaping of 'traditional' local forms of learning and modern education as part of modern nation-state building. While Joseph and Matthews' volume Equity, Opportunity and Education in Postcolonial Southeast Asia (2014) includes some historical context, its focus is firmly on the perceived inequality involved in the provision and delivery of education and the present policies that lie behind its perpetuation. It does this by aiming at understanding the cultural politics of Southeast Asian education through postcolonial theory. To a certain extent the contributions in this volume offer details that contribute to our understanding of the roots of the resultant 'inequality' or 'unevenness' in the access to or delivery of education and complement these interpretative studies with actual case studies. Additionally, the contributions to the present volume are different because they are not primarily concerned with the sociological development idea of the role of modern schools in leading to modernisation and transformation of rural societies. Instead, we look at the various forms of knowledge production and how these were adapted, manipulated and disseminated by state providers and citizen consumers alike as Southeast Asian societies changed from pre-colonial to colonial and post-colonial nation states.

Southeast Asia's history is usually divided between the 'maritime' and the 'mainland', and yet themes common to both and relatively unique to the region as a whole, such as betel chewing and wet and dry rice cultivation, bind the culture and politics of the region together in ways that distinguish it somewhat from the world outside[3]. The region has for millennia been linked with trade networks to the north, through the Himalayan range into the Chinese province of Yunnan; eastward by sea to the coast, islands and archipelagos of China and to Japan; westwards across the Bay of Bengal to India and the wider Indian Ocean trade network; and to the shores of Iran, the Arabian Peninsula and East Africa. Tropical products, particularly spices unique to the Moluccas, but also forest products, such as deerskins from the mainland bound for Japan, gave the region a status that resulted in the formation of Indic city-states, typologically labelled by Anthony Reid as *nagara*, inland, river-based rice producers, and *negeri*, coastal gateway ports, and their hinterland dependencies (Reid, 2015, pp. 39–47). In their adoption of the religions of power legitimation from at least the fifth century, Confucianism, Hinduism, Buddhism (both Mahayana and Theravada), and from at least the twelfth century, Islam, these polities were able to assert their independence and navigate a world becoming increasingly connected with improvements in transport technology and marketing. These religions were based on the transmission of written text and its fetishisation, and this created the earliest demand for formal education in the region (Andaya and Ishii, 1999, pp. 164–227).

The entry of Europeans into the trading systems of Southeast Asia, with such reliable ocean-going craft and the incentive to make such journeys, from 1509, contributed to a period of further political development. However, in no way during the so-called European 'Age of Discovery' did Europeans dominate the politics of the region, whose powers on the mainland were located inland and included Bagan and Ava (in modern day Myanmar), Sukhothai and Ayutthaya (Thailand), the Khmer Yaśodharapura, or Angkor (Cambodia), the Red River-based Vietnamese Confucian empires and the 'Malay' Champa Kingdom to its south and in sophisticated and assertive Malay Islamic sultanates of maritime Southeast Asia (SarDesai, 1997, pp. 63–73). The Portuguese, who arrived first among the Europeans, taking Melaka in 1511, but subsequently being reduced to small self-perpetuating trading communities; the Spanish (in the Philippine Islands permanently from 1564); the English (whose only lasting settlement from the earliest period of European involvement was in Bengkulu, Sumatra); and the Dutch (Batavia and other coastal trading settlements and spice islands in what is today Indonesia) were able to establish their own coastal trading communities, tolerated and made use of by the indigenous *negeri*. A number of the region's polities had upgraded into semi-gunpowder states in the fifteenth century and this process continued to accelerate in the seventeenth and eighteenth centuries (Andaya and Andaya, 2015, pp. 97–98). They prosecuted expansionist wars, the main aim of which was the capture of people to recruit into their armies and serve as rice producers and craftsmen (Andaya and Andaya, 2015, pp. 51, 150). These were states to be reckoned with. Ayutthaya, or Siam (modern day Thailand), was strong enough to easily expel the English and the French in 1688.

It was not until the nineteenth century, with the aid of technology, steamships and telegraphs, that European power and reach expanded significantly into the interiors at the expense of the indigenous *nagara*-based states. The British East India Company, and the Dutch Government, which took over the role of the Netherlands' chartered company in 1800, pioneered this new forward movement into the interiors of these states. The Spanish also consolidated their control over societies in the Philippine Islands, even as far as the Muslim south, the Sultanate of Sulu. The French began to make substantial interventions into the Red River- and coastal-based Nguyen empire (Vietnam) and the Khmer state and the Lao principalities (Cambodia and Laos) of the Mekong River. These interventions resulted in the creation of colonial Southeast Asia at the end of the nineteenth century, British Burma (from 1885), French Indochina (from 1887), the Dutch East Indies (not fully consolidated along the lines of the present day territory of Indonesia until the first two decades of the twentieth century, with Java being taken from the middle of the eighteenth century, Lombok from 1894, Sumatra from 1904, Bali in 1908 and West Papua in 1920). Only Siam (Thailand) escaped colonial control, the only major mainland polity with the nous to agree to an 'unequal' commercial treaty and *modus vivendi* with an ascendant Britain in 1855, which partly explains its survival. Colonial regimes brought European systems of administration, but they did not completely replace indigenous institutions – and certainly not indigenous conceptions of governance and power, and what became their attendant 'informal' networks and relationships. Indigenous rulers and religious authorities survived (with the exception of Burma), albeit subordinated to the colonial power, in Vietnam, Laos, Cambodia and the sultanates of the Malay Peninsula and Indonesia (Trocki, 1999, pp.77–79, 83–97). Along with colonial administration came European education, designed to provide administrators for the extractive regime. But European education was also provided, as recompense, as a perquisite, and/or respectful acknowledgement, to sons of the indigenous elite class.

Naturally, 'adjustment to change' (and its inverse, 'continuity') is the most general theme underpinning the chapters in this book. More specifically, we hope that the extent to which formal education has been setting the pace, and the extent to which it has been catching up with that change, is suggested therein. Social, political and economic change in Southeast Asia (in step with most of the world) over the last two hundred years has been faster and more substantial than in any previous age, as the impact of the Industrial Revolution intruded into the region in one way or another and, particularly over the last fifty years, manifested itself in patent and tangible measures of the region's productivity, reflecting unprecedented sustained economic growth. The population of the region grew thirteenfold, from roughly 37,465,000 in

1820 to around 506,718,000 in 1998, about eight per cent of the world's population (Maddison, 2001, p. 213). Productivity measured as gross domestic product (GDP) is not available for Southeast Asia as a whole over the *longue durée*. However, Indonesia's growth in productivity has been reconstructed, rising (in 1990 international dollars) nearly sixty-fold, from $10,970,000 in 1820 to $627,499,000 in 1998. Thailand's GDP has risen nearly one hundred-fold, from around $4,081,000 in 1870 to $372,509,000 in 1998. Even Burma/Myanmar and Cambodia, whose economic paths have experienced catastrophe, have seen increases in total GDP from $7,711,000 and $2,155,000, respectively, in 1950 to $48,427,000 and $11,998,000, respectively, in 1998 (Maddison, 2001, p. 214). This productive revolution has required the harnessing of the region's resources on a massive scale, with manpower, from the mid-nineteenth century onwards, sharing its formerly exulted place with capital. While the raw application of labour to new means of production and distribution account for part of the equation, the role of 'human capital' transformation – that is, the upgrading of the quality of the manpower, in this process, which fundamentally rests upon education, is less clear.

The correlation between economic growth and education is a long established convention, although not an easily measurable fact (Kuznets, 1966, pp. 81–82). The more stable link between education and higher personal incomes does not necessarily translate into economic growth (Blaug, 1972, pp. 61–100). Undoubtedly, much of the growth, including the harnessing of manpower, does not require increases in school enrolment and literacy to explain it. Anne Booth's examination of the role of education in aiding recent growth, particularly the more spectacular final decades of the twentieth century, has questioned its importance, even blaming poor government planning and delivery in education for growth retardation, mismatch and bottlenecks (Booth, 1999). We cannot measure, with any precision (and besides, this book is not a quantitative study), the contribution formal education has made to the variables associated with the region's development. According to figures harvested by the United Nations Educational, Scientific and Cultural Organization (UNESCO), the region spent an average of 3.6 per cent of its gross domestic product on education from 1980 to 2016 (this is a very incomplete series, and includes particularly high portions of Timor-Leste's budget over the last seven years). Malaysia spent the largest share of its GDP on education, with Vietnam a close second (at least from 2008), and the corresponding figure for Thailand stood at nearly four per cent (UNESCO Institute for Statistics).

Nevertheless, modern education has been a critical factor in economic as well as social change, of one sort or the other. Foreign-educated Marxists brought to a number of Southeast Asian nations the economics of retardation; conversely, foreign-educated technocrats in the non-communist bloc imported economic strategies that stimulated the rapid growth of the 1980s and 1990s (Christie, 2001). Domestic variants of 'liberal' or 'academic' education have fitted out bureaucracies and provided Southeast Asian nations with the public goods of relative security and authoritarian stability, but have perhaps equally served as an obstacle to entrepreneurial stimulation, which has been facilitated through other means (World Bank, 1993). Vocational education has been held up for the masses as the most direct means of achieving economic growth. Meanwhile, popular, or civic, education has been aimed at producing a compliant population, and, as a by-product, unquestioning fodder for factories (cf. Bourdieu and Passeron, [1970], 1977; Bowles and Gintis, 1977; Willis, 1977; Apple, 1995).

This reminds us that education is designed to serve purposes other than economic growth. Part of the process of Southeast Asia's regional transformation has required the forging of the region's population not just into the productive substance needed to man the region's expanding capital, but as citizens of new nation-states. Relatively few educational channels were explicitly designed for the purpose of improving productivity; the notion of 'human capital' only emerged fully formed in the 1960s (Becker, 1963). The practical needs behind modern education policy for both the colonial and post-colonial eras never constituted the sole rationale and have continuously competed with the social engineering aspect of a national curriculum. Nevertheless, these two objectives often overlapped. Missionaries may have had the aim of the ideological transformation of the population, but one signal for that change was the cultivation of industriousness in their pupils. Schools under direct colonial aegis were intended as incubators of productivity, in that the object was to train indigenous people to man the apparatus of the colonial extraction machine, and yet also demanded of their students certain rules of deportment and conveyed new understandings of territoriality that informed later national identities (Furnivall, 1948, pp. 376–377; Anderson, 2006, pp. 113–140).

Change has therefore been the result of contest and, in turn, resulted in further contest. The classroom has been a place for the dissemination of exclusive and rivalrous perspectives aimed at the specific socialisation of new entrants into the community for as many years as urban literate civilisations have prevailed. Literate Southeast Asia has been no exception, and premodern schools were firmly located in the *wat* and the *madrasah*. Later, various Christian denominations sought to contend for influence over the communities' perspectives with their own schools. For instance, in *Empire, Education, and Indigenous Childhoods. Nineteenth-Century Missionary Infant Schools in Three British Colonies*, May, Kaur and Prochner (2014) establish an understanding of historical patterns of interaction between missionaries and indigenous peoples in the early nineteenth century. The study examined the link between education, schooling and the missionary endeavour. In this way, the authors established a link between the historical 'lessons learned' and twenty-first-century developmental discourse in which Eurocentric beliefs continued to shape the lives of children in former colonial countries.

Brian Simon (1994) discerned periods of 'thrust' in histories of education; periods in which significant 'advances' or developments are made through a

Introduction   7

new conceptualisation of what can, and ought to be, achieved. If we can loosely apply such thinking to the region's history of modern education, it can be broken up into four periods, the latter three being periods of 'thrust': a traditional period (which is not fully dealt with in this book), the colonial period, a post-war nationalist development-oriented period, and, for want of a better term, a post-Cold War 'commodification' period. Needless to say, elements of the terms that define these periods are found in all of them, but they also reflect the changing priorities of states and citizens. The influence of 'traditional' pre-modern education was tenacious and pervasive. The colonial period constituted an injection of innovative technique and capital, though the 'thrust' was oriented toward the interest of colonial powers. Development and nationalism remain constant and concurrent themes throughout the post-colonial period, though in recent times it is becoming more and more apparent that nationalist agendas take precedence over economic prosperity. The 'commodified' period refers to the 'Washington Consensus' era, from the 1990s onwards, when a burgeoning middle class, with its growing purchasing power, and with aspirations for prodigious classical piano-playing, mathematically brilliant offspring, began shifting the initiative away from the state, whose monopoly was beginning to be more effectively challenged (Norris, 2011; Ye, 2016). The private sector in education in Southeast Asia has, however, been around even longer than nationalism. The commodification period has been marked by a diversification of the education sector, with private universities and cram schools springing up in or near the region's shopping malls.

Simon has equally argued for reactive periods where limits and reluctance to try new things characterise the prevailing mood. In his view this can be characterised, at least for the nineteenth century, as the jostling of classes, established and emergent, for the securing of their interests through the institutionalisation of education (Simon, 1994, p. 4). The modern age in Southeast Asia has not been one of smooth or harmonious transition, but one of violent contention as elites have sought to legitimise their rule by forging a favourable national narrative. This has meant exerting control over the production of vetted knowledge in curricula and its reproduction in the classroom. The struggle between the old elite and foreign missionaries to control female education and female expression is discussed by Natanaree Posrithong in Chapter 3, which examines the fractious social and political impact of the modernisation of education on women from 1870 to 1910, focusing on the competition between royal sponsored female schools and the private Christian missionary schools. In Chapter 6, Thomas Richard Bruce examines the efforts of Thai indigenous elites to capture modern industry (in his case modern shoemaking) from the migrant Chinese commercial class, through the establishment of institutionalised vocational education. In Chapter 12, Jeremiah Reyes explains that when Americans acquired the Philippines from Spain in 1898, one of their most immediate concerns was the establishment of an effective public school system to implement their colonial policy. The

American values, particularly of individualism, came into conflict with the 'Filipino Values' which paradoxically had first been systematised by American ethnologists keen to define and reproduce a malleable population, American style individualism was a danger to the *cacique* order as well. Through the analysis of Burmese history textbooks, Rose Metro demonstrates in Chapter 1 how history textbooks reflect the evolution of nation-building strategies in Burma/Myanmar. She traces the process of 'ethnification' of Burmese or *myanma* identity over the past two centuries by analysing continuities and changes in the way schoolbooks portray one king, Kyansittha. In Chapter 5 Aranya Siriphon and Sunanta Yamthap examine the export of the People's Republic of China (PRC)'s Chinese language-based education and modern Chinese culture into the 'Nationalist Chinese' communities in northern Thailand. Their data suggest that this transfer of knowledge challenges both the PRC and 'Nationalist Chinese' communities, thus causing tensions that are inherent in China's political history after 1949. In Chapter 2, Pia Jolliffe explains how the introduction of Western education and schooling to the peoples of Burma/Myanmar has historically been linked to Christian missionaries and British Empire building. Focusing on the Karen legend of the 'lost book', she analyses how transfers of modern knowledge relate to the value of accessing formal education in traditional oral traditions like myth-telling.

Additionally, the chapters in this book convey an idea of the sorts of obstacles that have prevented education making as full an impact on the region's rate of change. Zinoman (2014) has made the observation that colonial-era education accentuated divisions in society. The argument that colonial regimes brought pronounced and formalised social division is a familiar one, but is not without a measure of dissent. Wicks (1980) has been keen to emphasise the responsibility of pre-colonial groups in reproducing ethnic-based divisions in education. Elsa Lafaye de Micheaux's chapter, 9, on the development of education in Malaysia argues that the education system was retarded by the country's descent into racial categorising and positive discrimination in favour of the ethnic Malay sons of the soil, all of which had its firm basis in the structures built by British colonialism. While the economy has grown, Lafaye de Micheaux argues it has owed little to education which has remained muted under the burden of institutionalised plurality. This outcome can be compared with Theophilus Kwek's analysis of Singapore's history textbooks between 1965 and 2000. Kwek explains, in Chapter 10, how curriculum planning has come under increasing centralisation by state authorities, in conjunction with shifting official perceptions of the role of history in national identity formation. His data draw attention to the consolidation of an essentialised notion of 'race' as well as a retrospective reading of independent Singapore's official system of racial classification into its colonial history. In Chapter 4 Wasitthee Chaiyakan examines the problems that faced the Thai government during the Second World War in launching their adult education programme in recently annexed areas where Thai was not spoken, and reflects the wider issues of national integration, in a region of such diversity, that concerned educationalists across the region.

Conversely, the book provides an idea of the extent to which the growth and development of education, such as it is, has been facilitated by the region's indigenous configurations. Contestation and manipulation have not only been the preserve of the state. Simon (1994) also emphasised the active intervention and initiation of local communities, of the consumer, in appropriating, reinterpreting, or manipulating institutions and curricula for their own particular requirements. Such examples are given in this book; in fact this collection suggests that the state seldom gets its own way and that the periphery normally determines the centre's next move when it comes to education. Marta Lopatkova's analysis of women's education in colonial Vietnam in Chapter 7 argues that, although Vietnamese society was engulfed by modernism and modernity, deeply-rooted Confucian concepts prevailed in most schooling texts and were used by colonial authorities and nationalists alike to shape the role of women in their respective ideals of a Vietnamese future. Erich DeWald's chapter, 8, emphasises the students' rational evaluation of their economic environment and how they acted accordingly, using the tools of their training to assert their independence and negotiate and engage on their terms with a rapidly changing society. The reach and power of modern infrastructure, both physical and mental, constituted an opportunity for conservative forces wishing to resist or ride the waves of socially challenging change. In his discussion of State and Islamic education in Indonesia in Chapter 11, Kevin Fogg explains how, under Dutch colonialism, religious education and secular education were entirely separate enterprises in the Netherlands East Indies and how, since that time, nationalism (both anti-colonial and postcolonial), rising Islamic orthodoxy, and political exigency have pushed Islamic education and state education closer and closer together in Indonesia. The emergence of nationalism as the central organising principle for society provided the classroom with a new set of ideas for dissemination there. Nationalist formulae such as Indonesia's *Pancasila* were able to integrate the older 'religious' curriculum and compartmentalise the problematic, transnational nature of universalistic religion.

All of which brings us back to the central themes of manipulation and contest. The requirements and aspirations of state authorities and citizens inevitably differed and altered with the strains of the change that the region underwent. As new cultural – and potentially economically enhancing – tools became available to the population, there was a scramble for their utilisation and, if possible, monopolisation. Inevitably, much of this was played out in the classrooms of Southeast Asia, in ways which were nonetheless unique to the region by dint of its distinctive hysteresis, and resulted, as it so often has done across the globe, in an educational history characterised by manipulation and contest.

Notes

1 Unfortunately, however, Laos, Cambodia and East Timor (Timor-Leste) are not represented in this book.
2 One might also add Confucianism in Vietnam, and among the Chinese migrant communities.
3 Betel nut chewing has a slightly wider geographical reach (Sri Lanka) but is nevertheless relatively concentrated in SEA.

References

Andaya, B. and Andaya, L. Y. 2015. *A History of Early Modern Southeast Asia, 1400–1830*. Cambridge: Cambridge University Press.
Andaya, B. and Ishii, Y. 1999. Religious Developments in Southeast Asia, c.1500–1800. In: Tarling, N. ed. *The Cambridge History of Southeast Asia, volume 1 part 2, from c.1500 to c.1800*. Cambridge: Cambridge University Press. pp. 164–223.
Anderson, B. 2006. *Imagined Communities: Reflections on the Origin and Spread of Nationalism*. Revised edition. London and New York: Verso.
Apple, M. W. 1995. *Education and Power*. Second edition. New York and London: Routledge.
Becker, G. [1963], 1975. *Human Capital: A Theoretical and Empirical Analysis, with Special Reference to Education*. Second edition. New York: NBER.
Blaug, M. 1972. *An Introduction to the Economics of Education*. London: Allen Lane/Penguin.
Booth, A. 1999. 'Education and Economic Development in Southeast Asia: Myths and Realities'. *ASEAN Economic Bulletin*. 16:3. pp. 290–306.
Bourdieu, P. and Passeron, J.-C. 1977. *Reproduction in Education, Society and Culture*. Translated from French by R. Nice. London, Thousand Oaks, New Delhi: Sage.
Bowles, S. and Gintis, H. 1977. *Schooling in Capitalist America: Educational Reform and the Contradictions of Economic Life*. New York: Basic Books.
Christie, C. J. 2001. *Ideology and Revolution in Southeast Asia, 1900–1980: Political Ideas of the Anti-Colonial Era*. Richmond, Surrey: Curzon.
Clarke, L. and Winch, C. ed(s). 2012. *Vocational Education: International Approaches, Developments and Systems*. London and New York: Routledge.
Emerson, D. K. 1984. 'Southeast Asia: What's in a Name?' *Journal of Southeast Asian Studies*, 15:1. pp. 1–21.
Furnivall, J. S. 1948. *Colonial Policy and Practice: A Comparative Study of Burma and Netherlands India*. Cambridge: Cambridge University Press.
Halib, M. and Huxley, T. 1998. *An Introduction to Southeast Asian Studies*. London and New York: I. B. Tauris.
Harding, S. 1998. *Is Science Multicultural? Postcolonialisms, Feminisms, and Epistemologies*. Bloomington and Indianapolis: Indiana University Press.
Joseph, C. and Matthews, J. ed(s). 2014. *Equity, Opportunity and Education in Postcolonial Southeast Asia*. London and New York: Routledge.
Keyes, C. F. with the assistance of Keyes, E. J. and Donnelly, N. 1991. *Reshaping Local Worlds. Formal Education and Cultural Change in Rural Southeast Asia*. New Haven, CT: Yale Center for International and Area Studies.
Kuznets, S. 1966. *Modern Economic Growth: Rate, Structure and Spread*. New Haven, CT and London: Yale University.

Maddison, A. 2001. *The World Economy: A Millennial Perspective*. Paris: Development Centre Studies, OECD.
May, H., Kaur, B. and Prochner, L. 2014. *Empire, Education, and Indigenous Childhoods. Nineteenth-Century Missionary Infant Schools in Three British Colonies*. Surrey: Ashgate.
Norris, T. 2011. *Consuming Schools: Commercialism and the End of Politics*. Toronto, Buffalo, London: University of Toronto Press.
Reid, A. 2015. *A History of Southeast Asia: Critical Crossroads*. Chichester: Wiley Blackwell.
SarDesai, D. R. 1997. *Southeast Asia: Past and Present*. Boulder, CO: Westview Press.
Simon, B. 1994. *The State and Educational Change: Essays in the History of Educational and Pedagogy*. London: Lawrence & Wishart.
Trocki, C. 1999. Political Structures in the Nineteenth and Early Twentieth Centuries. In: Tarling, N. *The Cambridge History of Southeast Asia: Volume 2, Part 1, from c.1800 to the 1930s*. Cambridge: Cambridge University Press. pp. 75–123.
UNESCO Institute for Statistics. *UIS. Stat Database*. http://data.uis.unesco.org/Index.aspx. Accessed 24 March 2016.
Wicks, P. 1980. 'Education, British Colonialism, and a Plural Society in West Malaysia: The Development of Education in the British Settlements along the Straits of Malacca, 1786–1874'. *History of Education Quarterly*, 20:2 (Summer). pp. 163–180.
Willis, P. [1977], 1981. *Learning to Labor: How Working Class Kids Get Working Class Jobs*. New York: Columbia University Press.
World Bank. 1993. *The East Asian Miracle: Economic Growth and Public Policy*. New York: World Bank/Oxford University Press.
Ye, R. 2016. 'Transnational Higher Education Strategies into and out of Singapore: Commodification and Consecration'. *TRaNS: Trans-Regional and -National Studies of Southeast Asia*. 4:1. pp. 85–108.
Zinoman, P. 2014. Colonizing Minds and Bodies: Schooling in Southeast Asia. In: Owen, N. G. ed. *Routledge Handbook of Southeast Asian History*. Abingdon and New York: Routledge.

1 Myanma identity and the shifting value of the classical past

A case study of King Kyansittha in Burmese history textbooks, 1829–2017

Rosalie Metro

UNIVERSITY OF MISSOURI-COLUMBIA

Over the past two centuries, Burmese history textbooks have become progressively shorter. Although acquiring a full curriculum from any era but the present is difficult, today's history textbooks seem to be half the length of those from thirty years ago, and they are far pithier colonial schoolbooks[1]. Whether this trend will continue depends upon the outcome of the ongoing curriculum revision process, which the Myanmar government began under President Thein Sein in 2014 with the assistance of several governmental and non-governmental organisations. During this phase of political and educational transition, it is worthwhile to examine how and why history textbooks have changed over the past two hundred years.

Although new textbooks have been released for kindergarten and first grade, the rest of the curriculum in classrooms now is substantively identical to that under the former military dictatorship (the State Peace and Development Council, or SPDC)[2]. It is unsurprising that the SPDC instructed its Textbook Committee to limit information about the latter half of the twentieth century, given intractable ethnic insurgencies, pro-democracy demonstrations, condemnations from abroad, and categorisation as one of the United Nations (UN)'s Least Developed Countries. It is more difficult to understand why the SPDC would reduce the space devoted to the pre-colonial dynastic era that it classicised as the genesis of contemporary national identity, and from which it attempted to derive legitimacy (Schober, 2005). In Naypyidaw, large golden statues of three kings (Anawrahta, Bayinnaung, and Alaungpaya), tower over the parade ground. Before the transition to nominal civilian rule, state-controlled media often featured these kings, lauded as the founders of the 'Three Myanmar Empires', who united the 'national races', laying the groundwork for the current Union of Myanmar (see, for example, Tin Ka, 2006). If the dynastic era is so important to the country's present, why did coverage of it in state textbooks shrink down from hundreds of pages in the 1950s to several dozen pages today?

In his discerning meditation on historiography, *Silencing the Past: Power and the Production of History*, Michel-Rolph Trouillot (1995, p. xix) argues that studying history requires us to unearth the 'roots' of power by examining the production of narratives and the silences around which they grow. Tracking how history textbooks have changed over time provides a fruitful opportunity for such an examination. However, I shift Trouillot's metaphor from horticulture to arithmetic to suggest that the silences that structure Myanmar's national narrative are not simply subtractions, progressing cumulatively toward a blank history textbook. I envision an equation of national identity in which chosen terms are 'raised to a power' by the authorities who act as their 'exponents'. But the information that textbook authors cross out in order to balance the equation does not disappear. As silences multiply, larger-than-life (although not necessarily longer) explanations must take their place.

Thus, historians are always responding to previous claims in the same way mathematicians working collaboratively on a problem over many years recheck each other's work. Historians who revise textbooks are always beholden to existing narratives in ways they may not realise; they may both consciously manipulate the 'correct' answers and unconsciously reproduce the assumptions or miscalculations of earlier writers whose conclusions they may reject. Whether they negate, ignore, or appropriate what previous authors have written, they cannot help but assign it some *value*. In other words, they can attempt to overwrite or erase previous histories, but evidence of these alternate pasts remains beneath current versions, like traces on a chalkboard over which a new equation has been inscribed.

With this metaphor in mind, my aim is to examine the shifting importance, or 'value', that history textbook authors assign to the classical past in narratives of Burmese nationhood. I also investigate how this value correlates with an understanding of ethnic and national identity, as expressed in the use of the Burmese terms *myanma* and *báma*[3], and the English terms 'Burman', 'Myanmar', 'Burma', and 'Burmese'. The diglossia of literary and spoken versions of the Burmese language, as well as a variety of political, historical, and semiotic factors, complicate the use of these terms. I use 'Burman' to refer to the majority ethnic group, and 'Burmese' to refer to the language and to the multi-ethnic national identity conceptualised in the colonial era but only partially realised in the present. I use 'Burma' to refer to the territory annexed by the British in the nineteenth century and existing until 1988; I use 'Myanmar' to refer to the current country and to the post-1988 nation-building project that the military regime undertook. I use *myanma* in three ways, which I will clarify in this paper: to refer to a) the majority Burman ethnic group (the written equivalent of the spoken term *báma*); b) a multi-ethnic national identity existing since the nineteenth century (called 'Burmese' in English); and c) the post-1988 multi-ethnic national identity that the military regime indicates by using the English term 'Myanmar'. See Houtman (1999, p. 45) for an extensive typology of these meanings.

14 *Rosalie Metro*

According to Thant Myint-U (2001) and Michael Charney (2006), *myanma* identity emerged during the Konbaung Dynasty (1752–1885), centered on Buddhism, Burmese language, and Burman ethnicity. Mikael Gravers (2007, p. 2) points out that over the past century, identity in Burma has been 'ethnified' as nationalists have adopted colonial racial paradigms that linked ethnicity to territory and national character, thereby replacing earlier, more flexible notions of identity. Finally, Gustaaf Houtman (1999) and Mary Callahan (2004) theorise a process of 'myanmafication' undertaken by the military regime after 1988 to transform earlier, more varied conceptions of *myanma* identity into a unitary culture. For this chapter I have searched for evidence of these phenomena in textbooks, their source material, and their authors' stated aims. In this manner, I analysed how ideologies of ethnic and national identity have been reproduced and transformed under monarchy, imperialism, nationalism, socialism, and military dictatorship.

I undertook this project through a case study of one figure who has appeared in history books in a variety of guises: King Kyansittha (1084–1112), a venerated leader from the Pagan Dynasty (1044–1287). I consulted inscriptions and dynastic chronicles that are the primary sources of information about Kyansittha; and a selection of textbooks by British historians from the colonial era, by Burmese nationalists before and after independence, by the socialist state following the 1962 coup, and by post-1988 military dictatorships. I analysed how these texts assign meanings to King Kyansittha's life, how historians silence certain interpretations while amplifying others, and how these shifts illustrate changing conceptions of *myanma* identity and re-valuations of the classical past.

I examined these sources not as a historian, but as an anthropologist of education, in the tradition of scholars who analyse the discourse of curriculum in order to understand its ideological consequences (Apple, 1979). I assume that education is never politically neutral, and that formal schooling tends to reproduce dominant ideologies (Bourdieu and Passeron, 1977). History curricula in particular bestow legitimacy on contemporary power structures (Tosh, 1984) – this is as true in my own country, the USA, as anywhere else (Loewen, 1995). In post-colonial contexts, however, this legitimacy is often connected to a 'golden age' that serves to unite the nation on the basis of ethno-cultural identity (Chatterjee, 1994).

I also assume that curricula, like all texts, are discourses with both intended and unintended social effects evidenced by their grammar, vocabulary, figures of speech, and meta-narratives (Fairclough, 2003). This does not mean that texts affect readers mechanistically: meaning is created dialogically between readers and writers within ideological frameworks they share (Voloshinov, 1986). My readings, like all discourse analyses, are incomplete and limited by my own biases (Fairclough, 2003), as well as by the fact that I approach Burmese texts as a non-native speaker. I present an analysis of how textbook authors are in dialogue with each other, not an empirical investigation of how their audience interpreted them.

Kyansittha as a universal monarch in the Myakan inscription

The earliest surviving records about Kyansittha are inscriptions and court records created during his reign. All history textbooks about him are, directly or circuitously, based on these sources. The fact that they are already packaged for posterity highlights the elusiveness of value-free history. This section of what historians refer to as the Myakan inscription, which is contemporaneous with the first surviving records in Burmese language, was carved in Mon script on a pillar in Pagan:

> The king of the Law, who was foretold by the Lord Buddha, who is great in love (and) compassion towards [...] all beings, – to the end that all beings may obtain happiness, bliss, (and) plenty, (and) be free from famine of tillage, – (in) every place that lacks water, lacks arable land, lacks strenuous cultivation, our lord the king of the Law dams the water, digs a tank, (and thus) creates arable land (and) strenuous cultivation.
> (Duroiselle and Blagden, 1962, p. 142)

This inscription is no neutral chronicle of Kyansittha's deeds, but a narrative crafted to commemorate him as a *dammaraza*, or 'King of the Law', who upholds Buddhist principles through his good works. This presentation of Kyansittha also calls to mind the *sek-kya-mìn* (Houtman, 1999, p. 351), or universal monarch (Tambiah, 1976), in that he acts on behalf of 'all beings' rather than a specific ethnic group in a clearly defined territory. It seems that the concept of *myanma* identity was not yet extant; an antecedent of the term was used for the first time in Kyansittha's reign to describe the style in which his palace was built (Houtman, 1999, p. 53). During the Pagan Dynasty, Burmese, Mon, Pali, Pyu, and Sanskrit languages were all used, indicating the coexistence of multiple ethno-linguistic groups and a hybrid culture rather than a homogenously Burman polity or one in which ethnicity was a salient division (Thant Myint-U, 2001, p. 84). In keeping with this ecumenical spirit, the inscription describes Kyansittha as the ruler whose authority extends in all directions.

Kyansittha as a *myanma* king in the *Glass Palace Chronicle*

Inscriptions like this were among the sources for later chronicles that presented the 'sacred biographies' (Schober, 1997, p. 4) of kings by tracing their unbroken lines of succession to the Buddha. Among the most influential has been *The Glass Palace Chronicle of the Kings of Burma* (GPC), commissioned by King Bagyidaw in 1829, just after the British won the First Anglo-Burmese War (Burma Research Society, 1923). The GPC may have been used as a textbook in monastery schools (Thant Myint-U, 2001, p. 92; Kyan, 2005, p. 3), but Charney (2006) argues that it was directed at educating the British even more than Konbaung subjects; he asserts that the primary purpose of the

'Buddhist literati' who wrote it was to defend the monarchy's territorial claims and to convince encroaching colonial powers of its legitimacy.

The GPC's portrayal of Kyansittha illustrates these goals and provides our first example of silence: the irrigation works mentioned in the Myakan inscription are not referenced in the twenty-plus pages devoted to Kyansittha. While it is difficult to know if the GPC's authors were aware of that particular inscription, they seem more intent on illustrating Kyansittha's spiritual pedigree than his agricultural works. The vast majority of the information about him provides evidence of his good karma: the Mahagiri *nat* (spirit) intervenes on his behalf; an image of a wheel appears on his forehead; a sour lime tastes sweet to him; and he is able to vault over a high fence. The GPC's authors also establish an unbroken line of succession from the Buddha to the Konbaung monarchy by refuting previous chronicles' supposition that Kyansittha was the son of a *nagà* (mythical snake) and insisting he was sired by King Anawrahta.

This focus on spiritual lineage is accompanied by a concern with regional identity and territorial boundaries. For instance, the GPC's authors find an excuse to list the extent of Kyansittha's kingdom (which included some of what was, by 1829, part of the British empire) by claiming that his baby grandson wailed until this information was read out loud: 'Eastward the Panthe Country, also called Satteitha; south-eastward the country of the Gywans, also called Ayoja; southward to Nagapat Island in mid-ocean; south-westward the Kala country, also known as Patteikara [...]' (Burma Research Society, 1923, p. 106). This description contrasts with the Myakan inscription in that it associates certain *lu-myò*, or 'kinds of people' with specific places.

The *lu-myò* around which the GPC is centered, and which is bounded by the peoples and places above, is called *myanma* (or *báma* in spoken Burmese). Thant Myint-U (2001, p. 88) argues that the concept of *myanma lu-myò* was consolidated around Burmese language, Buddhism, and the political and legal institutions based in the Konbaung court at Ava during the late eighteenth century. This identity was spread by itinerant monks in what was later described as a process of 'Burmanisation', in which non-*myanma* people were given incentives or pressured to adopt *myanma* customs (Houtman, 1999, p. 137). Because *lu-myò* was more flexible than twentieth-century conceptions of ethnicity, people could 'become' *myanma* by changing their political allegiance or behaviour; the category *myanma* was capable of retaining its purity while incorporating other groups (Charney, 2006). However, Charney (2006) and Thant Myint-U (2001) agree that the history of *myanma* kings presented in the GPC reflects the reduced scope of the early nineteenth century kingdom at Ava rather than the long tradition of multi-ethnic empires indicated by sources like the Myakan inscription.

The still-fluid yet solidifying nature of *myanma* identity is apparent in one of the GPC's anecdotes about Kyansittha. When deciding on a marriage partner for his daughter Shwe-einthi, Kyansittha chooses his handicapped nephew over a prince from Patteikara, after his advisors worry that Pagan might become 'naught but a Kala country' (Burma Research Society, 1923, p. 105). The term *kulà* was used in the nineteenth century to refer to 'an "overseas person", a person from south Asia, west Asia, or Europe, and probably insular south-east Asia as well' (Thant Myint-U, 2001, p. 89). The fact that *kulà lu-myò* could encompass such a variety of peoples illustrates how different the nineteenth-century concept of *lu-myò* was from a twentieth-century concept of ethnicity or race. *Kulà* is a catch-all term for otherness, defined in opposition to *myanma*, and its valence changes depending on the context. For instance, while Kyansittha rejects a *kulà* son-in-law, he brings *kulà* slaves to the capital after conquering some *kulà* territory[4].

In sum, the GPC presents Kyansittha and other *myanma* kings as main characters in history, while *kulà, talaing*[5] (Mon), *tayok* (Han Chinese), *rakhaing* (Arakanese), and *gywan*[6] leaders took supporting roles. The GPC also evidences a new consciousness of competition among these *lu-myò* that emerged in the Konbaung era (Gravers, 2007, p. 12). While the Myakan inscription presented Kyansittha as a universal monarch, Konbaung Dynasty historians re-calibrated this legacy to shore up the court's legitimacy as the inheritor of thousands of years of good karma accrued to *myanma* people. For these historians, the value of the classical past lay in its potential to glorify the Konbaung monarchy and thereby protect it from British designs. *Myanma* emerges from this discourse as a proto-national identity that classicises a limited subset of regional history while silencing a past in which *lu-myò* was less politically salient.

Kyansittha as a Burman imperialist in colonial textbooks

The GPC and other chronicles provided source material for the Burmese history textbooks that British authors began writing for use in their new colony's schools in the nineteenth century. Yet as Jacques Leider (2009) has argued, the British were not equipped to understand the cosmology or royal idiom of Konbaung monarchs' self-representation. In particular, the omens and divine interventions designed to convey kings' karmic credentials struck the British as merely fanciful. One colonial official characterised the chronicles as 'a mixture of fabulous tales, mythical imaginings, pedigrees, dry records of fightings [...]' (Scott, 1921, p. 429). Therefore, they saw fit to remove the supernatural interventions and astrological details that figure so prominently in the GPC and other chronicles. In this way, the GPC's Kyansittha, whose birth is accompanied by auspicious omens, who is visited by the Mahagiri *nat*, is transformed into an empire-builder with more worldly concerns.

While the British may not have absorbed all of the GPC's intended messages, they did unwittingly reproduce some of its silences. Thant Myint-U (2001) and Charney (2006) both argue that British historians, with less access to historical sources that revealed Burma's cosmopolitan past, accepted the GPC's positioning of *myanma* people as protagonists while neglecting the political legacies of other *lu-myò*. At the same time, the colonial passion for classification led them to conceptualise groups in Burma as discrete races, each with a distinct language, culture, character, and territory (Thant Myint-U, 2001, p. 243). They translated *myanma lu-myò* as a race called 'Burmans', while dividing other *lu-myò* such as *gywan* into Shan, Kachin, and many subgroups. This re-classification enabled British historians to read a new plot into the GPC's silence about non-*myanma* power structures: racially-motivated warfare dominated but never decisively won by the Burmans. This observation confirms the insight that while colonial historians did not *invent* the concern about group identity in Burmese history, their fascination with it led them to spotlight it in misleading ways (Aung-Thwin, 2005; Lieberman, 2007).

Arthur Phayre's 1883 *History of Burma*, an archetypal work used as a school text (Bagshawe, 1976), provides an example. Phayre portrays Burmese history as a struggle for supremacy among bounded, coherent, and timeless groups: Burmans, Mons, Shans, Indians, and Arakanese. Phayre devotes only two pages to Kyansittha, excising ninety per cent of the material available in the GPC and other chronicles and zeroing in on Kyansittha's hesitation to marry his daughter Shwe-einthi to the *kulà* prince. In Phayre's version of the story, unlike in the GPC, the prince commits suicide but nonetheless Shwe-einthi bears his child, Alaungsitthu, who succeeds Kyansittha on the throne. Phayre (1883, p. 38) translates *kulà* as Indian, titling the section on Kyansittha 'An Indian Prince Comes to Pagan,' thereby prioritising a concern with racial purity in a way the GPC had not. Other section titles, such as 'Shan kings in a divided Burma', reveal how Phayre (1883, p. 58) projects 'Burma' hundreds of years into the past while defining it as a Burman country in which non-Burman rule was anomalous. This conceptualisation of Burmese history both enabled and justified the British practice of ruling the supposedly Burman-dominated 'Burma proper' separately from the 'Frontier Areas', which were blocked out as the territories of Shan, Kachin, Chin, and other non-Burman races (Gravers, 2007, p. 13).

G. E. Harvey's (1926) textbook *Outline of Burmese History* retains this focus on race and dramatises the competition it supposedly engenders. Harvey uses the GPC as a source, but what the Konbaung literati were trying to sell as a triumphant tale of a *myanma* monarchy glorious enough to control vast territory, he buys as a tragedy in which Burman kings act as romantic heroes doomed in their attempt to unify a country that is too large and ethnically divided (Phillips, 2005, p. 19). Harvey (1926) embellishes the GPC's tales of Kyansittha in order to craft a psycho-realist narrative. He describes one military campaign this way:

> The news that he [Kyansittha] was present in person spread dismay among the Talaings [Mons] marching eastward to bar his road – they remembered his exploit against the Laos ... [Kyansittha's] men burned to avenge [a previous battle] and free their homes ...
>
> (p. 28)

Harvey not only echoes Phayre by referring to all people from Pegu as 'Talaings', while assuming those at Pagan to be Burman, but he also dramatises their battles as an ongoing saga, stitching together a narrative of Burman aggression that drives the plot of his book. The GPC's missions to expand territory, gather religious artefacts, and shore up dynastic power becomes a series of racial grudge matches.

In the process of heroising Kyansittha, Harvey justifies British rule. Although this may seem paradoxical, Harvey (1926) characterises Kyansittha's goal – establishing 'undivided sway' (p. 32) over the diverse groups in Burma – so it anticipates the colonial project. Harvey's (1926) classicisation of Burman dynasties is linked with his celebration of colonial renaissance:

> The English conquest came not to destroy but to fulfill. Racial character cannot develop so long as the government is unstable. [...] [Burma's] was seldom a true unity, for whenever it was more than nominal it was maintained by means so terrible that they destroyed the end [...] The empire came to give her [Burma] that unity, and the reform scheme to give her power to make it a true unity welling up from within, not an artificial unity imposed from without.
>
> (p. 185)

In other words, the British have done with law what the kings failed to do by force, and Burma's democratic future is the colonisers' gift. In this narrative, British presence is the only reason that internecine warfare has subsided. The GPC's idiosyncratic description of *myanma* identity, transformed by Phayre into a concern with Burman racial purity, becomes in Harvey's hands a vicious competition among the indigenous races of Burma from which the British emerge as heroes. For Harvey and other colonial historians, the value of Burma's classical past lay in its ability to justify British intervention.

This attempt to narrate Burmese history in order to prop up British rule was not unique to Harvey, but was actually an educational policy. The 1916 *Report of the Committee to Ascertain and Advise How the Imperial Idea May be Inculcated and Fostered in Schools and Colleges in Burma*, released in the decade after the first Burmese nationalist organisations had formed, concludes that loyalty to the crown would best be promoted by co-opting Burman patriotism. Its slogan, 'Burma for the Burmans within the Empire' (Taylor, 2009, p. 119), illustrates the British attempt to keep Burmans in line by marginalising non-Burman groups. In the GPC, non-*myanma* groups' presence in *myanma* empires proves the glory of *myanma* rulers like Kyansittha; in colonial textbooks, non-Burman ethnic groups are cast as spoilers of Burma's unity. Colonial authors' reinterpretation of the classical past fostered the growth of a national identity that excluded non-Burmans.

20 Rosalie Metro

Kyansittha as a *myanma* unifier in nationalist[7] textbooks

Even while Phayre's and Harvey's books were still in use, Burmese authors were writing textbooks for the parallel National School system that the British were forced to allow after students' protests of the colonial 'slave education' system in the 1920s. Although the Burmese men who wrote this new curriculum decried colonial pedagogy, they had been weaned on the British textbooks described above. Like the British authors who reinterpreted the GPC's contents to suit their own political world view, nationalists selectively absorbed British messages even while condemning imperialism. They rejected Harvey's comparison of the British Empire with Pagan, but they accepted Burman kings as unifying heroes whose accomplishments prefigured the modern nation-state. Harvey's Kyansittha may have been a British person dressed up in Burmese clothing, but that did not stop the young men who read his textbook from imagining themselves in a similar role.

Although Burmese scholars followed the British in making the dialectic between racial unity and disunity their main theme, they introduced a new category of analysis that seems to have emerged in the early twentieth century: a *myanma* people (*báma* in spoken Burmese; 'Burmese' in English) who included not only Burmans but all *taìn-rìn-thà lu-myò*, (indigenous people or 'national races') (Houtman, 1999, p. 49). However, *myanma* and *báma* continued to be used to refer to Burmans alone. To add to the confusion, even in its most inclusive sense, *myanma/báma* was often linked to Buddhism and the Burmese language shared by most Burmans. For instance, the 1930s nationalist Dobáma ('We-*báma*') organisation took as its slogan a series of phrases that can be translated as '*Báma* country, our country; *báma* literature, our literature; *báma* language, our language ...' (Khin Yi, 1988, p. 5). Although this 'Burmanisation', as it was called, was primarily an attempt to combat the dominance of 'foreign' English and Hindi languages (Khin Yi, 1988, p. 6), it also excluded non-Burmese speaking ethnic groups from nationalists' conception of *báma/myanma*. Moreover, the nationalist movement was so deeply connected with Buddhism that one of its earliest incarnations, the Greater Council of Burmese [*myanma*] Associations (GCBA) was mistakenly referred to as 'General Council of Buddhist Associations' by several of its founding members (Houtman, 1999, p. 49). Non-Burmans did join *Dobáma* (Khin Yi, 1988, p. x), but given that many were Christian, Muslim, Hindu, or animist, the elision of *myanma* with Buddhism subtly excluded them.

Despite *myanma*'s ambiguity, nationalist history textbooks used it to refer to an overarching national identity. Ù Ba Than's 1929 *Myanmar History Textbook,* republished in 1963, is one example. First, Ba Than reclaims the chronicles that the British had maligned as unreliable, exhaustively reproducing the details of kings' lives presented in the GPC. However, he purges many references to the supernatural, perhaps out of deference to the British ideas he had absorbed in colonial schools. Although most of Ba Than's text faithfully duplicates the GPC, he replaces the GPC's veneration of

Kyansittha's spiritual pedigree with more worldly praise, describing Kyansittha as a hero 'with outstanding courage who brought honour to all *myanma lu-myò*'[8] (Ba Than, 1963, p. 69). Ba Than uses *myanma* in the early twentieth-century nationalist sense described above to include all the *taìn-rìn-thà*, rather than in the GPC's more limited sense. However, he also includes *myanma* alongside Mons and Shans among the *lu-myò* indigenous to *myanma naing-ngan* (country) (Ba Than, 1963, p. 21). This double meaning of *myanma* hints at the impending re-valuation of the classical past that nationalist historians would effect over the next few decades, while indicating the ambiguous nature of the national identity they would promote.

Although Ba Than's textbook was reprinted in the 1960s, and British texts were used well into the 1950s, a new type of schoolbook began to appear with independence. Bó Ba Shin's 1948 *Myanmar History* is one of the earliest textbooks to make this trend toward nationalist classicisation explicit by explaining that the birth of the Union was the fifth incarnation of a sovereign *myanma* nation following the four[9] dynastic empires. Former Prime Minister Ú Nu, who wrote the introduction, elaborates on this point, inviting students to realise 'how down the country was when it was divided and how glorious were the periods of unity during the reigns of Anawrahta, Bayinnaung, Thanlwan Mintheya, and Alaungpaya', although he adds that 'construction of the Union should rely on heart, and not on force like the empires of the kings'[10] (Ba Shin, 1948, p. 10). In other words, Nu agrees with Harvey that these kings' goals should be emulated while their methods should be foresworn. However, Nu diverges from Harvey by blaming the British for dividing the *taìn-rìn-thà* rather than uniting them. This concern with ethnic division was timely; by 1948, separatists had already rebelled. An army colonel who wrote a preface to *Myanmar History* acknowledged the need for a re-presentation of the classical era that was less *myanma*-centric, noting that accounts of *myanma* kings' military exploits in chronicles had caused other *taìn-rìn-thà lu-myò* to 'naturally fear *myanma* people and not trust them' (Ba Shin, 1948, p. v). Thus, Ba Shin's textbooks continued Ba Than's tradition of using *myanma lu-myò* to describe both Burmans and Burmese, while using the term *myanma naing-ngan* to project the contemporary Union of Burma hundreds of years into the past.

This new impetus to promote inter-ethnic unity is apparent in Ba Shin's (1948) sections on Kyansittha. First, he claims that Kyansittha composed inscriptions in Mon language instead of Burmese in order to promote Mon-*myanma* friendship and to please his Mon queen by following her customs. While debate continues about when Burmese script was first used, the dominant theory in the colonial era was that it did not join Mon, Pali, Pyu, and Sanskrit among literary languages used in Pagan until the end of Kyansittha's reign (Lieberman, 2007, p. 379). Thus Ba Shin's reasoning about Kyansittha's linguistic choice is not entirely convincing, and it seems designed to build inter-ethnic unity in his time rather than to reflect historians' understanding of the past.

Furthermore, Ba Shin includes a different version of the story told in the GPC and in Phayre's textbook about Kyansittha's decision concerning Shwe-einthi's marriage. Ba Shin (1948) asserts that 'for the cause of *myanma naing-ngan*'s unity, and to promote friendship with the Mon', Kyansittha married his daughter to a Mon prince (p. 70). Alaungsitthu, Kyansittha's successor and the result of this union, is described as satisfying all parties with his 'mixed *myanma* and Mon blood' (Ba Shin, 1948, p.71). There is no mention of the *kulà* prince, and Ba Shin apparently draws on other chronicles to arrive at this account. The fact that he chooses this version of the story, and that he interprets it as signifying Kyansittha's desire to build up inter-ethnic unity in *myanma naing-ngan*, illustrates the new value that nationalists assign to the classical past as the genesis of the post-colonial Union.

Kyansittha's heroisation continues, but on new terms. The Myakan inscription commemorated Kyansittha's benevolence to all people; the GPC recognised the karmic reserves that allowed him super-human strength; and colonial texts commended his ability to unite different ethnic groups while labeling his tactics too harsh. Nationalists such as Ba Shin praise Kyansittha as a diplomat who unifies ethnic groups in *myanma naing-ngan* through alliances. Sometimes these re-figurations are rationalised overtly, as in U Nu's preface to Ba Shin's textbook, but often authors do not acknowledge that they are revising history at all.

Regardless of whether these authors thematise historiographical change, traces of earlier conceptions of ethnic identity remain. First, the GPC's prioritisation of *myanma* people is preserved, although its more limited yet also more flexible conception of *lu-myò* is overwritten by a twentieth-century idea of races as bounded and competitive. Thus, even while explicitly rejecting the British meta-narrative of ongoing racial war in favour of one of unity, nationalists implicitly preserve the colonial understanding of ethnicity. This disjunction points to a key question that nationalists faced when trying to place a value on the classical past. Did history show that Burma had always been unified, except for the colonial interruption? Or did it show that Burma's challenge had always been, as it was in the 1940s and 1950s, the threat of disintegration into its constituent ethnic parts? These two answers coexisted uneasily in nationalist textbooks.

Kyansittha as a *myanma* socialist in the BSPP curriculum

Kyansittha underwent another transformation after the 1962 coup, when the Burmese Socialist Programme Party (BSPP) nationalised schools and the Committee on Curriculum Outlines and Books for School Use took over the writing of textbooks. This transition from textbooks written by private scholars to those written by a government-controlled committee marked a new era in which pedagogy was even more closely linked to political goals. As the military regime had promised shortly after the coup, they 'resort[ed] to education, literature, fine arts, theatre and cinema, etc., to bring into vogue the concept that to serve others' interests is to serve one's own' (Revolutionary Council, 1962, section 16). The conception of history also changed; according to the 1967 syllabi for primary and middle schools, it is 'not the chronological accounts of rulers as has been accepted generation after generation. It is rather a study of the human or the events of the working people' (quoted in Zar Ni, 1998, p. 136). Inter-ethnic unity was still a political concern insofar as Shan leaders' proposal of federalism and the supposed threat of disintegration of the Union had been the justification for the coup. However, the rhetoric of inter-ethnic unity was somewhat overshadowed by the idealised unity of the workers and the peasants.

In this context, kings like Kyansittha were in an ambiguous category. On one hand, they provided examples of military prowess, which was aligned with the new leaders' ties to the army; Kyansittha was one of four 'warrior heroes' whose name graced the teams into which all students were organised (Zar Ni, 1998, p. 139). However, the dynastic era was tainted by the inequalities of the 'feudalist' system, and the BSPP wanted to include non-elite classes in history. As a result, the golden pagodas, jewelled palaces, and many slaves mentioned in earlier histories of Kyansittha are replaced by accounts of his work on behalf of the common people. For instance, the 1978 *5th Standard History* textbook explains that he 'expanded the means of production including farmland, irrigation canals, wells, and reservoirs' (Government of the Socialist Union of Burma [GSUB], 1978, p. 57). Kyansittha's agricultural works, memorialised in the Myakan inscription but left out of subsequent histories, finally re-enter the narrative as evidence of his socialist credentials. Yet unlike the Myakan inscription, the BSPP textbook asserts that the credit for Kyansittha's good deeds accrues not only to him and to the Buddha, but also to workers. For instance, his military victories are partly ascribed to the 'bravery and perseverance' of his soldiers, who are acknowledged in textbooks for the first time (GSUB, 1979, p. 25).

In another nod to contemporary politics that fulfils the syllabus's goal to 'drive home the importance of unity and mutual respect among Burma's indigenous national races' (quoted in Zar Ni, 1998, p. 136), Kyansittha reaches out to non-*myanma* people. In BSPP textbooks, the term *myanma lu-myò* remains both an ethnic group that strives for unity with others, and a national group that always-already includes them. For instance, while continuing to use *myanma lu-myò* to refer to Burmese people as a whole, the BSPP also describes them as distinct from other ethnic groups:

> Valuing and respecting the Mons' strong traditions and culture, Kyansittha successfully built Mon-*myanma* unity. Kyansittha did not encourage the Mon to feel inferior to the *myanma*. He wanted the *myanma* and Mon to relate as equals. He wanted the Mon to get benefits.
> (GSUB, 1978, p. 58)

The evidence for these claims is similar to that provided in Ba Shin's text – Kyansittha made inscriptions in Mon language and married a Mon princess. Yet this BSPP textbook goes even further in ascribing contemporary motives to Kyansittha by asserting that his actions sprung from his respect for Mon culture, not only from his desire to create an alliance with them, as Ba Shin had claimed.

In this way, both the valuation of the classical past as a time of inter-ethnic unity and the ambiguity about the double meaning of *myanma lu-myò* carry over into the BSPP curriculum. Yet the BSPP assigns new meaning to the classical era as a time of the common people's economic and military triumphs. In the Myakan inscription, Kyansittha had acted on behalf of all beings and the Buddha; in the GPC he acted on behalf of *myanma lu-myò* and the Buddha; in nationalist textbooks he acted on behalf of *myanma naing-ngan*. In the BSPP curriculum, Kyansittha acts on behalf of the people and with the people's aid.

Kyansittha as a Myanmar patriot in SPDC textbooks

After the 1988 coup ended both the socialist era and hopes of imminent democratisation, the new regime tried to resolve the ambiguity surrounding *myanma lu-myò* while subtly yet profoundly revaluing the classical era. Houtman (1999) describes this project as 'myanmafication', the creation of a unitary *myanma* identity, which parallels the Burmanisation of earlier eras. Callahan (2004) clarifies that myanmafication entails a simultaneous homogenisation and differentiation of ethnic identity, in which minorities are 'exoticized and infantilized' (p. 110) and difference is confined to superficial factors such as traditional costumes and dancing styles. Myanmafication is pursued by restricting the expression of minority languages and cultures (Callahan, 2004), a process that some ethnic minority activists connect to the military strategy of rape and forced marriage designed to genetically integrate the nation (Women's League of Chinland, 2007).

The rhetorical aspect of myanmafication was heralded by the 'Adaptation of Expressions' law of 1989, which changed the country's English name from 'Burma' to 'Myanmar', ostensibly to correct the misapprehension of colonists who had labelled the country by its spoken name rather than by the formal *myanma naing-ngan*. The law also claimed that *báma* – what the British had rendered as 'Burma' – was not and had never been a nation, but was instead one of the ethnic groups that made up *myanma lu-myò* (previous usages of *myanma lu-myò* to describe the majority ethnic group went unexplained). State media linked these terminological changes with a restoration of the dynastic era's glory (Houtman, 1999, p. 48). This re-prioritisation of the classical past involved renewed focus on unifying kings, and on 'submission to royalty and adherence to an unchanging tradition' (Douglas, 2005, p. 230) in public spectacles. At the same time, periods of 'disunity' (absence of Burman dominance) were de-classicised.

In history textbooks, the result of this recalibration has been to focus on the three 'Myanmar Empires' (*myanma naing-ngan-dàw-gyì*) led by Anawrahta, Bayinnaung, and Alaungpaya, who were most successful in expanding territory and tributary relations. A brief textbook is devoted to each of these empires in the 5th, 6th, and 7th Standards respectively. On the other hand, information about periods in which Shan, Mon, or Arakanese kingdoms were powerful has been reduced or eliminated (Salem-Gervais and Metro, 2012). As Callahan (2004) notes, non-Burman ethnic groups have an increased presence in textbooks since 1988, but only in such a way that reinforces their subordination to Burmans. Although textbooks promise to promote 'union spirit' and 'patriotism' (Myanmar Ministry of Education, 2008, forward), their content reifies the primacy of the people now called *báma lu-myò*. In the dynastic era, non-Burmans are portrayed as mostly passive. While Burmans annex their territory, build unity with them and occasionally raise them to high positions, non-Burmans themselves take little initiative.

Kyansittha's role is both reduced and reified. There are brief passages about him in the 3rd and 5th standard textbooks. The GPC's twenty pages, curtailed to ten pages by Ba Shin in 1948, now stands at two pages. Some of the information from the BSPP textbook is repeated, although instead of building up Mon-*myanma* unity, Kyansittha now strengthens Mon-*báma* unity, in accordance with the Adaptation of Expressions law. His actions are summed up thus:

> Because he struggled to build up unity among the national races, promote agriculture, and propagate Buddhist teachings, Kyansittha continued the peace and development of the first Myanmar Empire that Anawrahta had built.
> (Myanmar Ministry of Education, 2008, p. 33)

This trinity of activities – national unification, economic development, and religious patronage – is carried out by all kings lionised in current textbooks, and it aligns with the political, economic, and social goals that the SPDC had printed in all publications, including 'national reconsolidation', 'development of agriculture as the base and all-round development', and 'uplift of the morale and morality of the entire nation'. In most editions of the state newspaper during the SPDC's tenure (see, for example, Tin Ka, 2006), one could find the ruling generals carrying out exactly such activities: promoting 'union spirit', consulting about economic development projects, and making donations to Buddhist causes. The parallels between the kings and the SPDC is reinforced by the similar vocabulary and discursive patterns that are used to describe their activities (Salem-Gervais and Metro, 2012). This alignment points toward a revaluation of the classical past as a proto-dictatorship in which the firm yet benevolent rule of kings like Kyansittha prevents disintegration of the unity of *myanma lu-myò*, which is both always-already accomplished and perpetually threatened.

The ongoing transformation of Kyansittha and myanma identity

Reviewing the coverage of Kyansittha from the Myakan inscription to SPDC textbooks, what I call 'exponential silences' become apparent. The GPC's innovation of a *myanma* country has been raised to a power so that it appears eternal. Colonists' narrative of racial warfare has been cancelled out by nationalists who inscribed inter-ethnic unity in its place, but both terms have a common denominator of essentialised ethnic identity. Whether Kyansittha appears as a universal monarch, a king, an imperialist, a unifier, a socialist, or a patriot, he and his classical era offer legitimacy: to a Konbaung monarch who sought to expand territory, to British colonists who wanted to justify their rule, to nationalists who needed a precursor for the Union, and to socialists in search of a nascent people's republic.

The fact that the SPDC both modelled the Union of Myanmar on the Three Myanmar Empires and cast ancient kings in its own image is just the latest revaluation of the classical era, the most recent recalibration of the meaning of *myanma*. In the official equation of national identity, '*myanma* = *báma* + non-*báma taìn-rìn-thà*'. However, in current textbooks (as well as in conversation with many Burmans), *myanma lu-myò* is sometimes used to refer to the majority ethnic group rather than the *taìn-rìn-thà* as a whole (Salem-Gervais and Metro, 2012). If *myanma* = *báma*, then substituting this value back into the official equation yields *myanma* = *myanma* + non-*báma taìn-rìn-thà*, or *báma* = *báma* + non-*báma taìn-rìn-thà*. Either way, the equation can only be balanced if the 'non-*báma taìn-rìn-thà*' has an exponent of zero that cancels their value entirely.

This specious nullification of non-Burman groups in the equation of national identity is a new formulation of a long-standing trend. Textbook authors did not need to lie in order to serve their political goals, they only needed to carefully select and interpret the information they chose. Kyansittha's shape-shifting appearances illustrate the changing priorities of people with the power to write, distribute, and mandate schoolbooks. However, the unconscious continuities and accidental misunderstandings that persist in their accounts undermine any mechanistic alignment of political goals with ideological outcomes. Moreover, crossing out so much information requires the leftover points to bear exponentially more semiotic weight. While *myanma* kings loom ever larger in state discourse and in statuary, their significance has been boiled down to a trinity of factors that any child could memorise. As history textbooks are shortened and more became unsayable, what is left behind must speak more forcefully.

In this context, the revision of textbooks currently underway will signal the direction not only of the education system, but also of national identity. The new curriculum is being developed by the Myanmar Government in co-operation with international entities; kindergarten and first grade textbooks are already in use. Its aims include 'reduction of reference to the military', in order to 'delegitimise violence', as well as 'inclusivity by ensuring representation from different ethnic groups' (Higgins et al., 2015). It remains to be seen how Kyansittha will fare in this era. The effort to revise history textbooks is one of the most difficult and crucial for the country's future. The architects of this revised curriculum can learn not only from the past, but also from the way the past has been narrated, as they seek to tell a new story.

Notes

1 Comparison made based on a full set of current textbooks and a dozen used between 1975 and 1987.
2 There have, however, been cosmetic changes (Metro, 2014). An examination of the newly released textbooks is an important topic for further research.
3 I use Okell's (1971, pp. 66–67) transcription system. I do not capitalise Burmese language terms, because the Burmese language does not have a distinction between capital and lowercase letters.
4 See Bryce Beemer (2013) for an analysis of cultural hybridisation resulting from slave gathering warfare.
5 Some Mon people today consider 'Talaing' a slur originating in Burman racism against them.
6 Thant Myint-U (2001, p. 89) defines this category as including groups today known as Khmer, Shan, Kachin, and Thai – a category nearly as diverse as *kulà*.
7 I refer to materials created prior to independence for use in National Schools, as well in the parliamentary era (1948–1962).
8 This and other translations of Burmese sources are mine unless otherwise indicated.
9 The SPDC recognised only three Myanmar Empires, excluding that of Thanlwan Mintheya; historians continue to debate whether there were three or four.
10 This and other quotations from Ba Shin were translated by Nicolas Salem-Gervais.

References

Apple, M. W. 1979. *Ideology and Curriculum*. New York: Routledge.
Aung-Thwin, M. 2005. *The Mists of Ramanna: The Legend that was Lower Burma*. Honolulu: University of Hawai'i Press.
Ba Shin (Bó). 1948. *myanma naing-ngan-dàw thamaìn*. n.l.: n.p.
Ba Than (Ù). 1963. *kyaùng thoùn myanma yazawin, 1929*. Yangon: Eiqhsatháyá Press.
Bagshawe, L. E. 1976. *A literature of school books: A study of the Burmese books approved for use in schools by the education department in 1885, and of their place in the developing educational system in British Burma*. MA thesis. University of London, School of Oriental and African Studies.
Beemer, B. 2013. *The Creole city in mainland Southeast Asia: Slave-gathering warfare and cultural exchange in Burma, Thailand, and Manipur, 18th-19th century*. PhD thesis. University of Hawai'i.
Bourdieu, P. and Passeron, J.-C. 1977. *Reproduction in Education, Society and Culture*. Translated from French by R. Nice. London, Thousand Oaks, New Delhi: Sage Publications.
Burma Research Society. 1923. *The Glass Palace Chronicle of the Kings of Burma*. Translated from Burmese by Pe Maung Tin and Gordon H. Luce. London: Oxford University Press.

Callahan, M. 2004. Making Myanmars: Language, territory, and belonging in post-socialist Burma. In: Migdal, J. S. ed. *Boundaries and belonging: States and societies in the struggle to shape identities and local practices.* Cambridge: Cambridge University Press. pp. 99–120.

Charney, M. 2006. *Powerful learning: Buddhist literati and the throne in Burma's last dynasty, 1752–1885.* Ann Arbor, MI: The Centers for South and Southeast Asian Studies.

Chatterjee, P. 1994. *The nation and its fragments: Colonial and post-colonial histories.* Princeton, NJ: Princeton University Press.

Douglas, G. 2005. Who's performing what?: State patronage and the transformation of Burmese music. In: Skidmore, M. ed. *Burma at the Turn of the 21st Century.* Honolulu: University of Hawai'i Press. pp. 229–247.

Duroiselle, C. and Blagden, C. O. 1962. *Epigraphia Birmanica.* Volume I. Rangoon: Superintendent Government Printing.

Fairclough, N. 2003. *Analysing discourse: Textual analysis for social research.* London: Routledge.

Government of the Socialist Union of Burma [GSUB]. 1978. *thamain pyinsámá-tàn.* Yangon: Government of the Socialist Union of Burma.

Government of the Socialist Union of Burma [GSUB]. 1979. *myanma phat-sa-thit tátìyá-tàn.* Yangon: Government of the Socialist Union of Burma.

Gravers, M. 2007. *Exploring ethnic diversity in Burma.* Copenhagen: NIAS Press.

Harvey, G. E. 1926. *Outline of Burmese History.* Bombay: Longmans, Green and Co.

Higgins, S., Maber, E. J. T., Lopes Cardozo, M. T. A., and Shah, R. 2015. *Education and peacebuilding in Myanmar.* Research Consortium Education and Peacebuilding, University of Amsterdam.

Houtman, G. 1999. *Mental culture in Burmese crisis politics: Aung San Suu Kyi and the National League for Democracy.* Tokyo: Institute for the Study of Languages and Cultures of Asia and Africa.

Khin Yi (Dàw). 1988. *The Dobáma Movement in Burma (1930–1938).* Ithaca, NY: Southeast Asia Program.

Kyan (Dàw). 2005. Conditions of Burma [Myanmar] 1885–1886. In: Myanmar Historical Commission, ed. *Selected writings.* Yangon: Ministry of Education.

Leider, J. P. 2009. *King Alaungmintaya's golden letter to King George II (7 May 1756): The story of an exceptional manuscript and a failed diplomatic overture.* Hannover: Gottfried William Leibniz Bibliothek.

Lieberman, V. 2007. Ethnic politics; 'Excising the 'Mon Paradigm' from Burmese historiography. *Journal of Southeast Asian Studies* 38(2), pp. 377–383.

Loewen, J. W. 1995. *Lies my teacher told me: Everything your American history textbook got wrong.* New York: New Press.

Luce, G. H. 1966. 'The career of Htilaing Min [Kyanzittha]. The Uniter of Burma, fl. A.D. 1084–1113'. *The Journal of the Royal Asiatic Society of Great Britain and Ireland* 1(2), pp. 53–68.

Metro, R. 2014. Looks good on paper: Education reform in Burma. *New Mandala* [e-journal]. Available at http://asiapacific.anu.edu.au/newmandala/2014/02/25/looks-good-on-paper-education-reform-in-burma/. Accessed 7 October 2017.

Myanmar Ministry of Education. 2008. *pátáwiwin hnít thamain tátìyá-tàn.* Yangon: Myanmar Ministry of Education.

Okell, J. 1971. *A Guide to the Romanization of Burmese.* London: The Royal Asiatic Society of Great Britain and Ireland.

Phayre, A. P. 1883. *History of Burma: Burma Proper, Pegu, Taungu, Tenasserim, and Arakan. From the Earliest Time to the End of the First War with British India*. New York: Augustus M. Kelley.
Phillips, A. 2005. 'Romance and Tragedy in Burmese History: A Reading of G. E. Harvey's A History of Burma'. *SOAS Bulletin of Burma Research* 3(1), pp. 1–26.
Revolutionary Council. 1962. *The Burmese Way to Socialism*. Yangon: Information Department of the Revolutionary Council.
Salem-Gervais, N. and Metro, R. 2012. 'A textbook case of nation-building: The discursive evolution of state and non-state history curricula under military rule in Myanmar'. *The Journal of Burma Studies* 16(1), pp. 27–78.
Schober, J. 1997. Trajectories in Buddhist Sacred Biography. In: Schober, J. ed. *Sacred Biography in the Buddhist Traditions of South and Southeast Asia*. Honolulu: University of Hawai'i Press.
Schober, J. 2005. Buddhist Visions of Moral Authority and Modernity in Burma. In: Skidmore, M. ed. *Burma at the Turn of the 21st Century*. Honolulu: University of Hawai'i Press, pp. 113–132.
Scott, J. G. 1921. *Burma: A handbook of practical information*. London: Daniel O'Connor.
Tambiah, A. J. 1976. *World Conqueror and World Renouncer: A Study of Buddhism and Polity in Thailand against a Historical Background*. Cambridge: Cambridge University Press.
Taylor, R. H. 2009. *The State in Myanmar*. Singapore: NUS Press.
Thant Myint-U. 2001. *The Making of Modern Burma*. Cambridge: Cambridge University Press.
Tin Ka (Tekkatho). 2006. 'Toward everlasting union spirit'. *New Light of Myanmar*, 12 February.
Tosh, J. 1984. *The pursuit of history: Aims, Methods and New Directions in the Study of Modern History*. London: Longman.
Trouillot, M.-R. 1995. *Silencing the Past: Power and the Production of History*. Boston, MA: Beacon Press.
Voloshinov, V. N. 1986. *Marxism and the Philosophy of Language*. Translated from Russian by L. Matejka and I. R. Tiunik, 1929. Cambridge, MA: Harvard University Press.
Women's League of Chinland. 2007. *Hidden Crimes against Chin Women: The Preliminary Report*. n.l.: Women's League of Chinland.
Zar Ni. 1998. *Knowledge, Control, and Power: The Politics of Education under Burma's Military Dictatorship (1962–1988)*. PhD thesis. University of Wisconsin-Madison.

2 The legend of the 'lost book' and the value of education among the Karen people in Myanmar and Thailand

Pia Maria Jolliffe

UNIVERSITY OF OXFORD

The introduction of Western education and schooling to the peoples of Myanmar has historically been linked to the arrival of Catholic missionaries in the Kingdom of Ava and American Baptists in British Burma. However, the value of access to formal knowledge has already been enshrined in mythology. Focusing on the Karen legend of the 'lost book', my research examines how oral traditions like myth telling explain social inequalities related to access to formal education. According to this legend, education is a gift that the Karen once received in the form of a golden book from Y'wa, a creating godhead. The gift was received but lost to the Karen's younger 'white' brother. Until today, this legend has been told and retold in various ways, but in essence it explains an original injustice that caused the Karen to remain mostly engaged in subsistence farming whilst other peoples advanced in technology and modern knowledge. The legend became prominent during the Karen's encounters with nineteenth-century American Baptist missionaries who encouraged the Karen to see in the Bible their 'lost book'.

The Karen

The term 'Karen' includes around 20 subgroups of Karennic-speaking peoples. The group name 'Karen' emerged from colonial ethnography, missionary activities and policies related to ethnic groups in Thailand and Myanmar (Hinton, 1983; Keyes, 2003, pp. 210–211). The people called 'Karen' are one of the many 'ethnic minority' groups living in the hill regions of mainland Southeast Asia. Scott (2009) called this area 'Zomia'. The concept of 'Zomia', in turn, designates a genre of area studies which is not defined by national frontiers. Instead, the justification of the designation of the area as 'Zomia' is based on ecological conditions and structural relationships, such as the relation between hill populations and kingdoms or state authorities (Scott, 2009, pp. 26–32). Indeed, the border between the Karen State in Eastern Myanmar and the hills of the Karen in Western Thailand has only existed since 1890. Until the mid-nineteenth century, Siam was composed of hundreds of principalities. Single political units were classified by local lords and places of residence, and not by territorial boundaries, nationality or ethnicity.

Local lords requested peoples' labour as well as tributes in kind (Boonlue, 2012, pp. 22–23; Gravers, 2012, p. 348; Hayami, 2004, p. 46). These lords, in turn, were allied to supreme monarchs and elites in the ruling centres. Within this system, peripheral peoples, like the Karen, were called *chao pa* ('wild forest people'). They belonged to the realm of Siamese elites and northern princes and were closely interdependent with them. For example, local Karen chiefs paid tribute to the elites in Chiang Mai, who in return recognised the legitimacy of the Karen chiefs and granted them protection. Autonomy was an important characteristic of peripheral polities, such as the Karen chiefdom. For example, one chief could be loyal to different higher Thai authorities at the same time (Laungaramsri, 2003, p. 2; Winichakul, 1994, pp. 8–82). Therefore, the hill populations, like the Karen, need to be understood in relation to central authorities and their institutions, such as schools. At the time of writing this chapter, there were an estimated 400,000 Karen who were born and lived in Thailand and have Thai citizenship. The Karen in Myanmar live in Karen State, which is also called Kayin State or Kawthoolei, which literally means 'a land without blemish' (Rogers, 2004, p. 9). Because of the ongoing conflict in this area, less than a quarter of Myanmar's Karen population live inside the Karen State of Myanmar (Thawnghmung, 2008, p. 4). Instead they live as refugees and migrants in Thailand, Malaysia and other parts of Southeast Asia as well as in third countries of resettlement like the United Kingdom. In spite of political and economic changes, the Karen in different parts of the world share a cultural heritage, including the respect for the value of agricultural work and modern education.

The legend of the lost book

The value of access to formal knowledge is enshrined in Karen mythology, especially in the legend of the lost book. According to this legend, education is a gift that the Karen once received from Y'wa (read: swaa), the creator god. The gift was received but lost to the Karen's younger 'white' brother. Similar versions of the legend of the lost book exist among other Southeast Asian people, such as the people called Kayan (Bridget Craig Robinson, interview, 15 March 2015).

During fieldwork in various Karen communities I listened to oral and read written versions of the legend. I thus found two basic version of the story of the 'lost book'. The first version says the book originally belonged to the Karen and then fell into the hands of a 'white' foreigner. Zoya Phan, for instance gives this version in her biography: Y'wa, the creator god, created three sons. A Karen, a Burman and a white man. He gave a golden book to the Karen, a silver book to the Burman and a paper book to the white brother. While the Karen was at his rice field, he placed the golden book close by. His youngest brother, the white man, grew jealous and – while the Karen was absorbed in his work – replaced the golden book with his own paper book. Then the white brother escaped by boat to a distant land, taking the book with the divine knowledge with him. (Phan, 2009, p. 68). The second version says that the book was burned and a chicken ate the remains of it. For instance, Marshall (2009) provides a version according to which there were seven brothers, one of whom was a Karen. The Karen received the book because he was busy working on the field. When he burned off his clearing, the book was lying on a stump and nearly destroyed. The pigs and chickens ate the charred remains of it: 'Thus the wisdom contained in the book, which the ancestors of the race sorely needed after sickness and trouble came upon them, was nowhere to be found except in the pigs, chickens, and charcoal, and it was to these they turned in their distress' (Marshall, 2009, p. 288). Marshall also provides several Karen poems that summarize the legend of the lost book. One poem, for instance, tells of a Karen woman and a Karen man who both neglected the book that was given to them. As a consequence, the pigs ate the book. Another poem mentions that both a golden and a silver book were given to the Karen ancestors. However, due to their disobedience they lost both books to 'the foreigner' (Marshall, 2009, p. 288).

There also exist versions that mention both the chicken scratch-theory and the theory of the foreigner. For instance, during fieldwork in Thailand in 2015, Loo Shwe, a Karen refugee youth told the legend in a way that combines both versions. According to Loo Shwe, God had three sons: the Karen, the Burmese and the English. One day the Father asked all three to bring food. The English brought very delicious meat. The second brother brought fruit. Also the eldest brother, the Karen brought a tiny portion of food of a different, bittersweet taste. God felt best after eating the food the Karen brought. So, God said: 'Oh, you are the oldest and you are very clever. You are bringing nice food'. When the God father returned to heaven, he asked the Karen to come with him, but he responded: 'I am not free. Because I have to work in the farm'. So God asked the youngest English brother to come with him to heaven. There he gave him two books, one made out of gold and one made out of silver. The books contained all the knowledge in the world. God said, 'Give this book to your older brother and keep the second book'. The youngest brother took both books and promised to return the book to his elder brother. However, when he returned to the farm, he showed his oldest brother the book. But he was working in the farm. So, he put the book on a tree trunk and the younger brother went back to his house. The older brother went away, too. He thus forgot the book on the tree trunk: termites came and ate the book and then a hen arrived and ate the termites. When the Karen eventually returned, he only saw chicken scratch remains. Therefore, in order to regain access to the knowledge of the book, the Karen killed the chicken and looked at the chicken bone. This is the reason why the Karen to this day use chicken bones for divination. In the meantime, the youngest brother returned to his place, read the book and learned a lot from it. The older Karen brother remained, hoping that maybe one day the younger brother will return the knowledge to him (Loo Shwe, interview, 25 March 2015). Also in the UK, Nant Bwa Bwa Phan, a young Karen refugee woman, remembers the legend of the lost book being taught when she was at school in the Karen State of Burma: 'It's a long time ago. All I remember is: We got a book. And the Karen brother was not looking after it properly and so it got missing. It got lost. So they believe that the white man is going to bring the book back later' (interview, 10 April 2015). Clearly, in these versions of the story, the Karen was the originally favoured brother who was invited to ascend with the creator God to heaven. His lack of faith kept him bound to his farm work. Instead, his younger English brother accompanied God to heaven where he received a golden and a silver book. Again, God made it clear that the golden and thus more precious book needs to go to the Karen, whereas the English brother could keep the silver book. Although the English brother dutifully returned the book destined for the Karen brother, the latter neglected the divine gift. He left the book on a trunk where it was eaten by termites. Thus, the Karen brother lost the golden book and his privileged access to knowledge.

The legend of the lost book highlights the symbolic value of education and the importance of time and space in knowledge transfer. The passing of time and the crossing of geographical distances fosters interpersonal relations as well as social inequality. The history of Christian missionary education in today's Myanmar and Thailand highlights the profound meaning of the legend of the lost book. To this day, some Karen refer to the lost book in their encounters with Western missionaries and humanitarian aid workers and politicians (Rogers, 2004, p. 211). Also in the accounts of other anthropologists, the legend of the lost book was presented as an important representation of Karen self and other. It has been handed down by different generations of Karen in Myanmar as well as in Thailand (Hayami, 2004, p. 25). The legend clearly distinguishes between formal education contained in the book and practical tasks that eventually lead towards agricultural work. The knowledge written down in the book seems to be the key to progress and socio-economic development. Rather than chasing this knowledge, the Karen in the legend patiently wait for the gift of education to return to them.

The Karen and modern schooling in Myanmar

The Karen's distinctive socio-economic and cultural life has been noted by foreign visitors and missionaries to the Kingdom of Ava and British Burma. In *An Account of the Kingdom of Ava* (1800), Michael Symes wrote about the Karen or 'Carianers' as he called them: 'They lead quite a quiet life and are the most industrious subjects of the state [...] They profess and strictly observe universal peace, not engaging in war or taking contests for dominion, a system that necessarily places them in a state of subjection to the ruling power of the day. Agriculture, the care of cattle, and rearing poultry, are almost their only occupations. A great part of the provisions used in the country is raised by the Carianers, and they particularly excel in gardening' (Symes, 1800, p. 207). The first Western teacher training school was built under royal permission by the Barnabite missionaries in Syriam (today Thanlyin). These Catholic missionaries were, from 1721, called to the Royal Court of the kingdom of Pegu. There, King Taninganwe supported the arrival of Italian missionaries as teachers for the young people at court. The missionaries learned the local Mon and Burmese languages and as an outcome of their studies produced grammar books and dictionaries of these languages. Although the above mentioned Barnabite school was destroyed during the war between Ava and Pegu, it was rebuilt after the arrival of Father Nerini in Syriam in 1749. The students were of different ethnicity, including Burmese, Peguans, Armenians and Portuguese – descendants of the merchants and mercenaries who had visited the kingdoms of Ava and Pegu from the 16th century onwards (Myint Swe, 2014, p. 271). In addition to reading and writing, students were instructed in geography, arithmetic and nautical sciences. The school was self-sufficient thanks to the attached farms and workshops, poultry pens and pigeon cotes (Ba, 1964, p. 295). Father Nerini was also known for his enthusiasm for the culture and customs of the peoples of Burma, especially the Karen. From Sangermano we thus learn that: 'the zeal of Nerini took him among some savage populations who lived separate from others in full liberty, and are called Karens (Cariani)' (Sangermano, 1893, p. 283). Clearly, the Karen were perceived as a people that lived independently from, and yet in relation to, the political and economic structures of the realm.

At the beginning of the nineteenth century, American Baptist missionaries arrived in Myanmar. During the three Anglo-Burmese wars in the years 1826, 1852 and 1886, Burma was gradually incorporated into the British Empire. The Karen became close to Baptist missions and British officials. The American Baptist educational activities were influential in forming the first ideas of a 'Karen' national identity.

The first Baptist missionary who is said to have met the Karen was Adoniram Judson, the son of a Congregationalist minister. In 1812, he and his wife Anne went as missionaries to India. There, they met British Baptists, left the Congregationalists and joined the American Baptists. As such they went from India to Burma where they actively engaged in missionary work. Jonathan Wade (1798–1872) and his wife Deborah Wade (1801–1868) also settled in Moulmein, learning Burmese and Sgaw Karen. Wade built a church and a school in 1828 and his wife taught in a school, but without a fixed schedule, since the demands of the moment had priority over adherence to fixed schedules. Indeed, it was common practice for individual Karen teachers to send selected Karen students for English language instruction and Bible study to the homes of missionaries (King, 1835, p. 169). During one of these home visits, a Karen man called Ko Tha Byu discovered in the house of Adoniram Judson the Book of Common Prayer, and wondered whether this might be the legendary lost book his ancestors had told him about. He converted and, after his baptism in 1828, subsequently visited many Karen villages, announcing the return of the 'white brother' and of the 'lost book'. This news, in turn, is said to have caused the conversion of hundreds of Karen (Marshall, 2009, p. 305). John Wade's biographer also notes that a group of Karen asked Wade: 'Teacher give us the Karen books'. Wade was at first confused by this request because he thought the Karen had no written script and therefore no books. But the Karen told him that they believed God gave them his word, and that the Karen lost it. Western foreigners, they believed, also had access to God's word. Accordingly, generations of Karen hoped a 'white foreigner' would return 'the lost book' to them so that the Karen would 'again be prosperous' (Wyeth, 1891, p. 83). This episode is said to have caused Jonathan Wade to undertake the work of putting the Sgaw Karen language into writing (Wyeth, 1891, p. 79–80).

This episode explains how some Karen understood the Bible as their lost book. It appears that even before the Karen understood the importance of literacy and education, they identified the written word as a source of spiritual and political power. The American Baptists' offer of literature, together with health and the message of salvation, had a strong impact on the Karen. Because of the legend the missionaries thought the hearts of the Karen were well prepared to welcome the sacred book of the Bible. In this respect, Randolph L. Howard (1931) noted: 'the prophecy of the return of the white brother with the Lost Book, which inspired the Karen with the hope of a better future and furnished an admirable foundation on which Christian teachers could build in promoting the development of the Karen nation' (Howard, 1931, p. 58). From a Japanese point of view, anthropologist Yoko Hayami (2004) suggests that the Karen's eager reception of Christian sacred texts could be interpreted as 'a desire for civilization and the power that accompanies it, as represented by the book and the written word' (Hayami, 2004, p. 41).

Formal theological training among the Karen began in 1836 in Tavoy. In 1840, the Catholic missionaries started their education work with the Karen boys near the port town Bassein, located in the province of Pegu. In 1860, the construction of another Bassein school was started. At the time of its completion, the school was called St Peter's Institution. The school counted 62 students from Bassein and a similar number of boarder students who migrated from surrounding villages for education at St Peter's. At this school, Karen boys learned how to read and write in English and Burmese. In addition, the students – almost all Karen boys - were trained in several handicrafts, including photography, carpentry and smithery. The purpose of the school was the development of Karen and Burmese according to the rules of European schools. In this way, the Bishop hoped to train an adult generation of craftsmen, teachers and catechists. Very talented boys and girls even made the transition to a College in Penang where they studied Latin. In the surroundings of the school, a small novitiate was built. In addition, a printing press was installed next to the school building. For the use of letter press printing, the community received types, i.e. pieces of metal with raised letters or characters on their upper surface. So as to write in the English alphabet, the French missionaries in Calcutta donated the types for printing the alphabet and the Burmese types came from the Baptist Mission Press which was founded in 1816 in Rangoon (Howard, 1931, p. 38). In this way the missionaries printed a prayer book in Burmese and school books for the teaching of the alphabet, geography, arithmetic and religion (Bigandet, 1887, p. 99). Close to St Peter's School an English day school for girls was built, together with an orphanage and a Burmese school for the daughters of Karen Christians who dwelt in villages around Bassein. The teaching and management were entrusted to two Burmese nuns who arrived from Rangoon, and Bishop Bigandet prayed that 'under God's blessing it is to be hoped that the Institution will prove productive of much good for the benefit of the Karen population' (Bigandet, 1887, p. 100). Clearly, Catholic schools for Karen emphasized both practical learning and formal education. Together with other Christian schools they also provided the basis for the formation of a Christian-led Karen nationalism. For example, the famous Judson College began in 1872 as Rangoon College. The College was at first a middle and high school, until 1920, when, with the addition of a bachelor's degree, it became Judson College and a constituent part of the University of Rangoon (Hall Hunt, 2005, p. 350). Because many students were Karen, it was nicknamed 'Karen College' and became a centre for the development of Karen nationalistic ideas. Indeed, the wide-scale establishment of missionary schools was important for the formation of a growing sense of Karen-ness within and beyond local communities. During the nineteenth and twentieth centuries, many literate Karen assumed roles within and between different village communities. In 1880 the Burma Baptist Convention sent three Karen missionaries to Thailand, where they established a church in Chiang Mai province (Rogers, 2004, pp. 53–54). One year later, in 1881, the Christian Karen founded the Karen National Association, a forerunner of the Karen National Union. The principal aim of the Association was the promotion of Karen identity, leadership, education and writing, independent of members' religious belief. This emergent Karen nationalism was particularly promoted by those Karen who were allied with the British after their conquest of lower Burma, central Burma and upper Burma. Their joining forces with the British against the Burmese, especially during the Second World War, provided the ground for the future ethnic conflict between the Karen and the Burmans in Myanmar (Smith, 1999, pp. 44–45).

Under British rule, the Western education system in Burma expanded and continued to grow until 1962, the year when General Ne Win came to power. Ne Win nationalised all the mission schools, and teachers largely went into exile. The ethnic minorities at the margin of the Burmese nation suffered particularly from these measures, as government education did not reach far into their rural areas of residency. As a consequence many young Karen people left their rural homes in Burma and crossed the border into Thailand to receive education in refugee camps. This education has largely been promoted by Western aid-agencies and Karen refugee committees (Jolliffe, 2016).

In this respect, Rogers (2004) suggests that the Karen legend of the book that was lost to the white brother, only to be returned by him again, had become true. After the American Baptists, the 'white brother' has been seen in the shape of various foreigners who supported the Karen cause: 'Some are missionaries, others activists, some humanitarian relief workers. Some are Christians, others are not. Some engage in the armed struggle, providing military training, procuring weapons and equipment, and planning strategy. Others speak and write on behalf of the Karens' (Rogers, 2004, p. 234). Indeed, when teaching Karen refugees as a volunteer during my own most recent fieldwork in March 2015, the young Karen refugee, Loo Shwe, after telling me his version of the lost book, astonished me by saying: 'One day maybe the younger brother will bring the knowledge to them. Like this. And now you come and give the knowledge to me, to us. It is completed now' (Loo Shwe, interview 25 March 2015). The story of the lost book is thus still meaningful to the Karen as they make sense of various forms of Western knowledge transfer.

Concluding remarks

This chapter has thus highlighted the importance of legends and mythology to understand the symbolical underpinning of Karen values and attitudes towards education. Focusing on the Karen's legend of the lost book highlighted the cultural roots of the modern division of formal education and informal learning. In narrating different versions of this legend, the Karen explain how they gained and lost access to divine knowledge. Accordingly, access to literacy has been associated with access to power and wealth, whilst manual and agricultural work seemed less advantageous. The Karen thus explained other peoples' technological and scientific progress and justified their own rural livelihoods based on rice farming. When American Baptist missionaries arrived in today's Myanmar, some Karen believed that the revered book of the Bible was the legendary lost book. The missionaries encouraged this assumption, as it was favourable to the process of evangelisation among the Karen people. Like the Catholic missionaries before them, the American Baptists built Christian schools and offered the marginalized Karen real opportunities to access formal learning. As a consequence, throughout the twentieth century increasing numbers of Karen children accessed primary, secondary and tertiary education. The myth of the lost book is still told today, as different 'white brothers' transfer various kinds of knowledge to the Karen people in Thailand and Myanmar.

References

Ba, V. 1964. 'The Beginnings of Western Education in Burma – The Catholic Effort'. *Journal of Burma Research Society* 47/2, pp. 287–324.

Bigandet, P. A. 1887. *An Outline of the History of the Catholic Burmese Mission. From the year 1720 to 1887*. Rangoon: The Hanthawaddy Press.

Boonlue, W. 2012. Karen Imaginary of Suffering in Relation to Burmese and Thai History. In: Nakamura, S. and Yoshida Y. ed(s). *Present State of Cultural Heritages in Asia*. Kanazawa: Kanazawa University, pp. 21–26.

Gravers, M. 2012. 'Waiting for a righteous ruler: The Karen royal imaginery in Thailand and Burma'. *Journal of Southeast Asian Studies*, 43(2), pp. 340–363.

Hall Hunt, R. 2005. *Bless God and Take Courage. The Judson History and Legacy*. Valley Forge, PA: The Judson Press.

Hayami, Y. 2004. *Between Hills and Plains: Power and Practice in Socio-Religious Dynamics among the Karen*, Kyoto and Melbourne: Kyoto University Press and Trans Pacific Press.

Hinton, P. 1983. Do the Karen Really Exist? In: McKinnon, J. and Bhruksasri, W. ed(s). *Highlanders of Thailand*. Oxford: Oxford University Press, pp. 155–168.

Howard, R. L. 1931. *Baptists in Burma*. Philadelphia, PA: The Judson Press.

Jolliffe, P. 2016. *Learning, Migration and Intergenerational Relations. The Karen and the Gift of Education*. Basingstoke: Palgrave Macmillan.

Keyes, C. 2003. The politics of 'Karen-ness' in Thailand. In: Delang, C. O. ed. *Living at the Edge of Thai Society. The Karen in the highlands of northern Thailand*. London and New York: Routledge Curzon, pp. 210–218.

King, A. 1835. *Memoir of George Dana Boardman, late missionary to Burma*. Boston, MA: Gould Kendall & Lincoln.

Laungaramsri, P. 2003. Constructing marginality: the 'hill tribe' Karen and their shifting locations within Thai state and public perspectives. In: Delang. C. O. ed. *Living at the Edge of Thai Society: The Karen in the Highlands of Northern Thailand*, London and New York: Routledge Curzon, pp. 21–42.

Marshall, H. I. 2009. *The Karen People of Burma. A Study in Anthropology and Ethnology*. Wokingham: Dodo Press.

Myint Swe, J. 2014. *The Cannon Soldiers of Burma*. Toronto: We Make Books.

Phan, Z. 2009. *Little Daughter. A Memoir of Survival in Burma and the West*. London et al.: Pocket Books.

Rogers, B. 2004. *A Land without Evil. Stopping the Genocide of Burma's Karen People*. Oxford and Grand Rapids: Monarch Books.

Sangermano, V. 1893. *The Burmese Empire a hundred years ago as described by Father Sangermano. With an Introduction and Notes by John Jardine*. Westminster: Archibald Constable and Company.

Scott, J. C. 2009. *The Art of Not Being Governed. An Anarchist History of Upland Southeast Asia*. New Haven, CT and London: Yale University Press.

Smith, M. 1999. *Burma. Insurgency and the Politics of Ethnicity*. Dhaka: University Press.

Symes, M. 1800. *An account of an embassy to the Kingdom of Ava, sent by the Governor-General of India, in the year 1795. By Michael Symes, Esq. Major in his Majesty's 76th Regiment*. London. Eighteenth Century Collections Online. Gale. University of Oxford. 8 August 2018.

Thawnghmung, A. M. 2008. *The Karen Revolution in Burma: Diverse Voices, Uncertain Ends*. Washington, DC: East-West Center.

Winichakul, T. 1994. *Siam Mapped: A History of the Geo-body of a Nation*. Chiang Mai: Silkworm Books.

Wyeth, W. N. 1891. *The Wades. A Memorial*. Philadelphia, PA: C. J. Krehbiel & Co.

3 The Modernisation of Female Education and the Emergence of Class Conflict Between Literate Groups of Women in Siam 1870–1910

Natanaree Posrithong

MAHIDOL UNIVERSITY INTERNATIONAL COLLEGE

Introduction

The history of modern female education in Thailand begins its gradual development from the reign of King Mongkut (1851–68) with the employment of an English governess in the inner court, as described in Anna Leonowens' memoirs (Leonowens, 1870). Nevertheless, due to the lack of available literature, which mostly focuses on male education, the study of the history of female education in Siam is rather limited. Only in the immediate pre-revolution years from 1925 to 1932 did female voices begin to be heard in the public sphere through the growth of women's print media. Previous studies have failed to elaborate on the education for girls that existed in Siam before the era of intensive modernisation from the second decade of the twentieth century. Wyatt (1969) did mention in his work Sunanthalai Girl's School, first founded in 1892 and one of the earliest female schools in Siam (Wyatt, 1969, p. 166). Unfortunately, the author presented no further discussion about this school. Instead, he focused on Suan Anan and Suan Kulap schools, which were the first boys' schools in Siam (Wyatt, 1969, p. 166). Even though statistics exist and testify to a remarkable and unprecedented growth in the number of female students attending primary and secondary schools and higher education institutions in the early twentieth century, no further analysis of female education's origins or impact was made.

At the turn of the twentieth century, the literacy rate of Siamese women was considered high in mainland Southeast Asia, especially when compared to Burma and Vietnam, where female education did not emerge until the early twentieth century. Indeed, it was only from 1911 onwards that Burmese women gained access to primary and secondary education. Even though Burmese education expanded rapidly thereafter, the number of enrolled female students was still much lower than in Siam. The official statistics demonstrate that 235,465 female students were already enrolled in schools in Siam in 1925, while only 120,419 female students were recorded in Burma in 1921, and an even smaller number – 40,752 female students – in Vietnam by 1930 (Barmé, 2002, p. 153; Ikeya, 2011, p. 55). The origins of this striking growth in the number of literate women in Siam came from the initiatives of both the Siamese court, led by Queen Saowapha, and the Christian missionaries from the West, namely the American Presbyterians. In fact, Siam's *de jure* 'un-colonised' condition imbued Siamese elite women with a positive stance towards modern education, which was seen as a tool for safeguarding their traditions and Buddhist values. With this perspective, Siam offers a unique case study where female education developed from the initiatives of both the 'insiders' (the Siamese elite women) and the 'outsiders' (the Western missionaries).

This chapter studies the impact of the modernisation of education on women from 1870 to 1910. It concentrates on both the publicly funded form of female schools and the private missionary schools. While the skills of reading and writing were almost unheard of among non-elite women in Southeast Asia, by 1874 reforms in the administration of the Siamese *fai nai* (the inner court) under King Chulalongkorn (Rama V) equipped many royal elite women with skills and a level of education never previously enjoyed by Siamese women. Barbara Andaya (2006) has pointed out the importance of the women's quarters of the palaces around Southeast Asia in providing an additional mechanism for the generation of political activity and cultural standardisation in the early modern polity. Although the women's quarters were viewed as the secluded spaces that tied elite women to the concepts of 'inside' and 'femaleness', they were the places that offered opportunities for women to enhance their skills and literacy (Andaya, 2006, p. 173). This was particularly true for the case of Siam. During Southeast Asia's colonial period, the Siamese inner court had rapidly enlarged due to King Chulalongkorn's practice of polygamy. While the foreign account of the famous Anna Leonowens (1870), who served as the governess at the Siamese court from 1862 to 1868, viewed the women's quarters mainly as the harem of the Siamese monarch, the inner court was more complex in its structure and advanced in its administration than the court Leonowens publicly criticised. Saowapha, Queen Consort of Chulalongkorn (1864–1919; r.1878–1910), took initiatives to advance the place of women in wider society by using the women's quarters to promote public education for Siamese girls for the first time in 1884. Nevertheless, the queen, as a royal elite woman, faced two sets of tensions: firstly, resistance from Chulalongkorn to female education, and secondly, competition from foreign missionaries. This chapter aims to study the historical development of female education through the prism of social fragmentation between rival female elites of the early modern period of Siam, which emerged as a result of a bifurcation in the channel through which modern education arrived there, and as a parallel development to the rising literacy levels in Siamese society. This rivalry between elite women that emerged from their different social backgrounds (aristocratic and commoner) was later reflected in the nature of the events of 1932 that marked a major turning point in Thai history. The revolution that took place on 24 June 1932 not only overthrew the absolute monarchy, but it also challenged the monopoly of the nobility on power and supported the rise, to at least a parallel ascendancy, of an emergent bureaucratic-based middle class. During the last decade of absolutism, criticisms of the aristocracy and even the failure of King Prajadhipok's administration were dramatically voiced by a number of newspapers and magazines written by both male and female voices (Copeland, 1993). These critical voices arose from the rising middle class, who benefited from the modernisation of education in the 1890s.

Female education in Siam: Early-modern stage of the latter half of the nineteenth century

In the pre-modern era (defined roughly as the period before 1855, when Siam began establishing 'modern' commercial and diplomatic treaties with industrialising global powers), education in Siam was only available in Buddhist monasteries (*wat*), the palace (*wang*), and well-off domestic households (*ban*) (Sukanya, 2005). With the exception of the elite class, temples became the first schools for boys from the Ayutthaya period (the fifteenth to eighteenth centuries) onwards. The monks' tasks not only included the teaching of Buddhist principles but also prepared the boys with literacy skills for higher stages of Buddhist knowledge. While a male 'commoner' started to learn how to read and write at a temple, usually at the age of eight, princes, princesses, and children of the aristocracy were co-educated within the inner court of the royal palace, or *fai nai*, from the age of three (Waruni, 1981). Given that there was no barrier between boys' and girls' education within the inner court, aristocratic girls could obtain the same education as boys until they reached their teenage years, when girls were to receive training in domestic skills from older princesse,s according to court tradition. This evidence highlights a distinct advantage of the aristocratic class compared to 'commoners' in urban Bangkok and nearby urban centres in central Siam at the start of the country's early modern period.

The general perception of female education in Southeast Asia in the pre-modern era, especially for non-elite women, was viewed as unnecessary or even inappropriate. Nevertheless, exceptions were made for women of the aristocracy. Doan Thi Diem (1705–1748), and Mya Galay (circa 1780–1840), were both aristocratic women who were trained in the royal courts and later contributed to the education of court women in Vietnam and Burma respectively (Andaya, 2006, p. 54; Ikeya, 2011, p. 53). A similar situation applied in Siam, where women with royal affiliation had a higher chance of receiving education and training in Bangkok's inner court. Nevertheless, access to education in Siam was rather restricted for the daughters of people outside that small circle, meaning mostly the peasantry. The reason for this is related to the pre-modern belief in Theravada Buddhist cosmology and gender roles. According to the traditional Siamese interpretation of Buddhist teachings, a woman's position had always been subordinated to men, as women were represented as symbols of temptation and sensuality and thus obstacles in the way of men's efforts to ultimately attain *nirvana* (Waruni, 1981). As a consequence, women were prohibited from direct contact with Buddhist monks and had limited roles in monasteries. Therefore, monastery-based education was not an option for women in the pre-modern era. By contrast, for boys the monastery was the most common means of acquiring literacy. For villagers outside the urban areas, literacy was seen as unnecessary for women because of a lifestyle based on agriculture, and only their labour, with its related skills, was required of them.

Nonetheless, in the new urban areas of the nineteenth century, literacy slowly became a symbol of class status and an opportunity, at the turn of the twentieth century, for women finding themselves in an emerging modern metropolis to enhance their social positions. The route would primarily be taken through marriage to the new upper class men of Chulalongkorn's generation who sought to marry literate women. This encouraged many urban middle-class families to train their daughters in their homes in basic literacy and domestic skills in Siam's early-modern stage of the latter half of the nineteenth century.

Education for aristocratic women: *Fai nai* (inner palace)

Princess Phunphitsamai (1895–1990) was a daughter of one of the most influential figures in Thai history, Prince Damrong, a half-brother of Chulalongkorn and member of his inner circle, who was intimately involved in the country's education policy from the early 1880s. Born in 1895, the princess spent her childhood growing up in the residences within the inner court. Within these private quarters, daughters of high-ranking aristocrats were sent to royal residences of queens and royal consorts (chaochom) to obtain skills ranging from basic literacy to specialised domestic skills. Princess Phunphitsamai had lost her mother at a very young age and her father did as other aristocrats did at the time. He decided to send the princess to the inner court. The education within the inner court was similar to education offered at early female schools in Siam in the 1900s. As the princess later recounted, 'The inner court served as a college for young women where all kinds of skills were taught from literacy to fashion'. (Phunphitsamai, 1990, p. 212). Older princesses were teachers of the younger ones, and occasionally foreign missionaries and governesses were also hired on contracts to teach English within this restricted zone of the palace. Princess Phunphitsamai recorded that she received her education from several teachers. She learned French and English from foreign teachers, learned Thai from Princess Witthayaprichamat, and was trained in domestic skills, which were also known as *wicha kunlasatri*, from Princess Niphanopphadon, who was a daughter of King Chulalongkorn. *Wicha kunlasatri* (noble ladies' course) that the princess mentioned in her memoir included the learning of crochet, knitting, cooking, manners, and women's fashion (Phunphitsamai, 1990, p. 212).

Education for 'common' women

For non-elite women, the choice of education was rather restricted. Pha-op Posakritsana (1912–83), one of the first female graduates from the Faculty of Arts at Chulalongkorn University, wrote in her memoir that the only available school option for her primary education was a non-registered school where a literate woman opened her house to teach the children in the neighbourhood – this arrangement was also known as village school (*rongrian chao ban*) (Dutsadi 1993). Unlike girls who were born in aristocratic families, Pha-op did not have a chance to attend the most prestigious academy at the time, which was located within the royal palace. Apart from the village-schools set up by local Thais, education for women was also actively promoted by a group of American Protestant missionary women as early as 1837 when Mrs Emilie Royce Bradley, wife of Dr Dan Beach Bradley who brought modern printing technology to Siam and founded the first Thai newspaper *Bangkok Recorder*, started teaching local children in their residence in Thonburi (Phitsanu, 2004). Nevertheless, the missionaries' promotion of female education faced great difficulties, which mainly sprang from parents' concerns. Their two major concerns were: firstly, that the idea of sending their daughters out of their households to day schools was an act against the good custom of a proper lady; and secondly, the fear of the promotion of Christianity taught by the missionaries (Yupphaphon, 1987). To counter these obstacles, the missionary women taught without charging the parents when they first founded Kunlasatri Wang Lang School in 1874, located on the Thonburi side of Chao Phraya River opposite the Grand Palace. Students had to make a contract with the school for three or five years, as the school was also committed to providing students with accommodation, food, and clothes (Phitsanu, 2004; Yupphaphon, 1987). As the school's income was based solely on donations, financial instability was unavoidable.

Kunlasatri Wang Lang: The rival missionary girls' school

Missionary women had made efforts to open girls' schools throughout the reign of King Mongkut (1851–68). However, they did not succeed until 1874, when Mrs Harriet House founded the first girls' boarding school in Siam named after its founder, Harriet M. House School for Girls, with funds she had collected from donors in the USA. This school was later known by the name Kunlasatri Wang Lang, but more commonly known for short as Wang Lang (Samakhom-sitwanglang-watthana samai pi, 2005–2006, 2005). Although the school was fully operated by foreign missionaries, the name Kunlasatri Wang Lang associated the school with the values of noble women (*kunlasatri*) and its proximity to the palace (Wang Lang) (Ratchabandittayasathan, 1999, p. 135). Both terms gave an aristocratic sense to its name.

From the first day that the school opened, its major aim was to recruit students of all classes and family backgrounds. One example was one Tuan, born of Chinese origins but who had been converted to the Christian faith. She was one of the students in the first class of the Wang Lang School, and became a key figure in the school's history. Mrs House, the headmistress of Wang Lang School at the time, appointed Tuan as the manager of the school when she had to leave Siam due to health problems in 1877 (Phitsanu, 2004). This proved a difficult time for Wang Lang School, but Tuan managed to keep the school going. She was one of a few middle-class women at that time who had both a good command of English and a charisma that impressed the students' parents. The parents of the students of Wang Lang respected and trusted Tuan, and her stewardship was one of the reasons they sent their daughters to study at Wang Lang School. What was significant about Tuan was not only her skills, but also the improvement in her social position through her very public contribution to Wang Lang School. Given that Tuan was born with Chinese origins and came from a middle-class family in the provinces, it would be quite hard to imagine her as a manager of the school. While most literate women were concentrated within the palace, Tuan had revealed that opportunities for middle-class women from non-aristocratic backgrounds to elevate themselves in terms of social status were open to them through the channel of an institution like the Wang Lang School.

Wang Lang became even more popular among Bangkok's urban population, especially the wealthy merchant class, when Miss Edna Cole (1854–1949) became its new headmistress in 1885. The popularity of English language learning among the wealthy of Siam expanded widely from the palace in the last decade of the nineteenth century. The Wang Lang School transformed its curriculum to meet this growing demand by placing a greater concentration on the teaching of English and charging a school tuition fee (Yupphaphon, 1987). Before 1885, Wang Lang had taught children for free as Thai parents were not familiar with the concept of schools for girls. Nevertheless, Miss Cole realised that donations alone could not guarantee the financial stability of the school, and she introduced the tuition fee of five to six baht per month for the class of 1885 (Samakhom-sitwanglang-watthana samai pi, 2005–2006, 2005). Teachers were concerned whether there would be enough students when parents were obliged to pay for their daughters' education. However, the apparent increase in the popularity of English language learning among the urban population motivated parents to send their daughters to Wang Lang School. Apart from the increasing popularity of the school, Miss Cole also spent the school's profits on its renovation and expansion. The new modern building attracted well-off Bangkokians in even greater numbers than before. From 1885, Wang Lang School gained a reputation as a school of English, able to shape the modern image of Siamese women for the new era. As Miss Cole wrote in a school advertising poster, 'This is a place for children's learning. We welcome anybody who wishes to send their children here.' (Samakhom-sitwanglang-watthana samai pi, 2005–2006, 2005, p. 23.)

The opportunity of education for middle-class girls expanded with the relocation of Wang Lang School. The change of location from its original position adjacent to the palace (Wang Lang) to Bang Kapi was a challenging step for the school. Situated in the Wang Lang area, the school had a stronger possibility of attracting girls from aristocratic families. However, with the limited space and the founding of the publicly funded Rajini School, Miss Cole's only solution for the survival of the school was to move its location to the larger property she had purchased on the further east side of Bangkok. She had hoped that the new buildings, facilities, and even the new given name 'Watthana' would help promote the school. The new name 'Watthana' means progress and prosperity, which was sometimes also referred to as 'watthanakan' ('evolution' or 'development') (Ratchabandittayasathan, 1999, p. 1058). Miss Cole had developed a good knowledge of Thai, after having spent 44 years in Siam – enough to choose this modern term as a new name for the country's oldest missionary girl's school.

As Rajini School was seen as an extension of the inner court and an exclusive place reserved for aristocratic women in reproducing aristocratic domestic skills in a modern context, the new look of Watthana Academy might also have signalled a change in the group of girls targeted for enrolment at this institution. The growth of the urban middle class, which comprised a large group of Chinese merchants, was undeniably significant in Bangkok during the turn of the twentieth century. These families were willing to pay for school education for their children, especially when their daughters would be guaranteed full training in the English language. Moreover, the name-change to 'Watthana' also symbolised the school's independence from all affiliations it previously had with the Royal Palace: it signified a new era of institutions independent of the monarchy, and opened up a new kind of elite education for new groups of parents. The school's targeting of middle-class students eventually resulted in class tensions between groups of literate women in the pre-revolutionary years of the 1920s and the start of the 1930s.

Royal elite female initiative in the modernisation of female education

Reforms introduced by 1874 in the administration of the *fai nai* under Rama V (King Chulalongkorn) equipped many royal elite women with skills and a level of education never previously enjoyed by Siamese women. As the inner court expanded in size – with estimates of the number of women varying up to 3,000 in the reign of King Chulalongkorn (1868–1910) – palace women were obliged to enhance their skills in order to take up roles in the administration (Loos, 2005). Princess Naphaphonprapha (1864–1958), and Consort Wat (1841–1939), served in the newly-appointed positions of General Secretary (*somdet athibodi*) and Head of Personnel (*thao worachan*) of the inner court, respectively. Both of them exercised a level of power that not many aristocratic women had previously enjoyed. As the missionary-run school became the rival institution for the aristocratic elites, palace women transformed their domestic learning and informal literary teaching into formal education for the first time.

Although King Chulalongkorn himself might have been seen as a supporter of education, as portrayed in official historical accounts, his views on education for women were actually rather ambiguous. By the end of the nineteenth century, Siamese male authorities were taking a reactive position rather than a pro-active position in regard to the development of female education. This was in contrast to male education, which King Chulalongkorn was very keen to promote as a way to elevate the nation to an equal level with the West. The modernisation of male education arrived in Siam at the same time as other Western-influenced reforms, which King Chulalongkorn had launched as a result of his own ambivalent fear and admiration of the West. Wyatt (1969, p. 380) stated that 'Chulalongkorn learned only slowly the difference between Westernisation and modernisation'. Only later, in the 1880s, did Prince Damrong discover that Siamese education could be modernised without Westernisation when he launched thoroughgoing reforms of the flagship elite Suan Kulap School and the traditional monastic schools. In other words, Siam's rulers had adopted a more focused and purposeful stance towards male education with the goal of serving the Siamese state's specific needs. By the end of Chulalongkorn's reign in 1910, the ruling class had already established a firm grip of control over male education and its curriculum. However, in the case of women, the education system was less focused and more complicated as there was no wide public support for female education until the end of the nineteenth century. While males were already acquiring an education in publicly funded schools, female education was relatively discouraged by the king.

Under the leadership of Queen Saowapha, a publicly funded boarding school for girls, Sunanthalai Girls' School, was finally founded in 1892 in response to concern about the missionaries' motives to convert students to Christianity and the pressure from the 'civilised' West for a greater degree of female participation in society beyond the subservient roles associated with the Orient, such as concubinage. Following the opening of the school, junior members of the extended royal family responded positively to the idea of education for their daughters. Girls moved from the residences of prominent consorts within the inner court to board at the newly-founded Sunanthalai School. Nonetheless, the school never received full support from King Chulalongkorn, as he initially did not see the importance of girls' education. Even after the successful establishment of Sunanthalai, the king's ambivalent support for female education is evident in a letter from Miss Smith, the principal of the school, dated 6 October 1895 (Sunanthalai Girls' School, 1895–1902). She expressed her disappointment with the king's decision to close down Sunanthalai and wrote this letter as a petition to him by requesting the king to pay a visit to the establishment. Although King Chulalongkorn wrote in his reply to Miss Smith that he had no intention to shut down the school and what she had heard was only a rumour, he suggested to the Minister of Public

Instruction (*Krasuang Thammakan*), Phraya Phatsakorawong, that the Government should not spend too much of its revenue on girls' education. As a consequence, in 1902, the temporary closure of the school was proposed as a solution for the school's financial difficulty (Sunanthalai Girls' School, 1895–1902). Hence, despite being the King's chief queen, Queen Saowapha continued to struggle to modernise and stimulate public female education, while the missionaries were already outpacing her as numbers of girls enrolled at the Wang Lang School continued to rise.

Traditional elites and Sunanthalai/Rajini Girls' School

Although the first teachers at Sunanthalai School were Western missionary women, they were obliged to follow Thai customs. *Khunying* Sin Suphansombat (born c. 1890), a former student of Sunanthalai School from 1894 to 1900, recorded that the missionaries who taught at Sunanthalai had to adjust themselves to Thai practices such as prostrating themselves and learning royal greetings, which was not the case at the Wang Lang School, which was more Western and where foreign teachers did not have to follow these customs (Anonymous, 2010, p. 29). This was one of the distinct qualities of Sunanthalai Girls' School as promoted by Queen Saowapha. The queen wanted to make Sunanthalai a model for other girls' schools in Siam: it was not only to introduce the modern idea of literate and educated women but was also to imbue them with a sense of traditional Thai hierarchy. As a result, she accepted the proposal from the General Secretary of the Education Department, Prince Kittiyakon-Waralak, to start a training course for potential female teachers in 1896. Six students of Sunanthalai School were enrolled in the teacher training course and their tuition and all expenses were fully sponsored by the queen. Mrs Robertson, the headmistress of the school at the time, had agreed to train the six teacher trainees in that year (Sunanthalai Girls' School, 1895–1902, p. 43).

Another approach taken by Queen Saowapha took in developing the school was to concentrate on and formalise the teaching of (royal) domestic skills (housekeeping, cooking and knitting) as well as the teaching of academic subjects. Sunanthalai's innovative curriculum was designed to combine both academic and domestic training, and included reading, writing, mathematics, geography, and domestic learning of arts and crafts (Yupphaphon, 1987). Victorian period influences were also seen in the school in accordance with their general promotion within the inner court. Princess Chongchitthanom (2007) reported that each student had to take turns to have lunch with '*khru maem*' (female missionary teachers) in order to learn proper Western table manners. In the afternoon, they also played cricket, tennis, and croquet. All of these sports were commonly played within the inner court and were considered to be sports of the Victorian aristocrats (Chongchitthanom, 2007).

The Queen used this innovative hybridised aspect of Sunanthalai School to highlight its benefits in resisting the education commissioner's proposal to close the school in 1902 (Sunanthalai Girls' School, 1895–1902). Nevertheless, the school was temporarily closed for financial reasons as in this particular year, the number of students declined to 17 from the 110 students who had been enrolled in 1894 (Yupphaphon, 1987, p. 25). The queen judged that the major problems of the school were related to the curriculum, which she considered too occidental for Siamese students (Anonymous, 2010, p. 32). As a consequence, Saowapha invited the Japanese educator Miss Yasui Tetsu (1870–1945) and her assistants, Miss Nakajima Tomiko and Miss Kono Kiyoko, to teach at the newly founded Rajini Girls' School that replaced Sunanthalai in 1903 (Anonymous, 2010, p. 40). In the same year, four palace women (*nang nai*), Khajon, Pit, Nuan, and Li, also received scholarships to go to Japan for domestic training (*wicha kan-ruean*). Queen Saowapha claimed in her reply to the commissioner that she had hoped that the newly hired Japanese teachers would include specialised domestic skills in their teaching, which would suit Siamese elite women more than the Western curriculum that focused mainly on the study of western etiquette and English language previously used (Anonymous, 2010, p. 40). Additionally, the employment of Japanese teachers was also a strategy to reduce the influence of Western missionaries on the cultivation of a modern Siamese mind. Whatever its ultimate merits, this conscious turning away from a 'Western' to an 'Eastern' curriculum was a strikingly forward-thinking attempt to make female education more appropriate to a Siamese setting, and which differentiated Sunanthalai Girls' School from the Christian missionary schools, such as the Kunlasatri Wang Lang.

Queen Saowapha's other contribution to the success of an aristocratic orientally-oriented girl's school was the use of her name; being sponsored by the Queen distinguished the institution from others. When the government's plan to build Rajini School in order to replace Sunanthalai, which had fallen into decline due to lack of interest and funds from the government as mentioned earlier, was approved, the queen agreed once more to be its main sponsor and the Ministry of Public Instruction granted it the title of *Rajini*, meaning 'Queen'. When compared to Wang Lang School, which effectively was its main competitor, Queen Saowapha's sponsorship provided a greater degree of confidence for parents to send their children to study at Rajini School. Moreover, under the queen's name, the school was able to raise funds from non-governmental sources for the further expansion of its facilities. Traditionally, Thai monarchs believed in building temples as a way to achieve merit, but Saowapha believed that sponsoring schools for girls was a modern way of doing so that would also enhance the status of women in Siamese society (Yupphaphon, 1987). Once again, Rajini School, in promoting its connection with the queen to exclusively recruit students of the aristocratic class, illustrated the efforts being made by elite women such as Queen Saowapha to ensure that modernity was firmly controlled by the traditional elite.

The consequential bifurcation of the elite

Both Sunanthalai and Wang Lang had opened up opportunities for women to acquire an education, but they also served as a prism of social fragmentation between old and new female elites. A recent study on the history of Thai education by Arwut Teeraeak (2014) suggests that there has always been a thin barrier in the access to receiving English lesson based on the western model in Siam, where it was reserved solely for potential government employees and those who could afford the tuition fee (Arwut, 2014). Accepting this assertion, I argue that the bifurcation of female education constituted a potent starting point for the class conflict, which consequently played out between the aristocratic and non-aristocratic elite and served as a basis for gradual development of the revolution in 1932. In the first decades of the twentieth century prior to the revolution of 1932, Rajini School constituted an extension not just of the inner palace but also of the new 'inner city', as its graduates made their presence known outside the palace walls. In contrast, but in a similar way, the Wang Lang School's openness to non-aristocratic, though well-to-do Bangkokian children, contributed to an extension of another 'inner city' made up of literate women, who attained their own distinct voice in the interwar period.

The decline of the aristocratic elites

The revolution in June 1932 is considered the most significant political and social transformation in Thai history, but only limited academic study has emphasised its impact on elite aristocratic women. As the reign of King Chulalongkorn ended upon his death in 1910, the roles of palace women began to decline in the reign of King Vajiravudh (Rama VI), his successor. The abolition of the inner court with the decline of the number of palace women, as a result of King Vajiravudh's opposition to polygamy, opened the way for female education to develop outside the boundaries of the palace, and this further stimulated the emergence of new non-aristocratic elite women in Siam. The former consorts and daughters of King Chulalongkorn and their retinues moved to their new residences in Suan Sunantha Palace in 1919, where they maintained their values and court etiquette even without King Vajiravudh's interest or attention. One of them, Princess Niphanopphadon (1885–1935), a former alumna of Sunanthalai School, turned to promoting female education herself by founding Niphakhan School within Suan Sunantha Palace to teach domestic skills to the younger generation of palace women in 1924 (Charuphan, 2007, p 38). Nevertheless, the space of elite women in Suan Sunantha including Niphakhan School could not survive the revolution that overthrew the absolute monarchy of King Prajadhipok in 1932. Some residences were turned into government offices after the revolution and the Niphakhan School was discontinued (Charuphan, 2007). The revolution not only impacted another royal sponsored girls' school, but also the lives of the women of Suan Sunantha Palace.

The People's Party's takeover of Suan Sunantha forced palace women to look for a new place to live. Princess Phunphitsamai Diskul (1895–1990) fled Siam after the revolution. The princess was one of the three daughters of Prince Damrong and *Mom* Chueai. She and her sister Chongchitthanom were both enrolled in Sunanthalai School. After years of exile in Penang, the princess and her family finally returned to Bangkok in 1942 during Field Marshal Phibun's regime and the period of his promotion of the Cultural Mandates[1]. Princess Phunphitsamai criticised heavily the new public norms that Phibun introduced by recording that 'we have witnessed the decay of Thai society by the ridiculous mimicking of Westerners [*farang*] amongst Thais...' (Phunphitsamai, 2003, p 226). Phunphitsamai further demonstrated her resistance to Phibun's leadership when she stated that his Cultural Mandates were confusing and impractical, such as the new dress code for women to wear only fitted skirts, which was extremely difficult for rural women to follow as they had to perform labour work in the fields (Phunphitsamai, 2003, p 220). These sentiments hint at a very real socially-based clash between the former aristocratic women and the post-revolutionary government. Unlike their pre-modern counterparts, they were literate and assertive, and able to articulate their opposition: the women were the product of a modern, albeit traditionally-oriented, education.

The rise of non-aristocratic elite women of *Kunlasatri Wang Lang*

A number of middle-class girls from non-aristocratic families who were enrolled in the previous Wang Lang School became politically active women in the post-revolutionary years. Tat Prathipasen was an alumna, having joined the school in the first years after its establishment. She became a spokesperson for the emerging community of middle-class Thai women by joining the first formal Association of Thai Women, founded in 1934. Roem Chanthaphimpha (born 1909) and Jirawat Phibunsongkhram (born 1921) were both active non-aristocratic elite women in the post-absolutist era. Roem was born in the province of Khon Kaen in 1909, and her father was a public prosecutor of that province. When she reached seven years old, Roem was sent to Bangkok to enrol at the newly established Watthana Witthaya School She finished her studies in 1928 and became a regular short-story writer for the newspaper *Prachamit*. In fact, Roem began to write from the time she was a student at Watthana, with her involvement in the eponymous *Watthana Magazine*. Her school years at Watthana greatly facilitated Roem's ability to become one of the most influential female writers in the post-absolutist era. Her works as a writer often reflect the social problems which were prevalent after the Second World War, such as economic problems, smuggling, and political corruption. Roem demonstrated a remarkable level of confidence and daring in writing these articles, which were controversial subject matter for women writers at that time. Another former student of the Watthana School who became a new voice representing Thailand's literate women was Jirawat Phibunsongkhram, daughter of Field Marshal Phibun, who was Prime Minister from 1938 to 1944 and again from 1948 to 1957, and his wife La-iad Phibunsongkhram. Throughout her childhood, she witnessed the political careers of her parents and became one of the prominent members of the Female Cultural Committee found in 1942 (Thai Post, 2005). Her task was to assist La-iad Phibunsongkhram, the chair of the committee, in reforming the cultural roles for women in accordance with the Cultural Mandates issued between 1939 and 1942. Both schools had contributed to the rise of literate women from aristocratic and non-aristocratic backgrounds in Bangkok society; and the differences between both schools had stimulated the sort of contested discourse found amongst women in the period of political change.

Conclusion

The reforms in the administration of the inner court under King Chulalongkorn examined in this chapter equipped many royal elite women with skills and a level of education never previously enjoyed by Siamese women. As a result, the aristocratic women within the royal palace, led by Queen Saowapha, were pioneers of public education for girls in the late nineteenth century. Nevertheless, the queen did not obtain the approval of King Chulalongkorn, who opposed the idea of female education until 1892. With the delay, a public girls' school was finally founded on the initiative of Queen Saowapha but it immediately faced competition from the already established missionary girls' school. The Thai-*farang* (Western) rivalry had a major impact on Siamese women. This bifurcation of elite quality women's education expanded the opportunity for women to access education on a wider social scale. When literacy was reserved only for aristocratic women within the inner court, the missionary school provided a chance for non-aristocratic women – including women of the merchant classes – to learn how to read and write. This eventually led to competition between Thai aristocratic women and the newly emerged non-aristocratic elite women in the field of education by the early twentieth century. The function of the term 'elite woman' (*ying phudi*) was then redefined with a modern connotation that includes both types of women whose elite status was determined by birth or by education. The non-aristocratic elites who earned their skills from private institutions emerged into the public sphere as writers in the interwar period. Access to education allowed these non-elite women to enhance their social status and they began to compete against the aristocratic elite women in the pre-, and immediately post-, revolutionary years of the late 1920s and 1930s.

Note

1 Phibun introduced the following twelve Cultural Mandates between 1939 and 1942: (i) Mandate on *the name of the country, people and nationality*, issued 24 June 1939; (ii) Mandate on *preventing danger to the nation*, issued 3 July 1939; (iii) Mandate on *referring to the Thai people*, issued 2 August 1939; (iv) Mandate on *honouring the national flag, national anthem, and royal anthem*, issued 8 September 1939; (v) Mandate on *using Thai products*, issued 1 November 1939; (vi) Mandate on *the music and lyrics of the national anthem*, issued 10 December 1939; (vii) Mandate on *urging the Thai people help build the nation*, issued on 21 March 1940; (viii) Mandate on *the royal anthem*, issued on 26 April 1940; (ix) Mandate on *language and writing and the duty of good citizens*, issued 24 June 1940; (x) Mandate on *Thai dress*, issued 15 January 1941; (xi) Mandate on *daily activities*, issued 8 September 1941; (xii) Mandate on *protecting children, the elderly and the handicapped*, issued 28 January 1942.

References

Andaya, B. 2006. *The Flaming Womb: Repositioning Women in Early Modern Southeast Asia*. Honolulu: University of Hawai'i Press.

Anonymous. 2010. *Phikunkaew, 105th Anniversary of Rachini School and 80th Anniversary of Rachini-bon School* [*phikun-kaew: 105 pi rachini 80 pi rachini-bon*]. Bangkok: Ammarin Printing and Publishing.

Arwut, T. 2014. *The Siamese State's Management of the English Language Education in the Reign of King Chulalongkorn* [*kan chatkan kan-sueksa phasa angkrit khong rat-sayam nai samai somdetphra Chunlachomklaochaoyuhua*]. PhD thesis. Chulalongkorn University.

Barmé, S. 2002. *Woman, man, Bangkok: Love, sex, and popular culture in Thailand*. Lanham: Rowman & Littlefield.

Copeland, M. 1993. *Contested Nationalism and the 1932 Overthrow of the Absolutist Monarchy in Siam*. PhD thesis. The Australian National University.

Charuphan, D. 2007. *The Influence of the Western Accoutrements on the Elite Women's fashion of Suan Sunantha* [*itthiphon khong khrueang-taengkai tawantok thi mi to kan-taengkai khong chaonai fai nai wang suan sunantha*]. Research Report. Available from ThaiLIS Thai Academic Reference Database.

Chongchitthanom, D. 2007. *The Memoir* [*banthuek khwam songcham*]. Bangkok: Samnakphim Siam.

Dutsadi, S. 1993. *The Royal Cremation of Colonel Pha-op Posakritsana* [*anuson nai kan phraratchathan ploengsob phantri-ying khunying Pha-op Posakritsana*]. Bangkok: Ammarin Printing and Publishing.

Ikeya, C. 2011. *Refiguring Women, Colonialism, and Modernity in Burma*. Honolulu: University of Hawai'i Press.

Leonowens, A. 1870. *The English Governess at the Siamese Court: Being Recollections of Six Years in the Royal Palace at Bangkok*. Boston, MA: J. R. Osgood.

Loos, T. 2005. 'Sex in the Inner City: The Fidelity between Sex and Politics in Siam'. *The Journal of Asian Studies*, 64(4), pp. 881–909.

Phitsanu, A. 2004. *Wang Lang – For the Honour and Dignity of Women: Pride of Kunlasattri Wang Lang School-Watthana Academy* [*Wang Lang – Watthana pheua kiat lae saksi khong sattri: kham phakphumchai kunlasattri wang lang-watthana witthayalai*]. Bangkok: Watthana Academy.

Phunphitsamai, D. 1990. *Things I have seen: In the royal cremation of Princess Phunphitsamai Diskul* [*sing thi khaphachao phop hen: nai ngan phraratchathan phloeng sop momchao Phunphitsamai Diskul*]. Bangkok: Watcharin Press.
Phunphitsamai, D. 2003. *Things I have seen: the ending* [*sing thi khaphachao phop hen: phak chop*]. Bangkok: Matichon.
Ratchabandittayasathan. 1999. *Dictionary* [*photchananukrom chabap-ratchabandittayasathan*]. Bangkok: Ratchabandittayasathan.
Samakhom-sitwanglang-watthana samai pi 2005–2006. 2005. *In Commemoration of Miss Edna S. Cole: 150 Years of Watthana Academy's Founder, 2005–2006* [*ramluek phrakhun Miss Edna S. Cole 150 pi phukotang watthana witthayalai*]. Bangkok: Dan-sutthakanphim.
Sukanya, J. 2005. *An Analysis of Thai Educational System from Literatures during the Early Time of Rattanakosin in the Reign of King Rama 1–3* [*wikro rabop kan-sueksa thai chak wannakadi samai ratthanakosin ton ton nai samai ratchakan thi 1- ratchakan thi 3*]. Unpublished M.Ed. thesis. Graduate School, Srinakharinwirot University, Thailand.
Sunanthalai Girls' School [*rongrian-sattri Sunanthalai*]. 1895–1902. [manuscript] Education of Rama V. M R. 5 S/17. Bangkok: National Archives of Thailand.
Thai Post. 2005. Heiress of General Phibun: Jirawat Panyarachun [*thayat chomphon po Jirawat Panyarachun*]. [online] 28 June 2009. Available at: www.thaipost.net/node/6921. Accessed 17 December 2012.
Waruni, O. 1981. *Education in Thai Society 1868–1932* [*kan sueksa nai sangkhom thai 2411–1932*]. Unpublished MA thesis. Graduate School, Chulalongkorn University, Thailand.
Wyatt, D. 1969. *The politics of reform in Thailand: Education in the reign of King Chulalongkorn*. New Haven, CT: Yale University Press.
Yupphaphon, C. 1987. *Education of Thai Women: Case Study of Rachini School 1901–1960* [*kan sueksa khong sattri thai: korani sueksa rong-rien rachini 2444–2503*]. Unpublished MA thesis, Bangkok: Thammasat University.

4 Thailand's Early Adult Education in Textbooks

Inclusion, Exclusion and Literacy, 1940–1944[1]

Wasitthee Chaiyakan

THAMMASAT UNIVERSITY

Introduction (1940–44)

After becoming Prime Minister in December 1938, Luang Phibunsongkram (Phibun hereafter) was in the ideal position to realise the principles of the *khana ratsadon* (The People's Party, or the 'promoters'), the select group of which he was a member and which had overthrown the absolute monarchy in June 1932. The sixth principle (of the six which constituted the objectives of the new Government) was to educate the country's citizens, and he set about intensively promoting education from very early in his tenure. This determination was reflected in an article in *Nangsuephim suphapsatri* (The Ladies' Newspaper), in a special edition to promote the Government's literacy campaign, published on 24 June 1943. Phibun's column was entitled; 'Studying literacy is the building of the pillars holding up our great Thai nation' (*Kan lao rian khian an, pen kan sang sao ruean hai kae chat thai*). Phibun wrote that 'those who do not study, cannot read and write, are considered incompetent [and] incapable of becoming the good citizens of the Thai nation …' At the end of his three-page article he stressed in his conclusion that '… Thai brothers and sisters, from every gender and age, have to repay our nation by quickly studying and becoming literate' (Phibunsongkram, 1943). This literacy drive was aimed at creating citizens who would be more effective at implementing their leaders' vision for their state.

Since quick results were required, the state naturally turned towards the country's adult population, which was largely a barely literate peasantry. The concept of adult education was therefore created, with the main objective being to encourage adults to learn the Thai language. Additionally, the Phibun Government also tried to shape people's attitudes and perceptions through the use of select content in the textbooks. This was the first time a Thai government had felt the need to directly indoctrinate adults through textbooks. The adult population to be targeted naturally consisted of those within Thailand proper but also in areas populated by non-Thai speaking people. The world's descent into war, particularly Japanese expansion, had afforded the Thai nationalist government an opportunity to restore its 'lost territories' allegedly lost to colonial powers in the nineteenth and early twentieth centuries. With France occupied, Thailand was able to secure parts of French Indochina (Laos and Western Cambodia) in May 1941 following their brief war with France; parts of the Shan States in August 1943, following the British collapse in Burma over 1942, and the four northernmost Malay states, transferred from the Japanese to Thailand in October 1943 (Reynolds, 1994; Office of the Secretary to the Prime Minister, 10 February 1941–27 July 1944).

Phibun and the formation of adult education

The faction of the *khana ratsadon* which had taken over in 1938 decided to mimic Italy and Germany – with their extraordinary executive institutions of *Duce* and *Führer*, respectively – and upgrade the position of Prime Minister to Leader. In practice, the Leader became the source of legislation and the executive, unilaterally able to make commands and change policy. In part, Phibun was able to be Leader because he happened to hold the position of Army Commander from January 1938 until August 1944. He additionally served as Supreme Commander of the Military and Police (Head of the Joint Chiefs of Staff) from November 1940 to April 1941. In the early 1940s, the young king, Ananda Mahidol or Rama VIII (r. 1935–1946), was also absent from the country, so no other leader-figure was available for a nationalistic political strategy.

A sense of Thai nationhood had been encouraged by King Vajiravudh (Rama VI, r. 1910–1926), but the nationalism now espoused by the Government was more confident, ambitious and aggressive. People who passed through the state education system would most likely identify with the state and implicitly follow the same aims, which were to obey the Leader, be a good citizen, and love the nation. This model of education could be seen in Mussolini's Fascist Italy, and Hitler's Nazi Germany (Welch, 1993, pp. 1–15; Yourman, 1939, pp. 148–163). The education systems of these states were often described in *Withayachan* (Journal of Teachers' Professional Development) from 1938 until the late 1940s. Most articles expressed their admiration for the education and training systems in those countries (Kanphai, 1939; Phongsathat, 1938; Chanthanapho, 1938). It is not clear how the information for the complex and lengthy articles was acquired, but they certainly would have served as the basis for policy formulation.

Unfortunately, it remained unclear what proportion of the population was able to read and write Thai. There are indications that practicable literacy rates were low, from the level of concern the Government displayed. A government resolution of 10 February 1938 decreed that every government employee must become fluent and literate in Thai by the end of 1943 (Office of the Secretary to the Prime Minister, 8 October 1940–29 January 1945). This announcement indicated that the Government was facing a significant challenge to its literacy drive, because not even their own administrators could write. The Government had to start forcing this group to acquire literacy skills before moving to the general population. Phibun's Government sought to achieve this with the issuance of *Rathaniyom chabap kao* (The Ninth State Convention) on 24 June 1939. The State Conventions or *Rathaniyom* were a series of twelve, launched under the Phibun Government from 1939 to 1942. They were one manifestation of the Leaders' new powers to order social change. The Ninth State Convention concerned language. The State Convention stated that Thai citizens must respect and venerate the Thai language. They must consider it a great honour to speak Thai, regardless of their different birth strata, their homeland, or their variable Thai accents. Accordingly, citizens were to conceptualise themselves as Thais whose speech, habit and clothing must also be Thai (Sukhumnaipradit, 1940). The policy of requiring clerics and officers to be fully literate in Thai was later imposed on the population in the newly acquired lands, which indicated that the annexations had brought new administrators into the system (Office of the Secretary to the Prime Minister, 10 February 1941–27 July 1944). It was with this in mind that the Thai Government decided to place a strong emphasis on the development of adult education in 1940, the main purpose of which was 'to offer education by the state in order to educate illiterate adults, making them literate and capable of complying with their civic duties'[2]. Subsequently, the Government established the Adult Education Department under the Office of the Permanent Secretary to the Minister of Public Instruction on 6 August 1940 (Office of the Secretary to the Prime Minister, 1940).

There were three main curricula for adult education: primary level, higher level and a special programme. The primary school and high school curricula were for native Thai- speaking adults. However, a separate programme was required for people in the provinces who mainly spoke non-Thai languages. The Ministry of Public Instruction launched a 'special education curriculum for adults' on 7 August 1941. This curriculum aimed at teaching people to speak Thai in the non-Thai speaking areas, such as the newly conquered areas in French Indochina, the northern part of Thailand in Mae Hong Son, north-eastern areas in Surin and Burirum (close to Cambodia), and the southernmost part of Thailand in Patani, Yala, Narathiwat, and Satun. Local people in these areas had not usually spoken Thai, and these areas tended to be on the vulnerable periphery of Thailand's borders, so it was important for the Government to target these people. In the Government's view, the distinct dialects of the people of the North, Northeast, and South were not dialects, but central Thai spoken with a different accent, which the Government considered accented variations of the central Thai language. This is because, they reasoned, people in those areas understood Thai. Thus, they did not have to use the same special curriculum as in the geographical areas mentioned above. The special curriculum, moreover, applied in the areas which were only approved by the Ministry of Public Instruction (Office of the Secretary to the Prime Minister, 17 April 1941–10 March 1942).

Reforming the Thai language

Alongside its drive to increase literacy, the Phibun Government also launched a campaign for 'Reforming the Thai language' in May 1942 (Ivarsson, 2007, pp. 193–194). Before the implementation of this reform in Thailand, this process had already taken place in Turkey in 1928 in order to make the Turkish language less Arabic and Persian, change the alphabet and simplify the language (Lewis, 1999) There are no sources demonstrating that the Thai Government acquired this model specifically from or were influenced by Turkey. The Turkish reform was probably the most radical and internationally well-known, and its allegedly nation-transforming success may have served as the most obvious inspiration. Phibun's Government certainly saw the advantages in simplifying the language:

> 'Thai language is an essential indicator of our nationality. The sovereignty is also indicated by language. The creation of our nation would be successful by having the language as a vital medium. If we do not support the use of our language, the language as well as the identity of Thai nation shall miserably perish.'
>
> (Petchlert-anan, 2006)

The Phibun Government tied the importance of language to independence and nation-building, and aimed at uniting people by using the Thai language. However, many studies of Thai language reform are mainly focused on the technicalities of the language changes themselves and not on the wider reasons – and, more importantly, the linkages with other aspects of national policy (Laksanasiri, June 1997–May 1998, pp. 5–21; Hudak, 1986). Phibun is usually criticised for attempting the reforms and the temporarily disastrous consequences for the Thai language (1942–1944). The Phibun Government established the Committee for the Promotion of Thai Language Culture (*Khanakammakan songseum wathanatham phasa thai*), a special committee for reforming and promoting the reformed Thai language across Thailand. The committee reduced the letters in the Thai alphabet from 44 to 31, and changed the spelling of words which had been faithful to their original Sanskrit or Pali roots by writing the words closer to the way they were pronounced, such as *ratsadon* (people) spelling of ราษฎร (literally *ras-dr*) became ราดสะดอน (literally *rat-sa-don*). Thamrongsak Petchlert-anan has argued that these changes made learning the language easier and increased the rate of literacy (Petchlert-anan, 2006, p. 300). The number of repetitions in the alphabet – *s, th, ph*, for example – and vowels were cut. During the war period, Phibun stated that the Thai language reform had helped Thai people to learn Thai. Nithi Eoseewong has argued that this simplification made people more socially equal in the country, because the social hierarchy in the former language had been removed. Royal words were no longer used for the royal family to show that they were different from commoners. For example, '*prasuti*' which is the royal word for 'to be born' was abolished, and all people used the same word, '*koet*' (Eoseewong, October 1984–March 1985).

Textbooks published after 1942 had to use the simplified version of the language. Because the annexation of parts of the Shan States and the four northern Malay states occurred in 1942, these areas were only ever issued with textbooks which used the reformed spelling. The Indochinese areas however, were incorporated before the reforms and ended up using a mixture of reformed and old spelling textbooks. Additionally, the lack of paper in the country forced printers to use poor quality paper to produce the textbooks. This is the reason why textbooks in the reformed language in the 1940s are incredibly difficult to find intact. Thus, the possibility for an analysis of the impact of the reform on textbooks specifically is limited.

Analysing adult textbooks in the early 1940s

Adult textbooks were a special case. Although there had already been some adult education initiatives in the late nineteenth century which were focused on literacy, no standardised curriculums or textbooks for adult education had been produced. There were no specially designed textbooks ready for the early stages of the campaign in 1940. The Ministry of Education had used the curriculum and textbooks for primary school students in an earlier adult experimental class. An official curriculum for adult education was launched on 13 January 1941, with the development of adult education textbooks specifically for adults having been begun (Sitthisurasak et al, 1990, p. 25). The main purpose of the early stage of adult education was to educate people to a basic level equivalent to *prathom* two, an early primary school level. During the period required to compile textbooks for adults, children's school textbooks were used for teaching adults. The teaching methods used were also the same as those used for teaching primary school children (Kriang Kiratikon, in Sitthisurasak, 1951, p. 38). This emphasises the extent of the Thai Government's determination and the sense of urgency to set up the adult education system for adults as quickly as possible, even though they lacked the materials.

The contemporary problems facing adult education can be seen in an interview conducted with Plueang Na-nakhon. He was a former adult education department officer from the 1940s, who explained the differences at the time between the method required for teaching adults and children. (Sitthisurasak et al., 1990, pp. 40–41). For instance, regarding the teaching method for children's spelling, the process was a gradual accumulative one, starting with the more basic words, and building up to the more complicated words. However, those in charge of adult education were reluctant to use the same method. This is because the Government wanted to educate people to a standard that would enable them to read and write properly within one year. Teachers felt that the children's method was too slow. Thus, producing textbooks especially for adults became a crucial issue, according to Plueang

Na-nakhon, one of the authors of the early textbooks (Sitthisurasak et al., 1990, pp. 40–41).

The Adult Education Division compiled textbooks for adults by copying a British-authored English language learning book called the *Basic Textbook*. The original version of Basic Textbook could not be found. However, Plueang explained that the Basic Textbook was apparently being used to teach foreign soldiers and civilians living in Great Britain during the Second World War. During the war a number of nationalities had congregated in Britain, mostly to join the war effort, or as prisoners of war, and it was important to teach English to them for communication purposes. This book was probably what would now be called a phrasebook. From this basic template, therefore, phrasebook-type textbooks were quickly compiled and published. Specific words and phrases used in daily life as well as war-related vocabulary were selected on the grounds that they were most relevant, and would more likely be considered useful by the readers. Meanwhile, children were still being taught the vowels and consonants in the original way (Plueang Na-nakhon, cited in: Sitthisurasak et al., 1990, pp. 40–41).

Each section, designed as one lesson, consisted of story-like descriptions of idealised daily life situations and their requirements, such as recognising the spelling of your own name, surname, address, the names of rulers, abbots, and the life of a farmer. The result of these deliberations between authors and the Division was the series called *Nangsue hat an khong phuyai phak ton* (Reading skills practice book for adults, first part) in four volumes, published in 1941 (Plueang Na-nakhon, cited in: Sitthisurasak et al., 1990, pp. 40–41). However, unfortunately, only the first two volumes have been recovered. Plueang Na-nakhon stated in an interview after the war that it was difficult to explain the reason for choosing the exact topic for adults to memorise words and phrases. He claimed that there was no research done before writing the textbooks and no curriculum within which they had to work. Plueang and his fellow authors, he claimed, had only chosen topics they felt that adults would have experienced in their daily life. The explanation is unlikely and perhaps reflects a reluctance to talk about a role in a political movement which has since been discredited.

Because the objective of adult education was to teach the Thai people to learn the Thai language as quickly as they could, readers were reminded of the links between their learning and the wider goals of the national community (Office of the Secretary to the Prime Minister, 26 April 1939–12 March 1949). The first page of every adult textbook before the beginning of the first chapter showed a message stating that one of the civic duties for Thai people was to study the Thai language, which was the national language. At a basic level, people should at least be able to read and write. This message was from *Rathaniyom chabap kao* (The Ninth State Convention) which also appeared in full on the back cover of every adult education textbook (Adult Education Division, Ministry of Education, 1941a).

After 1942, the spelling in textbooks had to follow the new rules. Chapters five and ten of volume two of *Nangsue hat an khong phuyai phak ton* explained the importance of knowing the Thai language at great length. Chapter five explained that studying is one of the duties of the good citizen (Adult Education Division, Ministry of Education, 1941b, pp. 9–10). Similarly, chapter ten described the benefits of knowing Thai, since it would allow the people to communicate with the government office in a more convenient manner without having to hire another person to write for them (Adult Education Division, Ministry of Education, 1941b, pp. 23–24). The practical and civic benefits and the important reasons and motivations for learning the Thai language were explicitly stated in adult textbooks. There was no attempt at subtlety.

The cultivation of the nation-state-based assimilation in adult textbooks

As noted earlier, content went beyond merely teaching literacy. Adult textbooks were used to teach people to become Thai, and such ideas were espoused in textbooks sent from the Adult Education Division. The strategy in the textbooks was to use a mixture of what were considered to be the stock components of nation-state-based assimilation. These components were race and culture, maps, a historical narrative regarding a great king, and national values exemplified by the *Rathaniyom*. Each example will now be examined in turn.

Race and culture

Chapter three of volume one of *Nangsue hat an khong phuyai phak ton* entitled '*khon thai*' (Thai people) reveals that in practice the idea of the Thai race was significantly compromised and perhaps never even attempted. For example this reading practice section simply recorded:

> 'We are Thais
> We were born in Thailand
> Thailand is our homeland
> I love my Country Thailand
> You will love my Country Thailand
> We all love our Country Thailand
> We dedicate our love to our Homeland.'
> (Adult Education Division, Ministry of Education, 1941a, p. 3)

The message is implied but is clear. If you are born within the frontiers of the Thai state, you are Thai. It is your duty to love your country, in practice to learn the language, and to identify with the Thai state. Unlike racial discourse in Germany and elsewhere, Thai nationalism was remarkably inclusive. Crucially, this meant in practice that the idea regarding the Thai race in its purest form was reduced to a background role.

However, inclusion had its limits. Another race-related strategy to define being Thai was to describe the otherness of neighbouring nation-states while defining which of the neighbours could be included in the nation. This is expressed in volume two, *Nangsue hat an khong phuyai phak ton lem song*, describing the neighbouring countries of Thailand, but stating that the Lao and Khmer (Cambodian) were also of the Thai race. Chapter fourteen of this textbook comes closest to the original Pan-Tai ideas, although the influence of Japanese Pan-Asianism is also apparent as there is no hint of mutual hostility between the countries of the Golden Peninsula.

> 'This land is called the Laem Thong [Golden Peninsula].
> In this land, there are many countries; Thailand is the largest of all. Our neighbours are Burma in the West, Malay in the South and Vietnam in the East. Moreover, China and Japan are considered our neighbours, but they are far away from our region.
> In the East, our country has Laos and Cambodia as our neighbours.
> The people of Laos and Cambodia are the same race as us.
> These neighbours have their ways of life similar to ours. For an example, they are all Buddhists and share similar cultures and customs with us.
> Our neighbours are not sovereign nations except for China and Japan.
> Thailand, China, and Japan are sovereign nations.
> We are autonomous, and have no overlords.
> In the countries that are our neighbouring, the Thai race thrives everywhere.
> If we are capable of uniting the Thai race, we shall become one glorious nation.
> (Adult Education Division, Ministry of Education, 1941b, pp. 34–35)

The notion that Thailand was the largest country of the Golden Peninsula region gave the Thais a special leadership status. Chapter fourteen showed that the Thai were scattered throughout neighbouring areas, so gathering and including all Thai together in one state was an ongoing process which defined the *chat* Thai (Thai nation) as one of the world's great nations.

The other device for differentiation, national costume, was also used to emphasise the existence of complementary races, in this chapter, portraying neighbours such as the Burmese wearing Burman *Gaung Baung* (traditional Burmese turban) and sarongs; the Malay people wearing turbans and batik sarongs, the Vietnamese wearing *Nón lá* (palm-leaf conical hats) and fisherman pants; and the Cambodians wearing *sambot* (the Cambodian sarong) and *krama* (a traditional Cambodian garment) around his waist. Although not a neighbour, the Japanese were also depicted, showing a Japanese woman wearing a kimono. Remarkably, Thai people were depicted by a man in a suit and tie. The implication went beyond race, as Thais were defined for their modernity (or civilised status), in stark contrast to their neighbours, including, oddly the Japanese. *Rathaniyom* or State Convention issue ten, announced on 1 April 1941, had ordered Thais to adopt what was described as the 'international style of dress'. The depiction therefore conformed to the State Convention.

Maps and annexed areas

People's identification with Thai national belonging was reinforced by the visual image of Thai territory through the use of maps. Volume one of *Nangsue hat an khong phuyai phak ton* depicted pictures of classrooms with maps on the wall in chapter one on 'studying' (Adult Education Division, Ministry of Education, 1941a, p. 1) and chapter six on 'soldiers' (ibid., p. 7). The ideal classroom as pictured in the reading practice textbook contained a map. In contrast, other images depicted of classrooms for adults, as shown in newspapers during the 1940s, did not display maps on the wall. In all likelihood, maps were present, but were excluded from the pictures. There was also the possibility that the ongoing war might have affected the production of maps, causing a shortage, thereby making supply to all schools difficult and possibly expensive.

A map of Thailand, as of 1941, including the newly annexed areas, appeared in chapter seven on 'career and work' and chapter nine on 'Thailand' of volume one of *Nangsue hat an khong phuyai phak ton* (Adult Education Division, Ministry of Education, 1941a, pp. 9–12). This marked the first time that the newly occupied areas comprising Phibunsongkhram, Phratabong, Champasak and Lan Chang provinces were portrayed as a part of Thailand in a textbook (Adult Education Division, Ministry of Education, 1941a, map 1). The fact that the shape of the country appeared multiple times in the textbook demonstrates the real purpose of the map, as argued by Thongchai Winichakul (1994), to create an easily recognisable form with which the viewer's identity was closely connected. While there were maps for serious geographical orientation, there were also maps for identity differentiation. It was the latter kind that was to the fore in these textbooks. However, there was no map of Thailand that included Saharat Thai Doem and Si Rat Malai in this textbook series. Due to the short occupation, these areas were not depicted in textbooks. Official maps of the country including these areas, as of 1943, are rare.

In contrast, although vital in winning public support for the invasion and occupation of the neighbouring areas in central Thailand, the 'lost territories' narrative was not mentioned at all in adult textbooks. This does not eliminate the possibility that the subject was raised by teachers. Moreover, maps and the section on King Ramkhamhaeng (see below) hint at the concept. However, it cannot be said to have been an important assimilation strategy. Authors probably realised that telling local people in newly conquered areas that they once belonged to the Thai state, where there was no popular 'memory' of such a situation (sometimes because it had never been the case), was pointless, and might even have made the other claims of the Thai authorities seem unconvincing. This clearly differs from children's textbooks in Thailand proper, which went on explicitly teaching the concept of 'lost territories'.

Historical narrative regarding a great king

In order to impress the greatness of the Thai race and of Thai territorial extent upon the readership, the authors made sure to include a brief historical narrative to serve as a shared historical narrative. Chapter two of the second volume of *Nangsue hat an khong phuyai phak ton* entitled 'Important People of the Nation' consisted of a ten-line summary of 'Thai history'. This was conveniently restricted to a description of Sukhothai:

> '600 years ago, the Thai capital was Sukhothai.
> Khun Ramkhamhaeng was King.
> He was a skilful and brave king.
> He fought with the enemy and was victorious, acquiring wide territory.
> At that time, Thailand was much larger than its present state.
> But all those years ago, there was no Thai alphabet.
> He was the one who invented the Thai alphabet.
> He improved the people's livelihood.
> All the Thais were happy and content.'
> (Adult Education Division, Ministry of Education, 1941a, pp. 3–4)

This was the only section of the first two volumes dedicated to 'history'. The 'history' presented was extremely brief, as the emphasis was on reading for beginners. Therefore, a neat formula was required that combined a shared past, greatness, and purpose. King Ramkhamhaeng, (r. 1279–1298) was the most convenient and perhaps the most obvious choice. The Ramkhamhaeng inscription became the very origins of the Thai past. It was where Thai writing had begun[3]. In this modern version, this became a powerful foundational narrative to give a sense of historical and symbolic meaning to learning. Additionally, the king had greatly expanded the territories of the kingdom, just as the present Government was doing. His kingdom represented the true extent of the Thai territory, and suggested the ongoing mission to restore it to its former glory. The king also presided over improvements in living standards and peace, which were an implicit result of his wars of conquest. This indicated a model strategy for the present. King Ramkhamhaeng was thus turned into an older and historical parallel of the present regime. King Ramkhamhaeng had fought enemies too, and the end result had been peace and prosperity. This therefore nudged its readers to draw similar conclusions about contemporary political processes.

Although the other volumes have apparently not survived, it is likely that King Ramkhamhaeng was the only king, and very possibly the only 'history', mentioned in this series of adult textbooks. The reigns of the other three kings associated with territorial aggrandisement were King Naresuan and King

Taksin, and the Bangkok period kings, especially King Rama I, were heavily associated with wars with their neighbours, so history of the other kings had been avoided or played down in adult textbooks. Although King Ramkhamhaeng fought against his 'enemies', it was more than six hundred years ago and the enemies were not specified. It would be much harder to discuss the other, later, kings without mentioning their enemy by name. Although the much more detailed children's school textbooks explained that the Siamese kingdom in these later periods included many parts of Burma, Cambodia, and Laos, they primarily focused on King Ramkhamhaeng's relationship with foreign countries, traders, and the creation of the Thai alphabet. Thus, choosing King Ramkhamhaeng as the national hero of the Thai was potentially more acceptable for people.

National values defined: the *Rathaniyom*

The fourth component, the encapsulation of national values in the *Rathaniyom* or State Conventions. These twelve edicts, issued by the Thai Government between 1939 and 1942, were described in detail in textbooks in order for people to perform the behaviour and duties of good Thai citizenship. The State Conventions were neatly summarised in chapter eleven of volume two of *Nangsue hat an khong phuyai phak ton* for adults to read and memorise:

> '*Rathaniyom* demands us, the citizens, to call the nation and the population as Thailand, the Thai Nation and the Thais.
> *Rathaniyom* tells us to love our nation and defend it from any threat.
> *Rathaniyom* defines the unity of Thai blood, and states that the Thai language is the only language [for Thailand].
> *Rathaniyom* commands us to pay homage to our glorious national flag.
> *Rathaniyom* tells us the Thais to purchase and consume products produced in Thailand.
> *Rathaniyom* demands that all Thais should become literate.
> *Rathaniyom* advocates that every Thai must work in order to build a strong nation.
> *Rathaniyom* commands that every Thai must be properly dressed.
> The Thais must love their nation and respect the Thai language; they must convey other Thais to do so. If they wish their country to become glorious and progressive, all Thais must comply with *Rathaniyom*.'
> (Adult Education Division, Ministry of Education, 1941a, pp. 26–28)

The inclusion of *Rathaniyom* in a practice reading book for adults illustrates even more explicitly that textbooks were more interested in inculcating new identities than in literacy. They effectively served as tools for the government to communicate their orders to the people. The beginning of each sentence starting with the word '*Rathaniyom* defines/tells/demands/commands ...'

could be interpreted as 'The Government orders you to ...' However, this cannot be interpreted as a threat, as it was probably felt that such orders from authority would simply be followed, in line with traditional indigenous understandings of 'patron-client' relations. Instead, there was a certain amount of incentivising, as one would expect from the reciprocal nature of such relations. Good citizenship would benefit the nation (*chat*) as suggested in the last sentence of the chapter. The extent to which adults in these newly conquered areas understood and interpreted this message is difficult to fully and accurately evaluate as no record of their experiences exist.

A notable absence in adult textbooks: Buddhism

Although people in Cambodia, Laos, and Kengtung were mostly Theravada Buddhists, the Thai Government did not use this shared religion in preparing textbook contents for adults as part of the Pan-Tai-based assimilation project. There was some mention of Buddhism, but the textbooks did not go as far as emphasising that the Thai people should be Buddhists. Although it was strongly implied, primarily through the occasional references and pictures in these textbooks, that Buddhism was an important religion for the Thai, the authors never directly stated that the definition of Thais was through their Buddhist religion. Nor did textbooks offer an explicit or even simplified description of the Buddhist religion.

Looking more closely at the relationship between Thai citizenship and Buddhism, volume two of *Nangsue hat an khong phuyai phak ton* does emphasise the duties that define good citizenship. In particular, one of these duties was related to Buddhism: 'On Buddhist Holy Days, people go to the temple to make merit and study at the Temple'. But being active and getting an education were the qualities that 'good citizens of the nation' most needed to possess (Adult Education Division, Ministry of Education, 1941b, p. 10). Similarly, where volume two of *Nangsue hat an khong phuyai phak ton* offered details of the calendar system, it stated that people must work for six days and rest on the weekly holy day, meaning Sunday, every week but implying by the choice of words – *wan phra* – that this refers to the Buddhist weekly holy day (pp. 41–42). Moreover, volume one of chapter ten portrayed a picture of monks and people who are offering food to the monks on New Year's Day. This chapter also explicitly stated that making merit was one of the activities that adult students should do on New Year's Day (Adult Education Division, Ministry of Education, 1941a, p. 14). Although the implication was relatively strong, through the occasional mention and pictures in the textbooks that Buddhism was an important religion for the Thai, they never directly stated that the definition of a Thai is their Buddhist religion or offered an explicit, though simplified description of the religion.

The main and obvious reason for the absence of an explicit emphasis on Buddhism in textbooks was that the annexed territories included people from other religions. This was particularly the case in the largely Muslim Si Rat

Malai province. The Thai Government was certainly aware that the promotion of Buddhism as an integral component of Pan-Tai ideas would have worked against the overall assimilation process. However, the temptation to draw upon Buddhism as a common bond between people of the largely Buddhist annexed areas to the north must have been strong. This may partly explain the occasional reference to Buddhism. Buddhism provided an opportunity for assimilation, but made the Thai authorities vulnerable. This is because the Thai Government did not have a monopoly on Theravada Buddhism which went far beyond Thai borders.

Conclusion

The attempt by the Thai Government to shape the world view of its citizens was clearly visible and overt in the contents of adult textbooks which condensed the Government's message, particularly during wartime in the early 1940s. This might have been the result of political expediency, as the Thai Government would have wanted adults both inside and outside the country to support the Thai Government in annexing neighbouring areas. The Thai Government could not simply wait and apply a sophisticated hidden agenda in textbooks during this time – it was a time in which they were rapidly attempting to take control of other areas. Therefore, adult textbooks in the 1940s served the Thai Government usefully. Subsequently, the study of these textbooks provides useful insight into the workings of the Thai political machinery during a period of wartime tumult and the redrawing of the territorial boundaries; enables an understanding of the interaction of education, power and ideology; and presents an analysis of how social and national identification are not simply formed as static products from a single political agenda but instead have multiple dynamic influences from religion, kingship, and local politics and histories. However, it is difficult to judge whether the Thai nationalistic propaganda via adult education would have been more successful over the longer run. Although the governments' records showed that the number of literate people increased significantly, other sources have not yet materialised to vouch for this alleged success of the adult education programme during the 1940s. However, despite these failings, adult education was first initiated by the regime of Phibun and its existence today in Thailand serves as a reminder of the remarkable contribution Phibun made to Thailand's development.

Notes

1 This chapter is based on research undertaken for a PhD dissertation submitted to SOAS, University of London, in 2018.
2 The Government formed a committee for this purpose. Prominent Promoter, statesman and educator, Pridi Phanomyong, then Minister of Finance, and from December 1941, Regent, and Wichit Wathakan, poet and pioneer nationalist, at the time Director General of the Department of Fine Arts and from 1942, Minister of Foreign Affairs, were also members of this committee, but it was dismantled in

February 1939. (Office of the Secretary to the Prime Minister (2) S R. 0201.24.5/1 Committees and Subcommittees for Adult Education).
3 The Ramkhamhaeng stele is a controversial topic. See more in Terwiel, 2010; Vickery, 1995; Krairiksh, 1989.

References

Adult Education Division, Ministry of Education. 1941a. *Nangsue hat an khong phuyai phak thon lem nueng* [Reading skills practice book for adults, first part, vol. one]. Bangkok: Yim si.

Adult Education Division, Ministry of Education. 1941b. *Nangsue hat an khong phuyai phak thon lem song* [Reading skills practice book for adults, first part, vol. two]. Bangkok: Yim si.

Chaiyakan, Wasitthee. 2018. *Pan-Tai Ideas and the Notion of 'Lost Territories' as Portrayed in Thai Textbooks, Late Nineteenth Century to 1944*. PhD thesis. London: SOAS, University of London.

Chanthanapho, T. 1938. 'Rongrian prathom nai yipun'. [Primary Schools in Japan]. *Withayachan* [Journal of Teachers' Professional Development] 38:3. March 1938. 448–455.

Eoseewong, Nidhi. 1985, 'Phasathai matrathan kap kanmueang' [The standard Thai language and Thai Politics], *Phasa lae nangsue* [Language and book], 17 (October 1984–March 1985), 32.

Hayes, C. J. H. 1926. *Nationalism as a religion*. Available at: www.panarchy.org/hayes/nationalism.html. Accessed on 3 March 2017.

Hudak, T. J. 1986. 'Spelling reform of Field Marshal Pibunsongkram'. *Crossroads: an Interdisciplinary Journal of Southeast Asian Studies*. 3:1. pp. 123–133.

Ivarsson, S. 2007. *Creating Laos: the Making of a Lao space between Indochina and Siam, 1860–1945*. Copenhagen and Abingdon: NIAS.

Kanphai, Kong. 1939. 'Kanphalasueksa nai prathet yoeramani'. [Physical education in Germany], *Waithayachan* 39:3. pp. 557–562. March 1939.

Kaysabutra, Prasnee. 1987. *Kanchadkansueksa phu yai kap nayobai sang chat khong rataban chomphon P. Phibunsongkram nai chuang pi ph. s. 2481–2487* [The organisation of adult education and the nation-building policy of the field Marshal P. Pibunsonggram government during 1938–1944]. MA thesis. Bangkok: Chulalongkorn University.

Krairiksh, Piriya. 1989. *Charuek phokhun Ram Khamhaeng, Kanwikhro choeng prawatisat sinlapa* [The Inscription of King Ram Khamhaeng, An Analysis from the Perspective of the History of Art]. Bangkok: Amarin Printing.

Laksanasiri, Churairat. 1997–98. 'Kanpatirup akson lea akkarawithi thai samai chomphon P. Phibunsongkram'. [Thai alphabet and spelling reform during Field Marshal Phibunsongkram], *Warasan aksonsat mahawithayalai sinlapakon* [Faculty of Arts, Silpakorn University Journal], 20. June 1997–May 1998.

Lewis, G. 1999. *The Turkish language reform: a catastrophic success*. Oxford and New York: Oxford University Press.

Office of the Secretary to the Prime Minister. 26 April 1939–12 March 1949. *General situations regarding adult educational administration*. (2) S R. 0201.24 5/6.

Office of the Secretary to the Prime Minister. 8 October 1940–29 January 1945. *Government officers and their families should be able to read and write by the end of 1943*. (2) S R. 0201.24.5/7.

Office of the Secretary to the Prime Minister. 10 February 1941–27 July 1944. *The adult educational administration in the Thai's newly occupied territories*. (2) S R. 0201.24.5/8.
Office of the Secretary to the Prime Minister. 1940. *Committees and subcommittees for adult education*. (2) S R. 0201.24.5/1.
Office of the Secretary to the Prime Minister. 17 April 1941–10 March 1942. *Curriculum, course syllabus, and examination regulations for adult students*. (2) S R. 0201.24.5/9.
Panyarachun, Jirawat. ed. 1997. *Chiwaprawat lae phonngan khong thanphuying La-aide Phibunsongkram* [Life and works of Thanpuying La-aide Phibunsongkram], Third Edition. Bangkok: Dan Suttha Printing.
Petchlert-anan, Thamrongsak. 2006. Chomphon P. Phibunsongkram kap kan 'sang wathanatham thai mai' [Field Marshal Phibunsongkram and the 'creation of the new Thai culture']. In: Yimprasert, S. ed. 2006. *Saithan haeng adit* [The Past Current]. Bangkok: Chulalongkorn University.
Phibunsongkram, P. 1943. 'Kan lao rian khian an pen kan sang sao ruean hai kae chat thai' [Studying literacy builds the pillars of the Thai nation]. *Nangsuephim suphapsatri* [The Ladies' Newspaper]. Special Edition. 24 June 1943, pp. 3–5.
Phongsathat, Siri. 1938. 'Rabop Kansueksa Nai Nana Prathet: Kansueksa Paitai Rabop Nasi Fatsit' [Education in other Countries: Education under Nazism System]. *Withayachan* [Journal of Teachers' Professional Development] 38:5. May 1938. 961–983.
Reynolds, E. B. 1994. *Thailand and Japan's southern advance, 1940–1945*. New York: Palgrave MacMillan.
Sitthisurasak, Phimchai. 1951. Interview with Kriang Kiratikon, former Minister of Ministry of Education. In: Sitthisurasak, P. et al., ed(s). 1990. *Wiwathanakan kansueksa phuyai lae kansueksa nok rongrian ph.s. 2482–2533* [The evolution of adult education and non-formal education, 1939–1990]. Bangkok: Non-formal Education Development Division, Non-formal Education Department, Ministry of Education.
Sitthisurasak, Phimchai. et al., ed(s). 1990. *Wiwathanakan kansueksa phuyai lae kansueksa nok rongrian ph.s. 2482–2533* [The evolution of adult education and non-formal education, 1939–1990]. Bangkok: Non-formal Education Development Division, Non-formal Education Department, Ministry of Education.
Sukhumnaipradit, Lung. 1940. 'Rathaniyom'. [The Eighth and Ninth State Conventions], *Withayachan* [Journal of Teachers' Professional Development] 40:10. October 1940. 1756–1759.
Terwiel, B. J. 2010. *The Ram Khamhaeng Inscription: The Fake that did not Come True*. Gossenberg: Ostasien Verlag.
Vickery, M. 1995. 'Piltdown 3: Further Discussion of the Ram Khamhaeng Inscription', *Journal of the Siam Society* 83. 103–198.
Winichakul, Thongchai. 1994. *Siam Mapped: A history of the Geo-body of a nation*. Honolulu: University of Hawai'i Press.
Welch, D. 1993. 'Manufacturing a consensus: Nazi propaganda and the building of a 'National Community (Volksgemeinschaft)'. *Contemporary European History* 2:1. 1–15.
Yourman, J. 1939. 'Propaganda techniques within Nazi Germany'. *Journal of Educational Sociology* 13:3. 148–163.

5 Contesting 'Chinese' Education
Schooling in the Kuomintang Chinese Diaspora in Northern Thailand, 1975–2015

Aranya Siriphon and Sunanta Yamthap

CHIANG MAI UNIVERSITY

The Kuomintang (KMT) Chinese, a distinct diasporic Chinese community, are the remnants of the KMT army who fled Yunnan into Burma and Thailand after the 1949 victory of the Communist Party of China (CPC) on the Chinese mainland. Over a 60-year period and up until the present day, three generations of this discrete community have dwelt in Northern Thailand and have maintained a distinct Yunnanese, Republican identity, expressed as anti-Communism and a loyal sentiment to the regime in Taipei, Taiwan, the Republic of China (ROC). At the same time, they maintained a strong traditional, pre-revolutionary Chinese (and Yunnanese) culture and Confucianism through schooling and education, as well as the popular religion and ritual of their daily lives. This monopoly over the provision of their education and the instilling of their values was challenged from two sources: one the Thai state and the other from the People's Republic of China (PRC) itself. The Thai state's education policy had been geared towards the integration of ethnically non-Thai communities by enforcing a uniform standard education system over its entire territory, prioritising Thai as the medium of instruction, and setting Thai cultural benchmarks as the standard. In the first decade of the twenty-first century, the PRC began exporting its own cultural, and therefore political, perspective through PRC Chinese language-based schooling and education, operated by the Confucian institutes run by the *Hanban* (the Office of Chinese Language Council International), and the *Qiaoban*, the Overseas Chinese Affairs Bureau (To, 2012, pp. 183–221) to overseas Chinese communities, including the KMT Chinese in Northern Thailand (Siriphon, 2016, pp. 1–17).

This chapter explores the changing dynamics of schooling and education in the KMT Chinese community in Northern Thailand. Particularly, it examines the influence of exported PRC education on local schooling, and how local efforts have contested mainland attempts to influence their identity formation through their own re-interpretation of Confucianism and Thai culture. Additionally, it contends that, although the KMT Chinese of Northern Thailand were closely connected to Taiwan politically and shared similar sentiments and perspectives, their daily cultural practices, including their interpretation of Confucianism manifested in their educational priorities, contrast with those not only of the PRC but also Taiwan. Under the pressure of marginalisation on Thai soil, KMT Chinese used education to help construct a *Kuomintang-Thai* identity, by selecting aspects of Thai national identity through selective engagement with and interpretation of prescribed textbooks and teaching in daily lives. By situating the performance of Chinese identity in particular local contexts, the chapter indicates that Chinese identity utilised by different dominant and subordinated actors at the local level, reproduced in education and schooling, demonstrates how the process of creating meaning was unstable and contested. In this sense, Confucianism, as revived in the last decade of the twentieth and first decade of the twenty-first centuries by the PRC state and KMT actors, seems to serve very different purposes in each case in defining traditional 'Chinese-ness.' In the case of the KMT Chinese diaspora in Thailand this has meant the appropriation and negotiation of imported intellectual resources and identity reconstruction to serve their own current objectives for ensuring their survival as a community in a foreign land.

Contextualising Kuomintang Chinese communities in Northern Thailand

The KMT Chinese generally live in the mountainous areas of the Northern Thai borderlands. They belong to the Han ethnic group but in many ways their 'ethnogenesis' story is now framed as their descent from the pioneer settlers of the Chinese Nationalist Army (Kuomintang-KMT). Within the changing circumstances of the Cold War, the Thai government was forced through its association with the anti-Communist Western bloc to take on the burden of accommodating and supplying the KMT Yunnanese troops who had refused to be evacuated to Taiwan, when the opportunity had arisen, during 1953–54, and then again in 1961. The Thai Government informally petitioned the Taipei regime for financial support for this group as their long-term resettlement in Northern Thailand became a reality. Between 1951 and 1952, the KMT gathered several of their army units in the border areas of Burma, and later settled in Northern Thailand where they established refugee villages in the 1960s (Huang, 2010; Chang, 1999, 2001, 2002).

The KMT troops and refugee villagers were composed of the two military units: the Third Field Army and the Fifth Field Army. In the 1960s the Third Field Army, with approximately 1,700 troops under the command of General Li Wen Huan, settled its centre around the villages near to the mountainous area of Fang District, in Chiang Mai Province. The Fifth Field Army, with approximately 1,500 troops under the command of General Tuan Shi Wen, settled in Doi Mae Salong, the mountainous area in Chiang Rai Province (Huang, 2010, pp. 6–12).

KMT schooling and education in Northern Thailand 1970–1980

It was not until the 1970s that the KMT troops and refugee villagers of the two military units (the Third Field Army and the Fifth Field Army) saw the predicament as somewhat permanent and looked to settle down along the Thai border in the provinces of Chiang Mai, Chiang Rai and Maehongson. During the 1970s the Thai Government, via the Supreme Command Headquarters of the Royal Thai Armed Forces, requested that the two KMT units gradually disarm in exchange for Thai citizenship and three hectares of agricultural land for each family, which, it was hoped, would allow them to make a living from farming in Northern Thailand (Prakatwuttisan, 1994); the measure aspired equally to stop their overland trade in opium and narcotic drugs, which was perceived by the Thai Government as a threat to Thai national security in their borderlands (Chang, 1999; Liulan, 2006, pp. 337–358). Subsequently, the KMT leaders and elderly members established schools in several communities which aimed to provide their children with a Chinese education and transmit their culture to successive generations as sojourners in a foreign land.

The Guang Huo School in Wiang Haeng district, Chiang Mai province, in the Thai-Myanmar borderlands, was among the clearest examples. The school was established in 1968 after the Thai government permitted the establishment of the village and gradually granted Thai citizenship or different types of legal status (of aliens, displaced people and independent immigrants) to the KMT forces and their dependents as a reward for their victories, in 1963–67, in the battles with Communist guerrillas of the Communist Party of Thailand (CPT) operating in mountainous areas (Chang, 1999, pp. 68–69). Another example was the Hua Xing School, established in 1971 when General Li Wen Huan, the head of the Third Field Army, and his troops established Ban Nong-Ook village and settled in the mountainous area of Chiang Mai Province.

These early schools followed the model of Taiwan-based Chinese schools, teaching Confucian orthodoxy and other subjects that cultivated a sense of anti-Communism in mainland China and the righteousness of the Taiwan Republic and Nationalist cause. The Chinese writing system also followed the traditional Chinese characters retained in Taiwan, Hong Kong and Macau, and among overseas Chinese communities. Teachers in these schools were educated KMT ex-soldiers and scholars. Textbooks, educational materials and other facilities were sent from Taiwan at the request of KMT leaders and community members in Thailand. (Two leaders of the Yunnanese Chinese Associations in Chiang Mai and Chiang Rai provinces, interview, 2014). The schools provided Chinese education not only to KMT children but also other to ethnic students, for example Shan, Lahu and Akha students, from within the village and surrounding villages. For those students whose home was outside the villages, the schools offered boarding school services, taking up residence when school was in session, without tuition fees and with free dormitory-lodgings provided for both male and female students (Prakatwuttisan, 2004, p. 248).

During the 1970s, not only were there an increasing number of Taiwan-based Chinese schools among KMT communities – and an increasing incidence of the establishment of Taiwanese-based education – but also, under the Thai assimilation policy of 1975, the Ministry of Education of Thailand sought to encourage KMT children and refugees to have a basic Thai education in Thai private or public schools. This authorisation by the Thai state, during that time, aimed, through Thai schooling and education, to integrate ethnic children along the borders into the Thai body-politic and secure its unstable frontiers. In 1975 the Ministry of Education, with the support of the Royal Thai Army, established the *rongrian chao thai phu khao*, the Thai hill-tribe schools, in the mountainous areas of the North, including in Chiang Dao District of Chiang Mai, selecting KMT children and other ethnic groups from Maehong Son, Chiang Rai and Chiang Mai to study at the school (Prakatwuttisan, 2004, pp. 306–307).

These hill-tribe schools were to be the primary mechanism for the Thai authorities to suppress mass kidnapping and counter the narratives of 'us and them', of insurgency and rebellion, being propagated by non-state actors along the Thai border. It was also hoped that these hill-tribe schools could help gain peripheral ethnic minority groups' loyalty toward Thailand, and then help safeguard the Thai territorial border, countering the ideological infiltration by Communist insurgents (Hyun, 2014, pp. 346–347). The Thai Ministry of Education built boarding schools at the primary level, and employed members of the military and border patrol police to teach ethnic minority children using central Thai as the medium of instruction. The curriculum promoted Thai culture and Theravada Buddhism within the framework of a modern Thai educational system. Apart from teaching, the military teachers were also tasked with gathering information for the authorities (Tapp, 2005, p. 11). Hyun (2014, pp. 332–363) noted that the involvement of the Royal Thai Army, and especially of the Border Patrol Police Unit (BPP) in the building and operating of schools served three main objectives: being able to communicate with the children, thus enabling the BPP to conduct intelligence-related tasks more effectively; establishing friendly relations with school children to help reduce the parents' fear of the BPP's presence; and gaining minority villagers' trust so that the BPP could set up surveillance systems in their communities with less resistance.

Apart from the educational projects mentioned above, the Thai authorities also sought to encourage ethnic minorities, including the KMT, to change or at least adapt their religious beliefs from animism, and in the KMT's case, folk-Taoism or Mahayana Buddhism, to state sponsored Theravada Buddhism, justifying this particularly intrusive measure by arguing that their traditional way of life, as non-Thai, constituted a threat to national security. Laungaramsri (1998, pp. 92–135) argued that such policies derived from a so-called 'hill-tribe discourse' which associated mountainous people with unstable population movements, ambiguous near-stateless identities, increases in narcotic drug use, opium cultivation, the violence of the drug trade, susceptibility to Communist ideals and infiltration, deforestation, and underdevelopment (Laungaramsri, 1998). External assistance helped increase the economic and social status of KMT Chinese, which gradually changed from the previous lowly status among the other marginalised ethnic groups on the periphery during the 1960s to one signifying upward economic mobility (Mote, 1967, p. 504, quoted in Chang, 1999, p. 132).

With the end of pro-Western bloc military rule in Thailand in 1973, a Thai civilian government, influenced by a resurgent left and the change in the international strategic environment between the US and China, and the regional change brought about by the Communist victories in South Vietnam, Laos and Cambodia, established diplomatic relations with the PRC in July, 1975. The opening of diplomatic relations led to Thai government cooperation with the PRC, and ended Thailand's longstanding diplomatic recognition of Taipei (Chinwanno, 2008). The return of a right-wing military-backed government in October 1976, however, led to a return to hostilities between mainland China and the Thai government. In the 1980s, the situation changed again, when the Thai and PRC governments sought to normalise their relations and the PRC withdrew its support for the CPT, in the interests of containing Vietnamese (and Soviet) influence in the region. This led to co-operation between the Thai government and that of the PRC, and a renewed distancing from the KMT (Bunbongkarn, 2004, pp. 52–54; Baker and Phongpaichit, 2013, pp. 233–275).

During the 1980s, while Thai schools established in the border regions were used as a political tool to assimilate KMT and other ethnic minority children, the KMT Chinese leaders – with the unofficial support of political leaders in Taipei – increasingly attempted to generate a patriotic sense of Chinese identity tied to the history of the KMT in Taiwan through their own schools. It was initiated after the arrival in Northern Thailand in 1982 of the Free China Relief Association (FCRA), a semi-official organisation that worked closely with the Nationalist Party in Taiwan (Chang, 2001, p. 1099). This organisation had been set up to provide aid to Chinese refugees in different parts of the world soon after 1949. Besides humanitarian considerations, the assistance was intended to provide political support to Chinese refugees abroad and overseas Chinese in general. In Northern Thailand, not only did the FCRA aim to improve the social and economic status of the KMT Chinese communities, but it also actively promoted a sense of loyalty toward the Taipei regime, fostering the image that Taiwan constituted the motherland of the KMT Chinese in Thailand (Chang, 1999, pp. 132–134). The FCRA worked to nurture the impression among KMT Chinese in Thailand that the Republican Chinese of Taiwan were committed to supporting KMT Chinese children, because of their shared inheritance and shared exiled (from the mainland) situation.

The FCRA was joined in its educational support efforts by the Yunnanese Chinese Associations in Chiang Rai province – these were one of the Kuomingtang's local organisations, established in 1981 by the KMT ex-general named Chen Mo Xiu or Charoen Prideepot. Together the two organisations helped provide financial aid and continued to bring about Taiwanese-based

Chinese curricula for schooling. This included the provision of images of Sun Yat Sen and Chiang Kai-shek in order that the communities could pay respect, as well as the supply of patriotic music tapes for distribution in the community (Chang, 1999, p. 137). They also offered scholarships for KMT children to study in Taiwanese curricula-based schools within their communities, full scholarships for study abroad in Taiwan for outstanding students, and textbooks and other educational facilities from Taiwan, and they paid frequent visits to the communities to offer educational assistance.

However, by the end of 1994, the FCRA's planned projects were terminated due to a decrease in funding and the changing political priorities in Taiwan. Additionally, the 1990s was a period of growing stability in Southeast Asia, conducive to economic opportunities and uplift, as insurgencies melted away and conflicts came to an end, a period which Thai Prime Minister Chatchai Choonhawan had proclaimed as one to be characterised as 'battlefields [being turned] into market places'. (Szalontai, 2011, pp. 155–172). The Taiwanese government of Taipei then informally arranged for the Tzu Chi Foundation, a Taiwanese Buddhist non-governmental organisation (NGO) led by Dharma Master Cheng Yen, a charismatic nun, to finance and assist the KMT communities (Chang, 1999, p. 133). Although the funding organisation had changed, the schools continued to operate extensively on the Taiwan-based model, teaching Confucian orthodoxy with traditional Chinese characters, emphasising the distinctiveness of a traditional and 'free' Han culture, and reflecting its goodwill towards Taiwan, all of which amounted to a residual anti-Communist theme.

Schooling and education of Kuomintang Chinese communities after the 1990s

During the 1990s, the international threat of the Communist alternative subsided and eventually evaporated as the PRC, under Deng Xiaoping, abandoned Leninist and Maoist economic strategies and adopted a Western free-market approach. The collapse of the Soviet Union in 1991 also removed much of the Vietnamese threat. In the 1990s, Thailand and its neighbouring countries shifted their international policies to focus on regional co-operation based on 'free-market' principles and relatively free trade by bolstering the Association of Southeast Asian Nations (ASEAN), and other regional and extra-regional co-operative structures. This included the creation of the Greater Mekong Sub-Region (GMS) in 1992 with the backing of the Japanese Asian Development Bank (ADB), to connect the borders of Thailand, Myanmar, Laos, Vietnam, Cambodia and China for economic purposes. Borders between Burma, China and Laos were properly demarcated, more co-operatively policed and opened up for trade (John, 1998, pp. 44–45). As a result, these structural interconnections facilitated a growth in the interconnectedness of China's and Thailand's polities, and generated a more confident and secure attitude regarding the cross-border environment. The opening up and state sanctioning of cross-border economic activity gradually attracted a number of members of ethnic minorities who were living along the border and those who had newly migrated from Myanmar. According to information compiled by the Chiang Mai Yunnanese Chinese Association, in 2014 (Chiang Mai Yunnanese Chinese Associations, 2015), 88 villages, comprising approximately 200,000 Yunnanese Chinese, existed in Chiang Mai and Chiang Rai provinces. This category of Yunnanese Chinese included both Muslim Hui and KMT Han.

Whereas Thai assimilationist education policy had been only ever partially realised in the borderlands because of security, logistical and funding difficulties, Thai national education policy, in more settled circumstances, tightened up in its borderlands at the end of the 1990s. The 1999 National Education Act of Thailand, designed and implemented by the Ministry of Education, required border ethnic minority children including those of the KMT to receive a Thai elementary education. This meant KMT children were required to attend Thai schools every day from eight in the morning to four in the afternoon during weekdays, using central Thai as the medium language, to follow the Thai national curriculum. This education policy, however, could not stop KMT children going to their Taiwan-sponsored schools, which were rescheduled to operate at weekends or weekday early mornings or evenings.

At the start of the twenty-first century, there remained approximately one hundred KMT Chinese schools (68 schools in Chiang Rai, 29 schools in Chiang Mai, three schools in Maehongson province and one school in Tak province), providing for different levels: primary, middle, and upper schools; and vocational colleges. They continued to adhere to the model of Taiwanese schools to provide a Chinese education, transmitting Chinese cultural content to their pupils. Apart from staples such as Mathematics, the subjects included Chinese History and global History, Geography, and Chinese calligraphy using the traditional writing system, a subject particularly popular with their parents. Many of the textbooks were brought directly from Taiwan.

Interestingly, the content of the textbooks used in the classrooms took a KMT-centred slant. For example, the history textbooks contained chapters covering the Ancient historical period to the Republic of China period, omitting historical content after 1949, when the KMT lost power in mainland China and was confined to Taiwan. Cultural events continued to be held at the schools, reaffirming the community's distinct roots. For example, parades were held each year, prepared by teachers and students, to celebrate the National Day of the Republic of China, and Sun Yat Sen, the first president and founding father of the Republic of China in 1912; and 'Memorial Day', both of which had been annual features of these schools since their inception. These communities also decorated their schools and community leaders' houses with images of Sun Yat Sen and other KMT leaders (Two leaders of the Yunnanese Chinese Associations in Chiang Mai and Chiang Rai provinces, interview, 2014; fieldwork on sight observations, 2015).

The situation changed in 2007 when the KMT Chinese felt increasingly challenged by 'soft power' activities of the PRC, which, in the form of the *Qiaoban* – together with its affiliated institutional organs, such as the Chinese consulate in Chiang Mai – attempted to reconnect with diverse overseas Chinese communities in Thailand (Siriphon, 2016). The *Qiaoban* was established in its modern form under Deng Xiaoping in 1978 and developed through the 1980s as overseas Chinese were reinvented in the mainland's eyes, from being the lackeys of counter-revolution to being a potentially patriotic (i.e. loyal to the PRC) resource (Thuno, 2001). The second institution was the Office of Chinese Language Council International, or *Hanban*, established in 1987 by the PRC's Ministry of Education as part of its policy of international outreach. The *Hanban* established the Confucius Institutes, with the first being founded in Seoul, Republic of Korea, in November 2004, as a PRC version of the Alliance Française or British Council, with aim of disseminating PRC-sanctioned Chinese cultural and language promotion (Paradise, 2009; Starr, 2009). These institutions began to collaborate with Chinese schools founded in diasporic Chinese communities, and even extended their own curricula and programmes into several levels of Thai formal education. Aimed especially at the KMT Chinese in Northern Thailand, in 2010, the *Qiaoban* established a large PRC-based Chinese school, called the Jiaolian School. The school was located in Ban Nong Ook, a KMT village in the borderlands of Chiang Mai, once the army base of the Third Field Army under the command of General Li Wenhuan.

The Jiaolian School and the *Qiaoban* enjoyed good relations with the Thai Government when the school decided to register officially as a private school. In 2011, the Private Education Commission of the Thai Ministry of Education granted a licence for their educational operations. Under the registered curriculum and the licence, the Jiaolian school taught multiple subjects: mathematics, English, geography (global and Chinese), and history (global and Chinese), using the simplified-character Mandarin writing system, as adopted by the PRC, in contrast to the use in KMT Chinese schools of Taiwanese Mandarin, using traditional writing characters, as a teaching language. Formal recognition helped the Jiaolian School certify its standards and this, in turn, secured its graduates' eligibility to pursue higher education or to find jobs outside the village. Thereafter, the school grew rapidly, and this became a challenge for leaders and elderly members of the KMT. There was concern that the PRC-sponsored school would separate their children from their KMT political roots and culture.

The two schools did not only differ in the use of different scripts but they crucially differed in their respective reinterpretations of Confucianism. While KMT Chinese used Confucianism as a source of moral and ideological support in providing persuasive explanations for a Chinese attachment to Taiwan and the maintenance of a traditional Chinese culture, the PRC government promoted Confucianism in its own way (Wu, 2014, pp. 971–991). Although 'Confucius' was the name given to the *Hanban*'s overseas language and cultural institution, Confucian thought and philosophy were rarely found in the textbooks of the Jiaolian School. The main goal of the *Hanban* textbooks provided was to teach foreign students PRC Mandarin Chinese. Therefore, the content of the textbook is focused on dialogue using everyday vocabulary so that students could practise PRC Mandarin. For example, the textbook for the second grade presented content about swimming, going to school and visiting the store; about how to talk with the doctor, how to attend school events, and about going to public parks. Only textbooks for the high school level mentioned Confucius' thought. For example, the textbook for the eighth grade showed a conversation between Confucius and his disciples about ethics and morality. Additionally, the Jiaolian School used a series on general Chinese history, culture and geography, but only to teach as auxiliary classes. Only these series had content concerning the history of China and presented Confucius as one of the key figures in Chinese history.

On the contrary, textbooks used at KMT schools were abundant with Confucian thought and philosophy, which appear at almost every educational level taught at schools. For example, the Chinese textbook for the first grade added several chapters on Confucius' teachings, for example: 'I see the sun is up early every day, and it does not stop until night'. Translated by a KMT teacher, (Yang Jinyu, a teacher at Hua Xing school, Chiang Mai, on 4 May 2014), it implied that children, as diligent and dutiful members of the community, should wake up early, work hard and industriously, which forms a part of the human virtues taught in Confucianism. The textbook for the second grade taught 'family ethics', in which parents and children were instructed in their roles. While parents were to take care of children, children were bound to pay respect and give gratitude to their parents. Also, the Chinese textbook for the third grade presented a 'mother's love', which was compared with the preciousness of the sunshine cultivating lives. The Chinese textbook for the fourth grade added more historical background about Confucius and his teaching, emphasising Confucius as the ideal man of knowledge and virtue; whose influence had endured for millennia and whose teachings constituted universal principles emphasising the non-negotiable elements of a successful community: loyalty, unity and forgiveness. The children were exhorted to practise these virtues daily in their relationships with other members of the community, the basic unit of which was the family. Chinese textbooks for the fifth grade taught the idea of patriotism, which was illustrated by the story of a Chinese king. By the application of Confucian principles the King was able to turn a chaotic city into a happy place of order within only three months and without criminality or conflict. The consequence of Confucian-based rule was peace. The other implication was that members of the community should love this kind of ruler and obey their rules, *if* their rulers were good and virtuous. This meant that all textbooks taught at almost every level in KMT schools maintained Confucian philosophy and principles in traditional interpretations in which the process of self-cultivation should be undertaken through the cultivation of human relationships (Fei, 1992). Human relationships were to be based on the principle of filial piety – a minister's loyalty to a ruler, which expected children to improve their individual self into a broader vision of themselves which generates affiliation with the wider community (Madsen, 2008, pp. 306–307).

According to Wu's (2014, 971–991) argument, the PRC government's renovation of Confucianism in the early twenty-first century was part of a political strategy with the purpose of securing its cultural leadership, while at the same time creating the impression that the PRC domestic and foreign policy strategies were in harmony with Confucian principles. The strategy also aimed to soften the image of the PRC as a military threat, especially to their near neighbours, and persuaded not just mainlanders but also overseas Chinese of the Party's leadership and legitimacy in the cultural sphere (Wu, 2014, pp. 990–991). In practical terms, the strategy was achieved by dispatching staff from the *Qiaoban* and inspectors from the Ministry of Education to visit Chinese schools in the Southeast Asian region and provide textbooks, grant-in-aid and teachers from the mainland.

Imagining Kuomintang Chinese identities in Northern Thailand

KMT Chinese in Northern Thailand, however, developed an identity that was neither PRC-based nor Republican-Taiwan-based. This is because they have also had to establish a narrative that accommodates a Thai identity as well. History textbooks used in the schools help demonstrate how KMT Chinese incorporate the Thai state's national identity into their own cultural identity. The new history textbooks which had been used in KMT schools since the 2000s were re-edited in 2011 by Thai-Kuomintang Chinese teachers in collaborating with the Overseas Compatriot Affairs Commission, ROC (Taiwan). They were not only to contain Chinese history, but also to emphasise the history of their involuntary KMT migration and their anti-Communist efforts in Thailand from 1949 up to the present. The textbooks included the history of *Doi Mae Salong* as an example of the settlement of KMT Chinese in Thailand, which Taiwan and the Thai Government benevolently helped support and sustain. Another component of the textbook narrative was the KMT's invaluable assistance to the Thai state during the 1960s and 1970s in its fight against the People's Liberation Army (PLA)-backed CPT and other Communist guerrillas in the region.

Additionally, one theme of the second grade history textbook was Thai nation-building. The Thai national narrative was taught through such devices as the explanation of the Thai national flag: each colour represented the three pillars of Thai society, the Nation (*chat*-people, land and language), Buddhism (*Satsana*-the religious dimension), and monarchy (*Phramahakesat* - king). Thai culture and social values, traditions and customs were also formalised within the context of the textbook. These included, for example, the value of the *Wai* (placing hands together at chest level) which served the purpose of both greeting and performing respect when applied in the right social situations, reinforcing the social hierarchy. There were also expositions of the qualities of Thai food which, again, sought to set a core culinary standard even for those, such as the mountain people and the Chinese, unfamiliar with this cuisine. The Thai national calendar was also taught: for instance, Father's Day on 5 December, which marked the birthday of His Majesty King Bhumibol (Rama IX) and stressed his role as Father of the Thai Nation; and Mother's Day on 12 August, which marked the birthday of Her Majesty Queen Sirikit and stressed her role as Mother of the Thai nation. Teachers and students were instructed in the correct manner of performing the paying of respect toward the portraits of the King and the Queen at school. Despite the ostensibly narrow definitions foisted onto the KMT children, these new loyalties did not compel them to exclude their former loyalties. The new ceremonies and rituals could simply be added on but given personal meaning through their Confucian understanding of the need to love the virtuous ruler, in this case the Thai King and Queen. These cultural additions allowed KMT children to form a 'double identity' – a hyphenated Kuomintang-Thai identity. Despite being Republican Chinese tied to their Taiwanese brethren, Thai-Kuomintang children faced the reality of being born and having to live on Thai soil. Buying into the Thai national narrative was therefore a survival strategy, and a necessity. This identity-adaptation was undertaken so that they could better bind their Thai citizenship and their Republican-Chinese identity together, and in so doing, maintain the latter. (Interview, Yang Jinyu, a teacher at Hua Xing School, on 4 May 2014)

An additional effect of the border opening process and the GMS regionalisation context was further economic improvement among the KMT Chinese, and this, coupled with improved communications generally, stimulated a reinvigoration of their connections with both Taiwan and the PRC, especially those in Yunnan province. Additionally, their historic close ties with Taiwan, through their personal connections with ex-soldiers and their dependents, often resulted in the facilitation of assistance from the capital abundant in high economically performing Taiwan for their various enterprises and projects. These conditions allowed many young KMT Chinese to migrate to study in Taiwan and work there. Their bilingual skills in Thai and Chinese also provided them with a major advantage in conducting either trade or tourism with China, Taiwan and Chinese-based language businessmen in and outside Thailand, and thus remit their wages back to their communities. The regional border opening conditions not only supported economic uplift of the KMT Chinese but, through their increased social mobility, it also helped reaffirm their shared commitment to pro-democratic (at least anti-CPC/PRC, and pro-Taipei) sentiments and a pride in holding a distinct KMT-based Chinese identity, strengthening a sense of imagined motherland – Confucianism. They were able to share in the success of Taiwanese modernity and allow it to generate a renewed sense of self-confidence and of being on the right side of history.

In the light of these conditions, it is interesting to find that Confucianism and traditional Chinese culture of KMT Chinese in Northern Thailand is distinctive from the manner in which Confucianism in mainland China and even in Taiwan had been renovated. While a sincere and more authentic Confucianism in mainland China and in Taiwan faded, due to the political and social changes wrought by modernisation, for the communities in Northern Thailand it was rigorously maintained in everyday life and in their programme of education.

Conclusion

Dynamic change in the education of KMT Chinese communities in Northern Thailand has revealed how the KMT Chinese communities in Thailand have strengthened and perpetuated their unique Chinese cultural identity, which became distinctive from both the PRC and even of Taiwan. Indeed, KMT Chinese claimed to be those Chinese who had most faithfully maintained their traditional originality by reproducing their traditional Chinese culture, as called by Huang (2010) 'the cultural reproduction of Chinese Diaspora', in their own way through continuously practising traditional Chinese rituals, cultural norms, Confucian orthodoxy, and Chinese education. That claim to authenticity became a defining component of their identity.

Under pressure of marginalisation on Thai soil, the KMT Chinese used education to help construct their Kuomintang-Thai identity, by selecting aspects of Thai national identity through a number of strategies recounted in textbooks and teaching. In this way, the KMT Chinese communities complied with the demands of the Thai educational curriculum. Ironically, this obligatory, but relatively undemanding, tolerant and accommodating approach, allowed them to compartmentalise – and therefore maintain – their KMT identity alongside their new Thai identity, by mentally adopting an unofficial, but widely accepted hyphenated status, Kuomintang-Thai, just as the Sino-Thai community had done before. The main vehicle through which this identity was formed was through the classroom, which appropriated textbooks and narratives from different political sources, and reshaped them for the needs of the community.

References

Baker, C. and Phongpaichit, P. 2013. Politics, 1970s Onwards. In: Baker, C. and Phongpaichit, P. eds. *A History of Thailand*. New York: Cambridge University Press.

Bunbongkarn, S. 2004. The Military and Democracy in Thailand. In: May, R. and Selochan, V. eds. *The Military and Democracy in Asia and the Pacific*. Canberra: ANU E Press. Available at: http://pressfiles.anu.edu.au/downloads/press/p33231/mobile/index.html Accessed 9 Dec 2017.

Chang, W.-C. 1999. *Beyond the Military: The Complex Migration and Resettlement of the KMT Yunnanese Chinese in Northern Thailand*. PhD, University of Leuven.

Chang, W.-C. 2001. 'From War Refugees to Immigrants: The Case of the KMT Yunnanese Chinese in Northern Thailand'. *International Migration Review*, 35(4), pp. 1086–1105.

Chang, W.-C. 2002. 'Identification of Leadership among the KMT Yunnanese Chinese in Northern Thailand'. *Journal of Southeast Asian Studies*, 33(1), pp. 123–146.

Chinwanno, J. 2008. *Thai-Chinese Relation: Security and Strategic Partnership.* Japan: International University of Japan (IUJ). Asia Pacific Series, 6 Available from: www.iuj.ac.jp/research/workingpapers/PIRS_1998_04.html. Accessed 13 December 2017.

Fei, Xiaotong. 1992. *From the Soil: the Foundations of Chinese Society.* Berkeley, CA: University of California Press.

Huang, S. 2010. *Reproducing Chinese Culture in Diaspora: Sustainable Agriculture & Petrified Culture in Highland Northern Thailand.* Maryland: Lexington Books.

Hyun, S. 2014. 'Building a Human Border: The Thai Border Patrol Police School Project in the Post–Cold War Era', *Sojourn*, 29(2), pp. 332–363.

John, R. 1998. 'The Land Boundaries of Indochina: Cambodia, Laos and Vietnam', *Boundary and Territory Briefing*, 2(6), pp. 1–47.

Liulan, W. 2006. 'Hui Yunnanese Migratory History in Relation to the Han Yunnanese and Ethnic Resurgence in Northern Thailand', *Southeast Asian Studies* 44(3), pp. 337–358.

Madsen, R. 2008. Religious Renaissance and Taiwan's Modern Middle Classes. In: Yang, M., ed. *Chinese Religiosities: Afflictions of Modernity and State Formation.* Berkeley, CA: University of California Press, pp. 295–322.

Mote, F. W. 1967. 'The Rural "Haw" (Yunnanese Chinese) of Northern Thailand'. In: Kunstadter, P., ed. *Southeast Asian Tribes, Minorities and Nations, vol. 2.* Princeton, NJ: Princeton University Press, pp. 487–524.

Paradise, J. 2009. 'China and International Harmony: The Role of Confucius Institutes in Bolstering Beijing's Soft Power', *Asian Survey* 49(4), pp. 647–669.

Siriphon, A. 2016. 'The Qiaoban, the PRC Influence and Nationalist Chinese in the Northern Thailand'. *International Journal of Asian Studies*, 13(1), pp. 1–17.

Starr, Don (2009) 'Chinese Language Education in Europe: The Confucius Institutes'. *European Journal of Education*, 44(1), pp. 65–82.

Szalontai, B. 2011. 'From Battlefield into Marketplace: The End of the Cold War in Indochina, 1985–1989'. In: Kalinovsky, A. and Radchenko, S., ed(s). *The End of the Cold War in the Third World: New Perspectives on Regional Conflict.* London: Routledge, pp. 155–172.

Tapp, N. 2005. *Sovereignty and Rebellion: the White Hmong of Northern Thailand.* Revised & Reprinted. Thailand: White Lotus Press, 1989.

Thuno, M. 2001. 'Reaching Out and Incorporating Chinese Overseas: The Trans-Territorial Scope of the PRC by the End of the Twentieth Century'. *The China Quarterly*, 168, pp. 910–929.

To, J. 2012. 'Beijing's Policies for Managing Han and Ethnic-Minority Chinese Communities Abroad'. *Journal of Current Chinese Affairs* 41(4), pp. 183–221.

Wu, S. 2014. 'The Revival of Confucianism and the CCP's Struggle for Cultural Leadership: A Content Analysis of the People's Daily, 2000–2009'. *Journal of Contemporary China.* 23(89), pp. 971–991.

Non-English language sources

Chiang Mai Yunnanese Chinese Associations. 2015. *Annual Report in 2014.* Chiang Mai: Chiang Mai Yunnanese Chinese Associations. (in Chinese).清迈云南华人社团. 2015, *2014.*年年报. 清迈: 清迈云南华人社团.

Laungaramsri, P. 1998. '"Hill Tribe" Discourse', *Journal of Social Sciences, Chiang Mai University* 11(1), 92–135 (Pinkaew Luangaramsri. 2541. wathakam wa duay chao khao. (worasan sangkhomsat 1(11), pp. 96–98)

Prakatwuttisan, K. 1994. *Brigade 93 Kuomintang Chinese Nationalist Immigrants in Doi Pha Tang.* Chiang Mai: Siamratta Printing. (Kanchana Prakatwuttisan. 2537. *kongphol 93 phu phayop adit tahan chin khana chat bon doi pha tang.* Chiang Mai: Sayam Rathana Printing).

Prakatwuttisan, K. 2004. *Kuomintang Chinese nationalists left in Northern Thailand.* Chiang Mai: Siamratta Printing. (2547) *kokmintang tahan chin khana chat tok khang phak nuea prathet thai.*

6 Vocational Education, Shoemaking, and the Emergence of a 'National' Economy in Thailand 1895–1973

Thomas Richard Bruce

PRIDI BANOMYONG INTERNATIONAL COLLEGE, THAMMASAT UNIVERSITY

Modern vocational education emerged because of the economic and social restructuring required by industrialisation and intensified global trade in the nineteenth and early twentieth centuries (Clarke and Winch, 2007; Weber, 1977, pp. 303–338; Sanderson, 1983, pp. 24–32). The gradual demise of the traditional providers of pre-modern vocational education – guilds, artisanship and apprenticeships – the introduction of new techniques, increasing mechanisation, and the expansion of modern methods of production, particularly factory organisation, reflected the dislocation of the workforce, and the increasing distance of the owners, from the processes of production (Gehin, 2007). This decline of the traditional means of technical, craft-based knowledge transmission entailed the creation of a state-sponsored system of labour force formation.

While the above rather general explanation is broadly satisfactory, the arguments made for vocational education have varied with the particular circumstances of different societies at different times. Changing approaches to vocational education, with its particularly potent association with the nation's future prosperity, are especially revealing of ambitions, anxieties and changes in ideological preference among state leaders. The debate over the effectiveness of a state-provided vocational equivalent of an academic education is an old and pervasive one precisely because success or failure has depended on changing aims and justifications (Foster, 1965; Wolf, 2002, pp. 56–97). Recent justifications for reinvigorating vocational education in Britain, for example, have been driven by the 1970s conversion of orthodox economic policy from Keynesian demand-side to 'neoclassical' supply-side strategies (Wolf, 2002, pp. 66–67; Sanderson, 1999, pp. 83–88). Vocational education first emerged in much of the non-Western world in the context of colonial rule (Headrick, 1988, pp. 304–351). Not only did these societies have to catch up in manning, and learning to manage, new state apparatus but they would have to navigate new products, many of which – such as modern footwear, the example on which this chapter will focus – became requisite markers of modernity. As a vehicle for the colonial extractive state, vocational schools effectively served as sites of technological or knowledge transfer.

The emergence of modern vocational education in Thailand, an independent yet vulnerable tropical state, was bound up with factors which were significantly different from those in both the colonised tropics and the Western world. Although bound by 'unequal' commercial treaties, beginning with that signed with the United Kingdom in 1855, which placed it in a precarious and subordinate position, Thailand's leaders, free of colonial rule, afforded additional significance to modern vocational education. Their concern was not merely with colonial encroachment but with the growing economic power of the Chinese migrant community and the correspondingly weak economic power of the agriculturally bound Thai. Thai rulers did not face the relatively straightforward task of building resistance to colonial rule: instead they went about the far more precarious task of maintaining their independence and constructing a nation-state. Survival meant the adoption of a number of strategies, as Larsson (2012) has illustrated in his examination of modern property rights policies. In the adoption of modern shoes, in seeking to nationalise their supply, and in upgrading their country's productive capacity, they found another tool for maintaining their survival and creating a sense of nationhood: through vocational education.

Education in Thailand

Barend Jan Terwiel has described the emergence of a modern centralised system of education in Thailand essentially as a process of separation of the secular components, namely literacy, of traditional monastery-based education, from the religious (Terwiel, 1977). Prior to the education reforms which began in earnest in the 1870s, Thai males received instruction in the monasteries as a part of their cosmological journey through a life of merit accumulation (see also McDaniel 2008). The monasteries were a convenient and cost-effective means of serving as the basis for the adoption of modern curricula until funds could be sufficiently generated to allow for a nationwide school-building programme (Wyatt, 1969). The building of schools came to be associated with merit accumulation, particularly under the sixth Chakri King, Vajiravudh (Rama VI). The first Western school, the Bangkok Christian College, was established by American Presbyterian missionaries in 1852 with the sanction of King Mongkut (Rama IV) (McFarland, 2011, pp. 209–211). State-led attempts at creating a national system of education based upon the models of Western countries began under King Chulalongkorn (Rama V) in earnest in the 1870s. His priority was the staffing of a modern bureaucracy and, aside from sending students abroad, a modern school was set up for this purpose called the Royal Pages School (*rong rian roi tahan mahatlek*) in 1882. A Department of Education (*krom sueksathikan*,) was founded in 1887 under the direction of the King's erudite half-brother, Prince Damrong Ratchanuphap, for the explicit purpose of promoting modern schools (Royal Thai Government, 1887). In 1892, along with a general radical reform of the administration into twelve ministries, a Ministry of Public

Instruction (*krasuang thammakan*) was created which absorbed the Department. The first national plan proper was drawn up in June 1898, and a plan specifically for the provinces in November of the same year. From the early decades of the twentieth century, the Chinese migrant communities independently began providing for their own educational infrastructure as well (Montesano, 2008). This initial fragmentary and incremental nature of educational expansion reflected the weakness and limited resources of the state.

Thailand's education was therefore organised into two levels at much the same time that Britain's education system was formally standardised (Sanderson, 1999, pp. 9–12; Searle, 1971, pp. 207–216) albeit with far less resources at the disposal of the Thai system. The two levels comprised elementary (*prathom*) and secondary (*mathayom*), which in turn was divided into lower (*tonton*) and upper (*tonplai*) levels[1]. The age of commencing education was generally seven. Three years of elementary or primary education (out of a total of seven years) became compulsory in 1921. In 1951, those three years were expanded to four years. From 1961 a series of five-year national education plans were launched with the overall aim of expanding secondary education enrolment rates and designing accompanying curricula which would best match the post-war period of 'development' and 'modernisation'. From 1962, the four years of compulsory primary education were expanded to seven years. From 1978, this was altered again with six years of primary education from age six upwards, followed by three years of lower and three years of upper secondary, creating the 6:3:3 formula. In 1987, the government began establishing free lower secondary education classes in rural primary schools, and in 1997, Thailand's most radical constitution to date enshrined the right of Thai citizens to twelve years of free schooling, although this remained aspirational until 2002. It was only in 1999 that a National Education Act made nine years of schooling, lower primary to lower secondary, compulsory[2]. Vocational education (*achīwasueksa*), not always known by that name, featured in this history from the 1890s, when the negative effects of economic integration into the global system and unintended consequences of the government reform process became apparent.

The early conception of vocational education and the fears of mismatch

The first serious discussion of vocational education occurred in 1898 when the Deputy Minister of Education, Phraya Wisut Suriyasak, drew a distinction between general education and what he termed 'special' education. The draft plan of 1902 went further and included the English term 'technical education', which it translated as 'extraordinary' (*wisaman*), as opposed to ordinary, *saman*, education, but also continued to use the term 'special' (*phiset*). This was defined as 'a variety of education in practical subjects or arts for which it is not necessary for the general public to know excepting those who are of a particular bent or have the desire and ability to practice specialised knowledge, and expressly in order to use as a tool for the relevant enterprise

...' (Royal Thai Government, 1902b). These early efforts laid considerable stress on fulfilling the needs of a modern state administration. The latter consisted of special purpose higher-level technical education schools that attempted to address the immediate and practical clerical needs of government departments and develop the country's given resources and their commercial potential. Such was the thinking behind the effort to reinvent silk weaving in the north-east as a modern industry from 1903 (Brown, 1988, pp. 157–164). The various government ministries and departments had taken their own initiative and set up their own 'schools', focused entirely on supplying their needs. These included a Naval College, part of which was an Engineer's School; a Law School, under the Ministry of Justice; a Gendarmerie School, under the Ministry of the Interior; and a Posts and Telegraphs School under the Ministry of Communications (Thailand Ministry of Finance, 1924). The need for the staffing of an expanding civil service, and the new clerical opportunities which an expanding state seemed to offer people from social echelons that had once never thought to take such roles, boosted the attraction of academic-cum-clerical education. In 1906, Prince Damrong explained the unintended consequences of this policy at a meeting of provincial officials:

'The number of positions in the civil service is insufficient to meet demand for them. When such a situation prevails, students will lose hope and their ambitions will be quashed. An example is that of the peasant's son who receives an education and then seeks a clerical position with a salary of just 20 baht per month; if it happens that his parents pass away, it is may well be that the son sells his parent's farmland and utterly abandons his homeland for good. Seen from this perspective, education is harmful! This error of education is not only ours. Even the British have made the same error in their organisation of education in India; they have trained a surplus number of graduates for the civil service for the sake of having BA and MA level degrees. The consequence is that the graduates cannot find work that fulfils their expectations and they are forced to travel around to find work of a much lower status than they hoped. The Indian government feels it has erred in inducing people to strive to enter the civil service. They have therefore sought to ameliorate the situation by changing the structure of education so that it is better suited [to local conditions] and they have only just recently begun putting this proposal into action. Our country should also quickly act to do this at this time ...'
(Charun Wongsayan and Pramot Chaiyakit, 1961, pp. 6–7)

The effect of this, according to the authorities, was what we now call mismatch: an overqualified population with little hope of its expected employment, which as a consequence might become troublesome, as had occurred in India. Nevertheless, due to the cost, separate and substantial vocational education was not initiated at this stage and instead the more convenient teaching of practical subjects appropriate to the student's local environment was adopted alongside the ordinary curriculum (Charun Wongsayan and Pramot Chaikit, 1961, p. 7).

The decline of traditional crafts

An equally powerful motive for the initiation of organised vocational education emerged from the perception that the country's arts and crafts were in decline in the face of competition from new Western imports (Thailand Ministry of Finance, 1899). In pre-modern Thailand, apprenticeships existed to the extent that the teaching of arts and crafts had occurred in the household of the *nai* (master) in which the craftsmen (*chang*) were employed (Ingram, 1971, pp. 18–19) but autonomous craft institutions, such as guilds, did not. Craftsmen or artisans were not free labourers and were bound to their patrons (Crawfurd, 1830, pp. 21–22). Outside of luxury production, basket weaving, textile weaving and the fashioning of tools took place at the village level largely for the producer's own use. These traditional arts and crafts had apparently declined with the opening of Siam to international trade from 1855 onwards (Resnick, 1970).

This perception of decline is apparent when talk of vocational education in government emerges in the eighteen-nineties. A proposal later emerged in 1899 from the Ministry of Public Instruction's British advisor, John Gordon Drummond Campbell, to introduce vocational subjects into the curriculum of new schools with the reasoning that:

> '... it is proposed to get a teacher who has made a special study of manual work and where services may also be utilised in teaching this brand of work to the students in the normal college and organising it in some of the schools. It will be found in the future to be of great importance that the boys in school should have some manual training, if as is hoped, a system of technical instruction be started in Bangkok. Only by such a system of instruction can the old industries of the country be revived and Siam take its proper place among the commercial and manufacturing countries of the world. A course of manual training is now looked upon as an essential part of the elementary curriculum in all the leading countries of Europe and I attach very great importance to introducing it into some of the schools in Bangkok.'
> (Thailand Ministry of Finance, 1899)

Furthermore, in 1906 Prince Wachirayan expressed the view that the import of manufactures had eroded traditional home-based vocational education, whilst leaving training in modern crafts to the Chinese (Thailand Ministry of Public Instruction, 1906, pp. 69, 71). None of these suggestions were acted upon, at least not immediately. Conservative fiscal policies and preference for security-related spending meant that the budget for education was never sufficient to allow for any great expansion (Wyatt, 1969, pp. 270–271; Brown, 1988, pp. 40–41).

State-sponsored vocational education emerges

The first concrete steps towards establishing specialised vocational schools were spurred on from a rather different source. In 1895, the government announced its intention of establishing what we might now call a vocational school, for children who 'lacked patrons' (*mai-mī-phū ūphatham*), perhaps orphans, in honour of the late Crown Prince Vajirunahis who had died that year: the Maha Vajirunahis School for Training in Various Kinds of Crafts (*rongrian mahawachirunahit samrap fuek hat kanchang tang tang*). The organisers had intended that the school should teach the following subjects: writing, sculpture, engraving, temple maintenance, woodwork and metal work. Woodwork was to be given greater emphasis because it had been of particular interest to the late Crown Prince. The idea behind the school in its first conception was to honour the late Crown Prince's memory, and in its choice of subjects it intended to help fulfil a need for craftsmen in an age when the forced system of labour that had governed Thai craftsmen had become redundant. However, it was felt that the school's limited budget would allow it to teach either only 60 boys the four subjects of writing, sculpture, engraving, and woodwork, or 40 boys woodwork and 20 girls embroidery (Thailand Ministry of Public Instruction, 1896). As was typical at that time, these budgetary challenges led to hesitation and, although more substantial plans were eventually laid in 1902, it was not until 1912, during the reign of King Vajiravudh (Rama VI), that the school was actually set up. When it was, there was no mention of the former Crown Prince.

In its second incarnation there were signs that the school was meant to usher in an age of modern productivity based upon independent craftsmen, practising but expanding the repertoire of the traditional crafts of the country. One of the heads of woodwork instruction was a European. The school was named the School for the Cultivation of Artisans (*rong rian pho chang* or Pho Chang School from hereafter) but translated as the School of Arts and Crafts. On opening the school, on 7 January, the King declared:

> 'At this time, our own Thai scientific knowledge has advanced considerably and it is now fitting that we all use the scientific knowledge that we have acquired from foreign lands to cultivate and nurture our trees. This means developing the Thai technical arts with the times. There are many ways to beautify and nurture our trees so that they may bring forth the fitting fruit of this season. When we can help one another nurture [these technical arts], it will be to the greater glory of our metropolis. Additionally, this will serve as an occupation for Thais most appropriate for the time and season.'
>
> (Charun Wongsayan and Pramot Chaiyakit, 1961, pp. 12–13)

Nevertheless, the curriculum neglected other crafts more translatable into modern-age production such as leather work and shoe making, with the sole exception of tailoring. As such, the curriculum differed little from the instruction proposed in the first incarnation, with some additions, such as wickerwork, although temple maintenance was not included. Nevertheless, the establishment of the school reflected the new King's desire for an expanded and diverse education system.

The changes ushered in by King Vajiravudh, which included compulsory primary education in the Act of 1 October 1921, also included the introduction of streaming: after three years of compulsory primary schooling from around seven years old, boys – and only boys – who were unable or unwilling to pursue the higher level of primary general education would be obliged to complete two years of vocational training; the nature of which would depend upon the specialisation of the district. These comprised mostly agriculture, but also included carpentry, sewing (perhaps tailoring), basketry, weaving and mat-making. More sophisticated or 'technical' courses were also made available for girls (usually the domestic science course), after their three years of upper primary and for boys on completion of their two years of vocational training (Thailand Ministry of Finance, 1924, p. 231). Schools of commerce, such as the Mahaphritharam School of Commerce, established in 1918, also emerged in the Sixth Reign, reflecting an attempt to reclaim the lucrative occupation of comprador (agent or intermediary) in *entrepôt* Bangkok from the Chinese middleman (Charun Wongsayan and Pramot Chaiyakit, 1961, pp. 12–17). This was aimed at children as young as twelve and thirteen to fourteen and fifteen – primary (*prathom*) levels 5 and 6, respectively. The school curriculum was highly specialised, committing all of its 27 hours per week to the teaching of commerce-related subjects. Although a further three-year secondary level of commerce education, regarded as mid-level, was made available, vocational education was designed at a low level because of the perennial problem of high costs in delivering higher-level vocational courses. Later, these lower levels were considered inadequate for actual application in the marketplace, and therefore useless. Aside from the commerce schools, the extent to which vocational education had been developed during this early period only allowed for a new generation to reproduce the economy of their fathers and not expand upon it (Charun Wongsayan and Pramot Chaiyakit, 1961, pp. 20–21). Yet new products were now being consumed and Thais found themselves outside the sphere of their production.

Footwear

This exclusion was partly due to divergences in the cultural inheritance of Chinese and Thais, which allowed the former group an easier passage into modern systems of production. The traditional place of footwear (*kueak* or *rongtao*) in Thailand was restricted as an indicator of class status and a marker of hierarchy and that, along with the tropical conditions, meant that

Thailand was primarily a country of bare feet. The king used a pair (*chalong phrabat*), identical to Persian pointed slippers, as one of the five coronation regalia (Wales, 1931, p. 86) and princes, *chaofa*, and *nai* used similar styles (de la Loubere, 1693). Some of this luxury shoe production occurred domestically. Forms of hide sandal were also produced domestically and used for functional purposes in certain areas among the peasantry. In a country with a population of under ten million by the start of the First World War and fourteen million at the start of the Second, the overwhelming majority of whom worked in the rice fields, the potential market for modern shoes was small. Shoemakers in particular were held in low esteem: for example, they were excluded from serving as legal witnesses (Crawfurd, 1830, p. 129). The stench and perception of dirtiness involved in tanning and leather work and the Buddhist injunction against taking life, particularly of cattle, no doubt increased the popular negative feeling toward the sector. The latter scruple had kept indigenous Thai from entering the lucrative pork trade (cf. Skinner, 1957, pp. 315–317).

Chinese shoemaking

In contrast, the Chinese had a strong pre-modern tradition of footwear use across social classes, and without the cultural sensitivities attached to feet and shoes shared by the Thai. Thus they brought not only their shoes with them to Siam but a commodified trade in them. Chinese migrants in Southeast Asia, and India, had long been noted for their tendency to enter the leather industry and occasionally to copy European styles for their European clientele. In late 1830s Burma, the American missionary Howard Malcolm noted the resident Chinese population's willingness and ability to manufacture European footwear: 'Foreigners, however, find no difficulty in getting [boots and shoes, in our mode] made by Chinese, who live in all the towns, and make almost any thing, if the pattern be furnished' (Malcolm, 1839, p. 210). It was in the manner of imitation, and learning by doing, or learning on the job, rather than any formal schooling, that modern shoe manufacturing became a Southeast Asian occupation.

The adoption and spread of *modern* leather footwear, particularly the dress shoe, the riding boot and the ceremonial court shoe, accelerated only with the reform of the machinery of state which began in the 1890s, the gradual establishment of a modern army from 1887, and the creation of a Western standard of schooling which hypothetically took the use of modern shoes deep into the interior. The group that took up modern shoe making in Thailand were the Hakka Chinese (Skinner, 1957, pp. 315–318). Around the 1890s, Chinese traditional shoemakers who had previously produced modern leather shoes as a by-line, began specialising in their manufacture. A migrant Hakka shoemaker, Seng Chong, from Meizhou in Guangdong, was one of the first (if not *the* first), specialising in modern shoe manufacture in Thailand, establishing his enterprise in Bangkok in 1899 (Thaksin Chučharin, in

Bruce, 2013; Acharit Praditbatuga and Chayasit Praditbatuga, in Bruce, 2017). The art of modern shoemaking was therefore a 'new' industry for which, as it became increasingly felt by state leaders, as the bureaucracy and state infrastructure expanded, there was a need to control supply.

The contribution of American missionaries

American missionaries began excursions into vocational education at the same time as the Thai Government. However, the contribution of the missionaries differed significantly for, in contrast to what happened in the government's initial programme, missionaries pushed the frontier of crafts outwards to include modern industrial goods such as leather shoes. Influenced by the notion of the 'lazy native', missionary motivation aimed to instil a Protestant work ethic into the population, concluding that:

> 'The Siamese need greatly the industrial element in education to break down the sense of the unworthiness of manual work, and the new plans of the government seek to meet the need by alternative industrial and general courses following the primary school. It is to be doubted, however, whether this will do more than provide two types of education, one of which will be regarded as inferior to the other ... Carpentering and sewing courses, attempted in some of our schools in lower Siam, have been found difficult, the government approving of them but parents objecting.'
>
> (Speer, Day, and Bovaird, 1916, p. 137)

Additionally, they also offered identical reasons to the Thai elite: that the Chinese had monopolised the trades of the country, leaving the indigenous Thais unemployed and indolent.

> 'Before her contact with the outside world, Siam had developed a civilisation of her own, including many arts and crafts; but with the incoming of the Chinese, they were gradually dropped until, today, practically all the trades are in the hands of the Chinese. They have their own guilds and a system of apprenticeship prevails. Since, perhaps, one-third of Bangkok, and the larger centers, are Chinese, and they are still coming into the country by the thousands, from the neighbouring Chinese ports, they will probably remain to be the skilled laborers of the country, and keep the trades in their hands.'
>
> (Speer, Day, and Bovaird, 1916, p. 138)

And finally, the missionaries were critical of the state's focus upon clerical education, which, they feared, would create an over-qualified population.

'Although the Siamese will probably never be able to compete with Chinese in industrial skill, the time is coming, and is fast nearing at hand, when there will not be such great demand for educated young men to fill the government and commercial offices and as teachers in the schools, as heretofore, and some sort of industrial work will have to be provided for the Siamese. As the supply of educated young men exceeds demand, salaries will decrease accordingly, and competition will increase. The time is not far away when the Siamese youth will have to show what he can do instead of merely producing a school certificate or diploma. Those who can not qualify for an office job or as a teacher in a school, will have to find some other way of earning a livelihood. Rather than educate all the boys for teachers and office jobs, attention should be paid toward developing the industries ...'

(Speer, Day, and Bovaird, 1916, p. 138)

Initial efforts in agricultural education failed because of a lack of understanding of Thai agriculture. In contrast, one school in Lampang (also known as Lakawn) in Northern Siam, specialising in leatherwork, was a relative success. It was founded by American Presbyterian missionaries in 1891, and from 1905 was named the Kenneth Mackenzie Memorial School for Boys. It was decided that the school would teach a vocational curriculum and in 1911, missionary Dr Howell S. Vincent incorporated a tannery into the school. A Chinese foreman, a Chinese shoemaker and a 'Lao' who became highly skilled, were engaged to run the factory and put twenty-six boys 'with 26 degrees of skill and willingness' to work. Here boys were trained in tanning and leatherwork and their products sold (United States Presbyterian Church, 1913, p. 378). The tannery was such a success that initially it was sold to its local manager and school teacher, Noi Khomsan in 1915, and then was turned into the Lampang Industrial Company with nine shareholders, although it continued to maintain its vocational schooling function (Kenneth Mackenzie School, 1990; United States Presbyterian Church, 1921, p. 375). Vincent's focus upon tanning and leatherwork served two purposes: firstly to inculcate a sense of diligence and industriousness in a population given to excessive leisure – an attempt to tackle the 'backwardness', as they saw it; and secondly to allow Siam to '[join] in the world's progress', fostering the modern habit of modern footwear use by introducing the entire process of leather footwear manufacture into the population. As for the school's success as a leatherwork producer, this was based upon the low capital requirements which contrasted with the cost of the machinery that it was felt was needed to improve agriculture, and perhaps crucially upon demand for the products the school turned out. The First World War was an important factor in its success when the Siamese military turned to the school to supply its leather needs with the shortages that resulted from drastic reduction in global trade brought on by the war (Speer, Day, and Bovaird, 1916).

The absolute monarchy period

King Vajiravudh's evident interest in promoting vocational education led to the establishment of an annual Arts and Crafts Fair in 1912, in which the students of the country's schools – none of which, apart from the Pho Chang School, specialised only in arts and crafts – were to exhibit examples of their own efforts (Thailand Ministry of Public Instruction, 1912). This was also an opportunity to sell these goods, to encourage the entrepreneurial spirit, and to broaden the market for these goods. Some regions were unable to produce sufficient numbers of products because the school had not previously taught or specialised in such activities. This meant the inclusion of goods that had been produced by young people who were not in fact students, 'in order to preserve domestic arts and crafts, and increase their commercial popularity in the country' (Thailand Ministry of Public Instruction, 1912, p. 51). The theme of the need to promote the idea of an alternative to academic education was also evident: '[Phraya Wisut Suriyasak] received his majesty and explained the efforts that are being made to extend technical training that will help [the pupils] to earn their living. The exhibits were drawn from many schools and classes, and showed the results of training that was not devoted to making boys clerks' (Thailand Ministry of Public Instruction, 1912, pp. 302–304). Leather goods, including shoes, were represented at the Arts and Crafts Exhibition from the Kenneth Mackenzie School. It is significant that the King himself presented the prize for the leatherwork category and did not do so for many of the other categories. It is also perhaps a little ominous for this infant industry's prospects that many of the leather goods, including the shoes, went unsold (Thailand Ministry of Public Instruction, 1912).

Shoemaking had been of particular interest to the King. As crown prince in 1902, on a visit to the USA, Vajiravudh had insisted on visiting a shoe factory in America's shoemaking heartland of Lynn, Massachusetts (The Evening Argus, 1902; The Milwaukee Journal, 1902; Asheville Daily Gazette, 1902). As king in 1916, and in part due to the wartime shortages, he bestowed his patronage on the local Hakka shoemaking establishment, Seng Chong, giving the proprietor the titular surname *Praditbatuga* (meaning 'the maker of my shoes') and the title *Luang* (Thaksin Chučharin, in Bruce, 2013; Acharit Praditbatuga and Chayasit Praditbatuga, in Bruce, 2017). This belied his ostensible hostility to the Chinese but also reflected the reality that if a domestic shoe industry was required, only the Chinese could at present fulfil that need.

Subsequently, however, the lead taken by the Siamese Government in developing the country's economy diminished, and citizens began to voice their concerns at the growing vacuum which was opening up in terms of adequate vocational training as new demands intensified. The lack of an educational facility for the teaching of leather manufacture was also pointed out by one Sim Sun (whose Thai name was Nguan Limpichāt) in a request to the Government to help his tanning enterprise. He implied that it was this absence of proper training that contributed to the poor quality of domestically produced leather, and had written his own manual on proper tanning techniques for distribution in Siam following his own research in Java (Thailand Ministry of Finance, 1924). In 1930, under the subsequent reign of King Prajadhipok (Rama VII), the last absolute monarch before the system's abolition, two young men of the Pho Chang School presented a petition pointing out the absence of shoemaking from the Pho Chang curriculum and requesting funds to allow them to travel to Italy for a year to train in shoemaking. As teachers they had recognised that with the growth of a modern schooling system, with rules regarding appropriate dress, that the required shoes were largely imported, and that those manufacturers who did produce them domestically were foreign (meaning Chinese). With 60,000 students in Siam, there was a considerable market for domestic production. On their return they would open a factory that would double as a school. The request, like so many others, was rejected and there may have been sound reasons for doing so other than conservative fiscal habits (Thailand Ministry of Public Instruction, 1930). Although the petition was turned down, the idea of vocational education as a means of indigenising what currently constituted a Chinese occupation was to be shared by young members of the succeeding regime.

The creation of the Leatherwork School

Following the coup d'état of June 1932, which abolished the absolute monarchy and brought an alliance of civilian bureaucrats and military men into government, a more aggressive economic development programme was adopted. While the National Education Plan of 1932 was in essence a continuation of the cautious policies of the absolute monarchy, the Plan of 1936 bore the more decisive and ambitious stamp of the new generation. For the first time in a national education plan, the term 'vocational', rather than 'special', education (*achiwasueksa*) was used. The consolidation of the young modernising faction among the promoters of the coup, under the premiership of Army General (*Phraya*) Phahon Phonphayuhasena, but with the growing influence of younger idealists such as *Luang* Phibunsongkram (Phibun) and *Luang* Praditmanutham (Pridi Phanomyong) after 1934, had allowed the Government greater freedom to act on its ideals (Stowe, 1991, pp. 83–142). The mainland political orientation of the Chinese migrant community and the allegation of remittances as a drain on the Thai economy informed the economic nationalism of Phibun and Pridi. This meant the indigenisation of the economy, requiring the excision of the Chinese, or self-identifying Chinese, from the economy so as to create a truly *national* one.

The opening of a school specialising in the manufacture of leather goods was part of a broader strategy to forge a modern citizenry and was one of a number of such nationally-oriented vocational schools, such as the Special Secondary School of Homemaking (*rong rian mathayom wisaman kan ruean*) for girls, established in 1934 (Charun Wongsayan and Pramot Chaiyakit,

1961, pp. 27–28). It is noteworthy that rather than expand the curriculum of the Pho Chang School, the new authorities felt the need to establish a separate college, teaching leatherwork and tailoring to both boys and girls. The Phranakhon Leather School was established as a public (state) school in 1936, in central Bangkok near Wat Suthat Thewararam. Its head teacher and school founder was one Annan Simtrakan. The school took in children who had completed a preliminary education up to the level of primary (*prathom*) four, around eleven years of age. The school moved three times in as many years: firstly to Suea Pa Road in 1939, which later accommodated a concentration of shoemakers; and secondly to the Chaloem Lok Bridge in the Pratunam area of Bangkok the following year. In 1941, the school was moved to the Rachadamnoen Klang Avenue, to focus entirely upon leatherwork, discontinuing its tailoring curriculum for females altogether and changing its name to the Ratchadamnoen Leatherwork School (*rong rian chang yeb nang ratchadamnoen*) (Sorachat Ritthirawong, 2012; Bangkok Arts and Crafts College, 2012). At least five other leatherwork schools were created in the provinces, in Chiang Rai, Lamphun, Uttaradit, Petchburi, and Lom Sak. To accompany this enthusiastic embrace of vocational education, and in the same year – 1941 – that the Ministry of Public Instruction was renamed the Ministry of Education, a vocational education department, the Office of the Vocational Education Commission, was set up for the first time. Despite this activity, the provincial leatherwork schools were gradually abandoned following Phibun's fall from the premiership in 1944, leaving just the Ratchadamnoen Leatherwork School.

Despite the creation of the Rathchadamnoen Leatherwork School, the problem of a lack of skilled shoemakers came up again during the shoe shortages brought about by the war, partly because of the end of foreign supplies and partly because of the exile of many shoemakers, all Chinese, to take up market gardening in the countryside to escape the vicissitudes of wartime Bangkok (Thaksin Chučharin, in Bruce, 2013). Phibun had become Prime Minister at the end of 1938 and in concert with Pridi had initiated a raft of essentially anti-Chinese legislation, including the prohibition of occupations for foreigners. This came at a time when the Government launched a campaign to end the culture of going barefoot so that the country, now named Thailand, could take its place among its Fascist allies as a 'civilized' country. According to the propaganda, shoes would build the nation (*rong tao sang chat*) (Royal Thai Government, Public Relations Department, 1942). The list of prohibited occupations did not include shoemaking, which indicated the impracticality of excluding the Chinese from an industry only they were engaged in (Chalida Tositrakun, 2006, pp. 4–5). Instead, the Army requisitioned tanneries to supply the army with its leather requirements at, so it hoped, a lower cost (Office of the Secretary of the Prime Minister, 1942, p. 75). The central justification, however, was that the industry, now regarded as a strategic one, ought not to be in the hands of the Chinese.

Post-war import substitution-driven vocational education

After the war, economic nationalism was rationalised into the import substitution industrialisation strategy (Skinner, 1957, pp. 353–355). This, coupled with the return of arch economic nationalist Phibun to the premiership in 1948, led to a reinvigoration of the Ratchadamnoen Leatherwork School with the purchase of new machinery from the Landis Machine Company of St Louis, Missouri, USA in 1951 (Bruce, 2016). The continued dominance of the Chinese in the industry continued into the post-war period, making it difficult for students of the Leatherwork School to set up as leatherwork manufacturers once they had graduated. Many became employees of the very foreigners they were meant to replace, effectively awarding the benefits of the state training programme to the Chinese. One graduate, Pradit Sapkaew, wrote to the Prime Minister complaining that although he and his 70 fellow graduates had worked for some eight years, none of them had found a permanent placement and none were their own masters, 'we are all Thai … when shoes don't sell well (usually during the rainy season) they lay us off and take on their own (*chek* or Chinese).' Pradit also complained of the treatment meted out to shoemakers and the disrespect shown by members of the public to the industry, an attitude which was pushing it to the margins of Thai society and ensuring its perpetual domination by the Chinese (Office of the Cabinet Secretary, 1951, pp. 4–7).

The response of the Ministry of Industry in 1951 was to propose the setting up of a factory to process tanned leather into leather goods and absorb the graduates of the leatherwork school. The Ministry's Tanning Organisation, established in 1955, would eventually take on the responsibility. But ironically owing to a shortage of graduates sufficient for staffing the projected factory, the enterprise would set up its own training programme. Orphans would be selected as trainees, again indicating the public's negative perception of the trade (Office of the Cabinet Secretary, 1951, p. 10). Nevertheless, the Tanning Organisation succeeded in becoming the main, if not the sole, supplier to the military, taking this potentially lucrative market from the Chinese, who despite the increasing adoption of Thai surnames and nationality, continued to be viewed ambiguously (Coughlin, 1960, pp. 11, 190–197).

Meanwhile, in order to deal with the problem of unemployed alumni, the Leatherwork School opened its own retail outlet, the Leatherwork School Old Boys Shop (*ran rong rian tad-yeb-nang luksit kao*), which supplied shoe-mending services to the police department. In 1956, the Old Boys Shop was asked to carry out its first shoe*making* duties in adjusting an order of boots from abroad to Thai specifications. The combat boots had been found to be ill-fitting for the Thai foot and it was proposed to replace the sole with a rubber one, provided by the Thai Rubber Company, and adjust the leather upper (Thailand Ministry of Industry, 1956, p. 18). The bureaucratisation of shoemaking had reached something of an apogee and although the private sector was to be given a more prominent role under Phibun's successors, from

1957, the military retained their leather tanning and shoemaking establishment.

From the decision to commit aid and armed forces to Korea in late 1950, Thailand's 'survival' was now increasingly framed within the context of the Cold War, as a geopolitical contest with the Communist bloc (Fineman, 1997, pp. 89–125). Thailand joined the Southeast Asia Treaty Organisation (SEATO) in September 1954, which secured the country within the Western bloc, and gave the USA a defining role in the country's path of development. The Cold War also informed Thailand's vocational education policy. The USA provided funding for a series of Technical Institutes, Arts and Crafts no longer being deemed sufficient. The first was founded in Bangkok in 1952, and three more such institutes were established in the south in 1955, the north-east in 1956 and the north in 1957. In 1958, SEATO provided funding to transform the simple carpentry schools of the earlier period of vocational education expansion into modern trade schools, while the United Nations Children's Fund (UNICEF) provided funds for the upgrading of their domestic science schools (Sobsan Utakrit, 1999). In the following year, the SEATO Graduate School of Engineering was opened, originally in the grounds of Chulalongkorn University with an initial emphasis on the teaching of hydraulic engineering, a fitting subject for a country with an abundance of water (USOM, 1962; The National Archives of the UK, 1957). In the same year, the Federal Republic of Germany set up the Thai-German Technical Institute, which was to be merged with other technical schools to form King Mongkut's Institute of Technology in 1971. In 1967, as war waged in Indochina and Thailand stood on its front line, the International Bank for Reconstruction and Development (World Bank), another tool of Western bloc prosecution of the Cold War, provided funds for the improvement of Thailand's ten agricultural schools and its fifteen trade schools (Sobsan Utakrit, 1999).

The focus had turned towards vocational or technical education aimed at upper secondary or tertiary level students. Vocational schools were now teaching 35 hours a week in order to resolve the problem of graduates being unable to compete in the market place without neglecting a broader education. The Leatherwork School's 1960 curriculum for lower secondary level had consisted of 16 hours of general education and 19 hours of a vocational curriculum. In the first two years students received 14 hours of practical training, which rose to 15 hours in the final year, with the remaining time allocated to theory. Subjects in the latter category included a brief history of leather goods, materials used, methods, dyeing studies, design, and draughtsmanship: each was taught for one hour per week. In the final year, these subjects were narrowed down to three hours of business studies and an hour each of design and draughtsmanship. Upper secondary level reduced general education to 12 hours, while the allocation given to practical subjects increased to 18 hours in the first two years. The final year allocated even more hours to practical lessons (Charun Wongsayan and Pramot Chaiyakit, 1961, pp. 52–56). This new availability of funding was crucial in enabling the Thai Government to take this long-desired step towards more substantial and meaningful vocational education. The Cold War had provided them a golden opportunity. The changing of the name of the SEATO Graduate School of Engineering to the Asian Institute of Technology (AIT) in 1967 and the establishment of the Institute of Technology and Vocational Education in 1975, which was to take the name of the Rajamangala (*ratchamonkhon*) Institute of Technology in 1988 – a name bestowed by the King, meaning 'royal auspiciousness' – as the Communist threat evaporated, signalled the greater sophistication, confidence and ambition that the country had developed in the provision of its vocational education (The National Archives of the UK, 1964, p. 10; Far Eastern Economic Review, 1972, p. 58; Sobsan Utakrit, 1999). Nevertheless, the inclusion of shoemaking for the first time in 1973, in a list of occupations reserved for Thais, reflected the completeness of the assimilation of the Chinese rather than the domestic production of ethnic Thai shoemakers (Royal Thai Government, 1973, pp. 14–19).

Concluding remarks

Although they followed a path replicated around the world, the origins of vocational education in Thailand were affected by idiomatic conditions of nineteenth and early twentieth century Siam and interpretations of a succession of rulers all seeking the survival of a Thai nation against the deluge of Western political and Chinese economic power. Vocational education served as one tool among others, keeping this imagined, but in some ways very real, Thai community afloat. This realisation had nevertheless been constrained by traditional understandings of artisanship and social hierarchy. The conception behind the first vocational school, the Pho Chang School, had been steeped in such thinking. The school was first and foremost a memorial to a prince; secondly, it was a charitable institution which specifically was to take in children lacking patrons (orphans); thirdly, it was a place where artisans working in the traditional crafts, as they had once as bonded labourers in the households of their masters before the abolition of slavery, could be returned to the service of the state. In its second manifestation, a step had been taken away from the traditional context for the production of such articles as the satisfaction of elite demand for luxuries. The use of vocational education as a means to muster a national citizenry was clearer in the efforts of missionaries and the economic nationalists of the twentieth century's middle decades to create a leatherwork school, so that indigenous people, as opposed to foreign workers abroad and local Chinese, could master the production of an explicitly 'modern' good. By 1954, the Cold War and US involvement in the country's development had led to a reinterpretation of the need for vocational education and placed the emphasis on higher level technical subjects which spoke more directly to serious industrialisation, but also reflected international concern for the growing technological gap between the developed and developing worlds. Successful assimilation of the Chinese shoemaker removed the original rationale behind the leatherwork school and, with the embrace of private sector-led export-oriented industrialisation from 1973 onwards, the survivalist 'nation-building' motivations that had underpinned technical education faded away.

Notes

1 This refers specifically to the British Education Act of 1902, which established Local Education Authority committees that ended the existence of multiple conflicting authorities with responsibility for the provision of education in an attempt to end a 'chaotic' system, and facilitated an expansion of secondary education.
2 Comprehensive overviews of the entire history of Thai education do not yet exist. This is compiled from the following: Wyatt, 1969, Dept. of Elementary and Adult Education, Thai Ministry of Education, 1970, Pin Malakul, 1975, Valenti, 1974, Thai Ministry of Education, 1976, Terwiel, 1977, Waruni Osatharom, 1981, Krisana Sinchai, 1982, Sukanya Nitungkorn, 1988, 2000, Sobsan Utakrit, 1999; and for a quantitative study, see Michel, 2010, and Michel, 2015.

References

Archival Materials and Other Primary Sources

Asheville Daily Gazette. 1902. North Carolina, USA. 31 October. 7:226. Available at: www.newspapers.com.

Bradt, C. E., King, W. C. and Reherd. H. W. 1920. *Around the World Studies and Stories of Presbyterian Foreign Missions.* Wichita, KS: Missionary Press Co. Inc.

Bruce, T. R. 2012. *Interview with Sorachat Ritthirawong of the Bangkok Arts and Crafts College.* 16 July 2012. Bangkok.

Bruce, T. R. 2013. *Interview with Thaksin Chučharin, son of a Bangkok shoemaker (b. 1941).* 9 September 2013. Bangkok.

Bruce, T. R. 2017. *Interview with Acharit Praditbatuga and Chayasit Praditbatuga, current owners of Seng Chong and great grandsons of Luang Praditbatuga, founder of the business.* 14 December 2017. Bangkok.

Crawford, J. 1830. *Journal of an Embassy from the Governor-General of India to the Courts of Siam, Cochin China Exhibiting a View of the Actual State of Those Kingdoms.* Volume II Second Edition. London: Henry Colburn and Richard Bentley.

The Evening Argus. 1902. 31 October. Available at: www.newspapers.com.

de la Loubere, S. *The Kingdom of Siam. 1693*969. Oxford in Asia Historical Reprint. Kuala Lumpur: Oxford University Press.

Malcolm, H. 1839. *Travels in South-Eastern Asia, Embracing Hindustan, Malaya, Siam, and China with Notices of Numerous Missionary Stations, and a Full Account of The Burman Empire; with Dissertations, Tables, Etc.* Vol. 1. Boston, MA: Gould, Kendall and Lincoln.

McFarland, G. B. 1928, 2011. *Historical Sketch of Protestant Missions in Siam, 1828–1928.* Bangkok: Bangkok Times Press, Ltd; this edition: Inter Publishing Enterprise.

The Milwaukee Journal. 1902. 31 October. Available at: www.newspapers.com.
The National Archives of the UK. 1957. FO 371/135659. *Telegram No. 108, From Clutton, Manila, to Foreign Office: 'SEATO Council Meeting, March 11 First Day'*. 11 March.
The National Archives of the UK. 1964. FO 371/180455. *Report of the Expert Study Group on the Future of the SEATO Graduate School of Engineering*. December 1964. Bangkok: South-East Asia Treaty Organization, p. 10.
Office of the Cabinet Secretary. 1942. (2) SR. 0201.22.2. 12/1 *Request for a Domestic Loan for an Industrial Enterprise to Prepare the Tanneries from the Minister of Finance to the Cabinet Secretary*. 10 October. p. 75.
Office of the Cabinet Secretary. 1951. (2) SR. 0201.22.2. 12/2, Shoes. *Request to Promote the Profession of Shoemaking* pp. 4–7.
Royal Thai Government. 1887. *Gazette (Ratchakichanubeksa—(RKB)*. 4:6. p. 48, 12 May 1887.
Royal Thai Government. 1902a. *Comments on the Organisation of Education* [kwamhen thi cha chat kansueksa, rattanakosinsok, 121].
Royal Thai Government. 1902b. *Draft Education Plan*. 21 July.
Royal Thai Government. 1964. *Royal Orders in the Fifth and Sixth Reigns in Context* [phraratchahatlekha song sang ratchakan nai ratchakan thi 5 lae 6 kap rueang prakop]. Bangkok, pp. 106–120.
Royal Thai Government. 1973. *Gazette (Ratchakichanubeksa—RKB)*. 90:24. pp. 14-19, 14 March.
Royal Thai Government, Public Relations Department. 1941. *Compendium of State Conventions and National Cultural Regulations* [pramuan rataniyom lae rabiab wathanatham haeng chat]. Bangkok: Public Relations Department.
Speer, R. E., Day, D. H., and Bovaird, D. 1916. *Report of Deputation Sent by the Board of Foreign Missions of the Presbyterian Church in the U.S.A. in the Summer of 1915 to Visit the Missions in Siam and the Philippine Islands, and on the Way Home to Stop at Some of the Stations in Japan, Korea and China*. New York: The Board of Foreign Missions of the Presbyterian Church in the USA.
Thailand Ministry of Finance. 7 December 1899. R. 5. Kh /22 Kh. 5 2/3: Campbell to Phatsakorawong, Bangkok.
Thailand Ministry of Finance. August, 1924. R. 6. Kh. 12. 3/18: Mr Sim Sun – Nguan Limpichāt to King Vajiravudh.
Thailand Ministry of Finance. 1925. *Statistical Year Book of the Kingdom of Siam (SYS) 1924–1925*. Tenth Edition. Bangkok: Department of General Statistics, Ministry of Finance.
Thailand Ministry of Industry. 1956. OK 0201.2.1/20 Collected Documents on the Thai Rubber Company Limited, 1953–1956: Quality Guaranty for Police Brand Rubber Shoe Soles and Heels. pp. 18–21.
Thailand Ministry of Public Instruction. 13 January 1896. R. 5. STh. 50.2/2: Her Majesty's Intention to Establish a Training College.
Thailand Ministry of Public Instruction. 2 January 1906. R. 5. STh. 5/32, 69. Wachirayan to King; 5/32, 71 Prince Wachirayan's Opinions on Education.
Thailand Ministry of Public Instruction. 29 November 1912. R. 6. STh. 17/1; Report on the Arts and Crafts Fair, p. 51; pp. 302–304.
Thailand Ministry of Public Instruction. 11 September 1930. R. 7. STh. 1/266. Teachers, Mr. Krachang Ūnhawait and Mr. Phū Niwatbūt, Royal Petition to Secure Funds for Training in Straw Hats, Shoe and Toy Manufacture. pp. 1–25.

United States Operations Mission to Thailand (USOM). November 1962. *Thai-American Economic and Technical Cooperation*. Bangkok: USOM.

United States Presbyterian Church. 1913. *Seventy-Sixth Annual Report of the Board of Foreign Missions of the Presbyterian Church in the USA*. New York.

United States Presbyterian Church. 1921. *Eighty-Fourth Annual Report of the Board of Foreign Missions of the Presbyterian Church in the USA*. New York.

Charun Wongsayan and Pramot Chaiyakit. 1961. *Documents from the Research Department; Educational Development Series; Number 3: Development of the Vocational Education Curriculum*, (kwampenma khong laksut achiwasueksa) Bangkok.

Secondary Works

Bangkok Arts and Crafts College. c. 2012. *General Conditions of the Educational Institution*. Bangkok: BACC.

Brown, I. 1988. *The Elite and the Economy in Siam c.1890–1920*. Singapore: Oxford University Press.

Bruce, T. R. 2016. *The Sole of a Nation: The Emergence and Development of Thailand's Shoe Industry, 1855–1997*. PhD thesis. Department of History, SOAS, University of London.

Chalida Tositrakun. 2006. *Labour Rights of Foreigners in Thailand: A Study of the Process of Acquiring Labour Rights in Thailand*. MA thesis. Faculty of Law, Thammasat University, Bangkok.

Clarke, L. and Winch, C. ed(s). 2007. *Vocational Education: International Approaches, Developments and Systems*. London and New York: Routledge.

Coughlin, R. J. 1960. *Double Identity: The Chinese in Modern Thailand*. Hong Kong: Hong Kong University Press/Oxford University Press.

Far Eastern Economic Review. 1972. Far Eastern Economic Review Yearbook. Hong Kong.

Fineman, D. 1997. *A Special Relationship: The United States and Military Government in Thailand, 1947–1958*. Honolulu: University of Hawai'i Press.

Foster, P. J. 1965. The Vocational School Fallacy in Development Planning. In: Anderson, C. A. and Bowman, M. J. ed(s). *Education and Economic Development*. London: Frank Cass & Co. Ltd.

Gehin, J. P. 2007. Vocational Education in France: A Turbulent History and a Peripheral Role. In: Clarke, L. and Winch, C. ed(s). *Vocational Education: International Approaches, Developments and Systems*. pp. 46–60.

Headrick, D. R. 1988. *The Tentacles of Progress: Technology Transfer in the Age of Imperialism*. New York and Oxford: Oxford University Press.

Ingram, J. 1971. *Economic Change in Thailand, 1850–1970*. Stanford, CA: Stanford University Press.

Kenneth Mackenzie School. 1990. *100 years K. M. S. Centenary 1880–1890*. Lampang: Kenneth Mackenzie School.

Krisana Sinchai. 1982. *Two Hundred Years of Thai Education: Some Important Events*. Bangkok: Chulalongkorn University Press.

Larsson, T. 2012. *Land and Loyalty: Security and the Development of Property Rights in Thailand*. Ithaca, NY: Cornell University Press.

McDaniel, J. T. 2008. *Gathering Leaves and Lifting Words: Histories of Buddhist Monastic Education in Laos and Thailand*. Seattle: University of Washington Press.

Michel, S. 2010. *The Burgeoning of Education in Thailand: A Quantitative Success.* In: Mournier, A. and Tangchaung. P. ed(s). *Education and Knowledge in Thailand: The Quality Controversy.* Bangkok: Silkworm.

Michel, S. 2015. 'Education in Thailand: When Economic Growth is no Longer Enough'. *London Review of Education.* 13:3, pp. 79–91.

Montesano, M. J. 2008. Capital, State and Society in the History of Chinese-Sponsored Education in Trang. In: Montesano, M. J. & Jory, P. eds. 2008. *Thai South and Malay North: Ethnic Interactions on a Plural Peninsula.* pp. 231–272.

Pin Malakul. 1975. 'Education during the Time when His Highness Prince Dhaninvat was Minister of Public Instruction'. *Journal of the Siam Society.* 63:1. pp. 9–27.

Resnick, S. A. 1970. 'The Decline of Rural Industry under Export Expansion: A Comparison among Burma, Philippines, and Thailand, 1870–1938'. *The Journal of Economic History.* 30:1.

Sanderson, M. 1983. *Education, Economic Change and Society in England 1780–1870.* London: Macmillan.

Sanderson, M. 1999. *Education and Economic Decline in Britain, 1870 to the 1990s.* Cambridge: Cambridge University Press.

Searle, G. R. 1971. *The Quest for National Efficiency: A Study in British Politics and Political Thought, 1899–1914.* Berkeley and Los Angeles: University of California Press.

Skinner, G. W. 1957. *Chinese Society in Thailand: An Analytical History.* Ithaca, NY: Cornell University Press.

Sobsan Utakrit. 1999. 'The Technical-Vocational Education and Training System in Thailand'. *International Journal of Sociology.* 29:1.

Stowe, J. A. 1991. *Siam Becomes Thailand: A Story of Intrigue.* London: C. Hurst & Co.

Sukanya Nitungkorn 1988. 'The Problems of Secondary Education Expansion in Thailand'. *Southeast Asian Studies,* 26:1.

Sukanya Nitungkorn 2000. 'Education and Economic Development during the Modernisation Period: A comparison between Thailand and Japan'. *Southeast Asian Studies,* 38:2.

Terwiel, B. 1997. The Development of a Centrally Organised Education System in Thailand. In: Orr, K. ed. *Appetite for Education in Contemporary Asia,* Canberra: Australian National University.

Thai Ministry of Education. 1970. *Education in Thailand: A Century of Experience.* Bangkok: Dept. of Elementary and Adult Education, Ministry of Education.

Thai Ministry of Education. 1976. *A History of Thai Education.* Bangkok: Ministry of Education.

Valenti, J. J. 1974. 'Current Problems and Developments in Thai Education'. *International Review of Education.* 20:1. pp. 71–82.

Wales, H. G. Q. 1931. *Siamese State Ceremonies: Their History and Function with Supplementary Notes.* London: Bernard Quaritch Ltd.

Waruni Osatharom. 1981. *Kansueksa nai sangkhom Thai: Pho. So. 2411 – Pho. So. 2475* [Education in Thai Society, 1868–1932]. Bangkok: Chulalongkorn University.

Weber, E. 1977. *Peasants into Frenchmen: The Modernization of Rural France, 1870–1914.* London: Chatto & Windus.

Wolf, A. 2002. *Does Education Matter? Myths about Education and Economic Growth.* London: Penguin.

Wyatt, D. K. 1969. *The Politics of Reform in Thailand: Education in the Reign of King Chulalongkorn.* New Haven, CT and London: Yale University Press.

7 Vần quốc ngữ: Teaching Modernity through Classics

Women's Education in Colonial Vietnam

Marta Lopatkova

CHARLES UNIVERSITY, PRAGUE

Women's traditional education in Vietnam

Until the launching of the education reforms of the twentieth century, Vietnamese women had no access to formal schooling. As in other Confucian countries, traditional Confucian schools (later called 'indigenous schools' by the French) were the only existing educational institutions. These schools were meant to prepare men from their childhood onward to climb a ladder of levels and exams to become officials in the Confucian state administrative system. The curriculum had changed only a little in centuries and consisted mostly of learning classical Chinese and Confucian classics, memorising and writing comments, and learning different literary styles. Boys' teaching was often provided at home by their fathers or private teachers. After reaching a certain level of knowledge, students attended Confucian schools in villages, towns and cities according to the level they needed. These Confucian schools were obviously not open to girls and there were no other schools for girls or women. In a culture strongly influenced by patriarchal and patrilineal Confucian philosophy, ethics and morals with an exclusive position for ancestor worship, girls were naturally relegated to the side-lines. Sons were preferred and needed to perform the rituals required to ensure family prosperity.

Despite this male-centred context, Vietnamese women could receive some degree of 'formal' education. However, as women were generally considered hard to educate, the instruction they received took place in the inner quarters of the house, behind public space and separated from the men's world. Additionally, if we speak about Confucianism and Confucian ideas of women's education, we mostly mean women from the elite strata of society – daughters of families of Confucian scholars and officials. The situation in the countryside was very different, due to the agricultural conditions there. It was simply not possible for girls to be separated from the men's world, because they participated actively in the livelihoods of their families. Even most of the male rural population was not educated and did not frequent any schooling institution because of the expense or lack of availability (Marr, 1981).

We will see later that the content of instruction to daughters of members of the highest echelons of society was in fact very similar to that given to peasant girls who were raised and educated at home. In both cases, tutors focused on practical household skills rather than 'trivia' and more sophisticated subjects. In the case of upper-class women, education and upbringing was much more delicate, and often, at the same time, narrower. 'Only in rich families, daughters knew how to weave, sew; the poor could merely know how to raise pigs, chickens, do rice husking, pounding, sifting and dishwashing'[1] recounted the column Nhờn đàn bà (Women's Voice) on women's education in the newspaper Đông Dương Tạp Chí in 1913 (Tran, 2010, p. 3).

Classical Confucian women's education consisted mainly of instructions on Confucian ethics, morality and practical skills to learn how to be a perfect housewife and wife to her husband and mother to her children. Girls had to learn how to behave properly in all possible situations, how to manage family finances, the household and the proper way to raise their offspring. According to Confucian tradition, girls were raised in order to attain the 'Four Virtues' (tứ đức): proper behaviour (hạnh), proper speech (ngôn), proper appearance (dung) and household skills (công); and being 'a subject of the three submissions' (tam tòng) – together called tam tòng, tứ đức. The three obediences, also called the 'three submissions', were a set of basic moral statuses for women to adhere to: obedience to her father as a daughter, to her husband as a wife, and to her sons in widowhood. Women who succeeded in these were praised as 'wholesome daughters, gentle wives, and caring mothers' (Tai, 1996, p. 94). Chastity – (trinh) was one virtue praised above the others and was one of the most praised qualities a woman could hold.

These moral instruction manuals, which served as their study materials, tended to be rather dull and uninteresting, due to their repetitive character. Although the oldest copy of these manuals for girls in Vietnam dates from the nineteenth century, it is highly probable that similar instruction books made their way from China to Vietnam much earlier. Most of the Vietnamese versions of these manuals took inspiration from Ming-era (1368–1644) manuals and morality books for women, as did other Vietnamese manuals for family rituals (Li, 2007)[2]. Only a few copies of these documents have survived the periods of war and harsh climatic conditions of Vietnam. In precolonial times, most popular books for women, among them the favorites, Nữ huấn – (Instruction for Women), Nữ giới (Restrictions for Women) and Nữ tắc (Rules for Women), were, according to a 1924 edition of the newspaper Nam Phong, 'boring; telling childlike stories, containing meaningless trifling stories, inspiring no elegance and charm'[3] (Tran, 2010).

Not only did the curriculum taught to boys and girls differ, but the language and style of each contrasted significantly. As boys were trained from early childhood in classical Chinese, which served not only as an official administrative language, but also as the language of high literature, books designated for boys were mostly written in classical Chinese. Considering the fact that most women were not educated and were not able to read and write, manuals for them were often written in what now we call *southern characters* – *chữ nôm* – in other words, Vietnamese vernacular script[4]. Although the *chữ nôm* was extremely hard to learn (it was necessary to know both classical Chinese and Vietnamese in order to do so), if it were read aloud, illiterate people could understand. Texts for women were often meant to be heard and not read by the women themselves. Most of these texts rhymed as they were supposed to be remembered, repeated and passed on by recitation. It was recommended that women murmur these verses to themselves while attending to housework or during other feminine activities such as embroidery, knitting or sewing. However, it would be incorrect to imply that all women in the pre-colonial era were illiterate. There were women whom it would be difficult to call uneducated during this period, for example Hồ Xuân Hương – one of Vietnam's most famous female poets – but such women were a mere drop in the ocean[5].

Education in French Indochina

The first *modern* or Western-style schools – it is probably more precise to refer to them as courses – were set up in the 1860s, shortly after the French arrival in the area in 1858. It was necessary to recruit interpreters to manage the newly acquired territory and facilitate communication between the colonisers and the locals. Even in the later periods of the French presence in Vietnam we should not consider the colonialists' interest in education reform as a sign of their philanthropy and altruism, but as a component of France's *mission civilisatrice* and thus as a means for controlling the population of the colony. Latinised Vietnamese script *chữ quốc ngữ*, and print media became the crucial tools in the processes of westernisation, modernisation, enculturation and bringing up new generations of Annamites to think of France as a 'nurturing mother, loving us like its youngest girl', as Sương Nguyệt Anh put it in the preface of her magazine *Nữ Giới Chung* (*Women's Bell*) (Taylor and Whitmore 1995, p. 182). For these reasons, education reform was among the colonialists' top priorities in French Indochina.

As an increasing number of French officials and private citizens came to Indochina, there was a growing need for schooling institutions in the colonies for French children, including girls. Because of those needs, the very first French schools were opened, firstly in Cochinchina, and later in the protectorates of Annam and Tonkin. These schools were intended for the children of French citizens residing in the colony. The curriculum was adopted from metropolitan schools in France and the language of tuition was French. New Western-style education attracted the attention of certain pro-Western and pro-French Vietnamese individuals, who started sending their children to these schools. In 1887 French Indochina was formed from three parts of Vietnam (Cochinchina, Annam and Tonkin), together with Laos and Cambodia. Officially only the southern part of the whole territory – Cochinchina – became a colony, whereas the other components held the status of a protectorate.

Early in the 1890s the traditional Confucian schools disappeared completely from Cochinchina, because the administration in the only colony proper of France's Indochina entity was completely French, as opposed to the administrative systems in the other components of French Indochina, and there was no need for Confucian-educated state officials, as remained the case in the lessdirectly governed protectorates. Unfortunately, there was not enough compensation for this loss in terms of other forms of education by the French authorities. For a long time, there was only one school, the French Lycée Chasseloup-Laubat in Saigon, established on 14 November 1874 as a *collège indigène*, to train the future cadres and interpreters for the administration's needs[6]. In Tonkin, the process of building new, modern, Western-style schools was slower. According to archival sources in the French colonial archives in Aix-en-Provence and the Archives of Vietnam *(Lưu trữ nhà nước)*, the first French schools were established in 1886 in Tonkin and in 1896 in Annam.

At the same time, the first proto-Franco-Annamite schools[7], combining elements of indigenous and French schooling, were opened. School inspector Gustave Dumoutier, an assistant to Resident-General Paul Bert and a strong advocate of Franco-Annamite education reform, refused to extend the abolition of the traditional education system which had occurred in Cochinchina to other parts. Instead of a complete replacement, he proposed a new system which would combine both – the indigenous schools with modern French education – in the new Franco-Annamite system. The importance he attached to the education of the indigenous population is reflected in the following statement:

> 'School is the strongest and most effective and convincing tool ... If we want to exercise our influence in these countries, to draw Indochinese people to follow our way, to liberate them and raise their spirit, we should deliver our ideas to them and teach them our language ... starting from the school'.[8]

Education of girls was high on the list of reform priorities; 'Girls' education is the most important, because women are a precious auxiliary for the education of small children', stated the director of a school in Sadec, a town in Cochinchina (Văn Thảo Trịnh, 1993, p. 178). The project of establishing Franco-Annamite schools was supposed to be launched subsequently in all areas, but due to the lack of finances it had to be postponed in these early stages and was only fully developed later.

The first modern schools and first schools for girls

At the beginning of the twentieth century, French Indochina's indigenous intelligentsia was convulsed by an intellectual turmoil, due to the formation of different intellectual circles with very different views on and responses to the French presence and their influence in the country. Under the influence of Chinese reformists, such as Liang Qichao and Kang Youwei, and Western philosophers, Vietnamese intellectuals, around the personalities of Phan Bội Châu and Phan Chu Trinh, founded a movement called *Đông Kinh Nghĩa Thục*, the famous Tonkin Free School.

The idea of modernisation (*hiện đại hoá*) was considered essential in order to compete with the French, and the intellectuals of the Tonkin Free School saw it as the only way in which the Vietnamese could possibly one day rid themselves of the colonists and rule their own country. The school was inspired by the example of Fukuzawa Yukichi, a Japanese modernist and founder of Keio University in the 1860s. The Vietnamese loose imitation was opened in March 1907. The aim was to create a modern school, to teach in the Latin script *chữ quốc ngữ*, by using modern textbooks, created and published specifically for the purposes of the school. The modernists perceived women as active participants in the modernisation of the country and society. It was desirable to educate the future mothers of new civilised and modernised generations. Therefore, they opened classes not only for men but also for women. Furthermore, the school was not meant to be an institution solely for children. Instead, classes were to be open for all who wanted to study, no matter what age they were. Those intellectuals who sought independence from French rule realised the importance of involving women in the movement, partly through the influence of Western literature but also because of the realisation that including women would greatly swell the ranks of those Vietnamese actively striving for independence. The curriculum was the most progressive Vietnam had seen up to that date. Science, mathematics, French, geography, history, literature, hygieneand other Western subjects were introduced. Soon after the school opened, it had to be moved to a larger building, due to the huge demand from prospective students. The French did not turn a blind eye to the independence-minded climate at the Free Tonkin School. It was shut down in 1908 due to suspicions of revolutionary activities, and some of the teachers were imprisoned.

Despite the school's brief existence, it caused a sensation which served as a warning shot for the French authorities. The colonial administration felt the urge to exercise a strict control on native education, for fear that the movement towards modernisation and Westernisation could get out of their control. The first Director-General of Public Instruction, Henri Gourdon, expressed this sentiment in the following way: 'Let's get hold of the movement towards Western civilisation in order to take charge of it and make it serve our goals so that it will not develop outside our control, and perhaps even at our expense' (Ha, 2014, p. 185)[9].

Neither of the two available ready-made educational systems was ideal for the French rulers. Supporting the traditional indigenous system based on classical Confucian learning would only encourage traditionalist-based anti-colonial and anti-modernisation movements to develop and facilitate the empowerment of traditional elites. Additionally, the traditional education system would produce graduates unable – and likely unwilling – to co-operate with the modern French administrative system. In contrast, the modern

French metropolitan system would create new generations realising their right to be included in that famous declaration of 'the natural, inalienable, and sacred rights of man', and demanding the same treatment as French nationals. Both were undesirable. Instead of opting for one or the other, a hybrid system was created: the new, more unified Franco-Annamite education system, which was a development of the earlier idea. The system also included women, not because they were its primary target, but because it followed the French-inspired trend which had introduced women's education in the early nineteenth century (Quartararo, 1995). After their introduction in the late nineteenth century in Cochinchina, Franco-Annamite Schools had been gradually opened in other areas. Even so, until 1906, there was no concept of a unified schooling system in French Indochina.

Education reforms and the Franco-Annamite education system

This situation – the lack of a unified education system – was supposed to be remedied by the establishment of a new institution, the Council for the Improvement of Indigenous Education. This aimed to create a new system, in part through the reform of that already existing in Cochinchina, which would then be applicable for the whole of French Indochina. In 1906 the Governor-General of French Indochina, Paul Beau, launched what became the first comprehensive set of reforms that laid the basis for the Franco-Annamite schooling system, built around French needs and involving both boys and girls. The first step was intended to be allowing girls to attend classes in indigenous Confucian schools. This was meant to give them rapid access to education while other elements of the reforms were gradually implemented (Ha, 2014, p. 188). But since Confucian indigenous schools had always been customarily closed for girls, families were not ready to send their daughters to these schools. Therefore, this arrangement proved completely useless.

According to Văn Thảo Trịnh, the rest of the reform programme was accomplished in three phases:

1 1906–17: The division of all existing schools into three new categories: French, Franco-Annamite, and indigenous Confucian schools. All schools in each of the categories were to follow the same curriculum.
2 1917–24: The abolition of the system of indigenous Confucian schools and the opening of only Franco-Annamite or French schools; this was accompanied by plans to abolish the Confucian examination system which remained valid until 1917.
3 1924–45: The extension of this system to, and the opening of, new schools in farther and more remote areas of Vietnam.

(Văn Thảo Trịnh, 2009, pp. 52–69)

The result was that by the end of the 1920s the system had reached its final form with two parallel systems, Franco-Annamite and French metropolitan, both with a different structure and curriculum. The French system offered mostly to French citizens a metropolitan curriculum from kindergarten all the way to the lycée, whereas the Franco-Annamite system, designated for natives, comprised four levels: vocational, primary, primary superior and secondary. (Ha, 2014, p. 186.) In the 1920s the Franco-Annamite schooling system comprised three years of elementary education in Vietnamese, three years of primary education in French, four years of primary superior education in French, and three years of French-language secondary education, leading to an Indochinese baccalaureate[10] (Zinoman, 2014, p. 23). Alongside these options, there were also three to four years of vocationally oriented primary superior education.

A year after launching the reform programme, the very first Franco-Annamite public primary school for girls was opened in Nam Định. And in 1910, by Decree No. 2436 of the Governor-General of Indochina, two more schools for girls were opened in Haiphong and Hanoi, including the famous Ecole Brieux on Hàng Trống Street (Tran, 2010, p. 4). (Later, in 1910, the school was moved to Hàng Cót Street, because the demand for placing girls into classes exceeded the existing capacity of the original premises[11].) Although the director of l'Ecole Brieux was a Frenchwoman, most of the staff were local. The usual practice was to hire teachers to teach *chữ quốc ngữ* from southern Vietnam where Latinised script had been adopted earlier. As capacity was limited, the initial measures to educate women were very partial in their application. In addition, due to the limited location of the schools the students came mostly from higher middle-class urban families.

In her family memoirs, Duong Van Mai Elliot describes her grandmother, a famous silk vendor with a house on the prestigious Hàng Gai Street, as a very modern woman – 'ahead of many women in her generation' – because she sent her daughters to l'Ecole Brieux to be educated (Elliott, 1999, p. 64). Unfortunately, Duong Van Mai's father made her mother abandon her education after the wedding. This family story illustrates how the idea of modern education for girls and women was still revolutionary, and conservative sentiments within the home could potentially influence the outcome of the education reform programme.

By 1913 there were already nine girls' schools in Tonkin. This trend continued in other parts of Vietnam as well. Some of the most famous institutions for girls, like Đồng Khánh upper primary school in the royal city of Huế (currently called Trường Trung học phổ thông Hai Bà Trưng), which opened in 1917, or the famous Áo Tím school, founded in Saigon in 1915, formed a part of this wave. In the school year 1922–23, 35 females attended the elementary level and 358 the secondary level of the Đồng Khánh upper primary (Dang Thi Van Chi, 2016). In 1917 Đồng Khánh School, the present-day Trưng Vương School on Hàng Bài Street, was the first upper primary Franco-Annamite school for girls to be founded in Hanoi. Đồng Khánh School provided the highest level of education available for girls within the female-only sector institutions in Hanoi (Tran, 2009, p. 6). There was no separate secondary school for girls, and those who wanted to continue studying after graduating from upper primary school had to enrol in the *Collège du Protectorat* (present day *Trường Bưởi*) with their male schoolmates. The number of girls studying there compared to boys was very low. According to the *Annuaire Statistique de l'Indochine* (9th volume, 1939–40), in 1940 there were just 10 female students at the *Collège du Protectorat*, together with 192 males.

The curriculum at the Franco-Annamite schools for girls

Despite the initiation of reforms that for the first time included women in education, a curriculum specifically designed for girls took some time to develop. The curriculum at the first Franco-Annamite school for girls was an abridged version of a boys' school curriculum. Major parts comprised subjects which prepared girls for their future careers as mothers and wives. Apart from those exclusively 'female' subjects, girls were trained in French, music and basic mathematics. The extent to which the school offered an excessively simplified and superficial course of study was reflected in the criticism it received in popular newspapers such as *Đông Dương tạp chí*[12], where the author pointed out somewhat sardonically that 'It is hard to be civilised with this rudimentary practice' (Tran, 2010, p. 9). It took a considerable amount of time to create a unified education programme for girls' schools, and it was only in 1917 that Albert Sarraut implemented the General Code of Education (Règlement Général de l'Instruction Publique en Indochine), which defined the rules and curriculum in all Franco-Annamite schools for girls:

> '… the organisation of primary schools for girls in principle obeys the same rules as that of municipal schools for boys. There will be at least one primary school for native girls with the full cycle of primary education (Écoles primaires de plein exercice) in the capital of each province. At the moment, if a separate school for girls could not be built, native girls can go to mixed schools but should be seated in a separate class'.[13]

In 1917 Đồng Khánh, the first upper primary Franco-Annamite school for girls, offered two study programmes. The first focused on general education (morals and etiquette, *chữ quốc ngữ*, French, hygiene, arithmetic, accounting and geography; while the second focused on domestic skills like household management, sewing, embroidery and other such activities. (Tran, 2010). Finally, in 1918 a new unified curriculum for boys and girls was launched and differed only in the classes on domestic or manual work and hygiene, according to gender. Hygienic obsession was a central feature of the *mission civilisatrice* in French colonies. According to Albert Sarraut's 1925 *La mission civilisatrice de la France*, it was necessary to combine and to focus on three main areas of policy. Creating a hygiene programme that promoted the health of the indigenous people was considered a priority, alongside the improvement of justice and the judicial system, and the development of educational policies to adapt the indigenous mentality to new ways of thinking in order to build up a generation of educated Francophile colonial subjects (Tran, 2015). As can be seen from the following sketch of the curriculum in the period from 1917 to 1945, hygiene and morals were represented at every single level.

Years 1–3: Morals, Vietnamese, French, Chinese characters, History and Geography of Tonkin and Indochina, Hygiene and Physical education, Arithmetic, Rudiments of Manual skills.
Years 4–6: French[14], Vietnamese, Chinese characters, Moral, Arithmetic, Elements of Geometry, Basic Physical and Natural Sciences, Geography of Indochina, Vietnamese History, Hygiene and Physical Education, Manual Skills.
Years 7–10: French, Vietnamese, Chinese characters, Morals and Psychology, History and Geography of Indochina and France, Natural History, Hygiene and Physical Education, Mathematics, Technology.
Years 11–15: French, Vietnamese, Morals and Psychology, History and Geography of Indochina and France, Mathematics, Physics, Chemistry, Natural History, Drawing, Technology.

(Tran, 2009, p. 13)

Additionally, hygiene was an important feature of education and policy. This was because of the significant medical advances and discoveries of the late decades of the nineteenth and first decades of the twentieth centuries, but also because of the fear of epidemics and diseases which the French had experienced in the first decades of their Far Eastern conquests and continued to struggle against over the course of the whole colonial period. Hygiene was also a frequently discussed topic on the pages of popular newspapers such as *Đông Dương tạp chí, Nam Phong, Phụ Nữ Tân Văn* or *Phong Hoá*, where the old society, its manners and its outdated customs were a target for harsh criticism[15].

The other subject represented at all levels of education was 'morals' (*luân lý*), and this concept was rooted in precolonial Vietnamese Confucianism. During the reign of the last Vietnamese dynasty, the Nguyễn dynasty (1802–1945), Confucianism became even more rigid than in previous centuries by the adoption of Gia Long's new code, which was basically a copy of a code from Qing dynasty China. Confucianism was therefore deeply rooted in society, and it would not be possible to rapidly change it. In fact, French colonisers saw an opportunity to exploit this inflexible system. Vietnamese living in a strict hierarchical society were raised to have a strong sense of duty, loyalty, respect and obedience to the rulers and people of a higher social rank. It was believed that it would only be necessary to change the object of this duty, loyalty and respect. After the French conquest, France and its representatives – the French administrators and colons (colonial settlers) – were supposed to become the object of Vietnamese social deference to whom the Vietnamese were to express these useful sentiments of loyalty and obedience. This ideological programme, '*la conquête des esprits*' or 'conquest of the minds', was meant to create a man, an economic individual who shared similar principles and beliefs to French nationals, while manifesting a strong sense of submissive obedience and loyalty to the colonial system and *la mère-patrie* – the motherland.

Textbooks and study materials

Until 1906 there were no special materials for students in French Indochina, and textbooks and teaching manuals were imported from France. Additionally, pedagogical reviews, such as *Học báo* in the North and *Sư phạm* in the South, were published. The content of these materials strictly followed the colonial ideology of a unified Indochina where the French were described as wise rulers who had managed to make Indochina more prosperous (Tran, 2010, p. 15). Teaching materials praised Confucian concepts of duty, obedience and respect, and family duty was considered the most valued virtue. In the Confucian world, the family was extremely important because it symbolised a microcosm of the world and these family relations were applied to the whole of society. As a son was bound to his father by filial piety, in the same way the subject was unreservedly loyal and bound to his ruler and expressed his respect for him. This Franco-Confucian-colonial setting formed the basis for the teaching materials for both boys and girls.

After the education reform of 1906, the French administration started producing textbooks and study materials designated specifically for Annamite students. It was necessary to create a set of textbooks teaching the Latinised form *chữ quốc ngữ* and other Western subjects which until then were unknown in Vietnam. While these schools exposed their students to some of the most fundamental aspects of the changing society and to modernisation, their existence and their proliferation of *chữ quốc ngữ* even affected people with much less contact with the schools. Those who did not go to French-Annamite schools, or those who dropped out after the first few years (which in fact constituted the majority) learnt at least enough *chữ quốc ngữ* to be able to function in colonial-oriented Vietnamese society. Some people studied at schools and some by themselves at home, or were taught by their parents or by voluntary organisations. Some, especially from upper and middle class families, had private teachers to teach them basic *chữ quốc ngữ* (Marr, 1981).

Besides the officially organised schools and classes, numerous informal study groups and organisations were set up in all three parts of French Indochina in the 1920s and 1930s. One of the more well-known was the Women's Labour-Study Association (Nữ Công học hội) founded by Đạm Phương, a passionate advocate of women's education. Its aim was to spread the idea of the educated woman and the Latinised form of Vietnamese. Following this development, young Vietnamese intellectuals started creating their own study materials and textbooks in order to spread not only ideas of modernisation but also of patriotism. All of the texts in French Indochina had to pass through strict French censorship; many of those books were banned, and their authors fined or imprisoned, due to their subversive character, with content appealing to patriotism and national identity, and calling for independence.

As French authorities did much to preserve and promote select Confucian ideas, it was natural that truly progressive groups promoting women's emancipation were few and far between. Modern girls behaving à *la mode*, adopting French fashions and lifestyle trends, were considered by most Vietnamese intellectuals as a bad example of adaptation to the French cultural opportunity, and a negative form of Westernisation. One of the products of this period was a growth in romantic fiction, eagerly consumed by these new 'modern girls', which in turn was blamed for their corruption. Being labelled as *cô gái mới* [modern girl] was not considered desirable, and led to calls for textbooks that stressed traditional values by some Vietnamese (Marr, 1981). Partly as a result of this disorientation of the Vietnamese female, the number of educational morality books increased throughout the interwar period in the whole of French Indochina; one example among the many produced was *Vần quốc ngữ*.

The textbook *Vần quốc ngữ*

Although, Vần quốc ngữ, a tiny book, was just one of the many 'textbooks' from this period, it is a particularly pertinent and practical example, illustrating previous theories on the dissemination of Western knowledge, the Latinised script of Vietnamese, *chữ quốc ngữ* and modern concepts such as hygiene, while at the same time conserving and promoting the classical Confucian concepts and ideas at the same time. This short textbook was designed to teach girls to read *chữ quốc ngữ*. It was published in 1929 in Gò Công, Cochinchina by the female writer and publisher Phan Thị Bạch Vân, a well-known pioneer in woman's education and emancipation.

Phan Thị Bạch Vân (real name Phan Thị Mai) was born in a small village, Bình Trước, in Biên Hòa province in 1903 as the fifth of seven siblings. As a district chief, *tri huyện*, her father was an educated man, but he died young, leaving his wife and children behind. Phan Thị Bạch Vân married at the age of seventeen, but it is said that the marriage was not a happy one. The marriage did not last and Phan Thị Bạch Vân started to write as a way to overcome her despondency. After she had published her first newspaper articles in 1928, she established the publishing house Nữ lưu thơ quán (Women's Press), and an office on Chủ Phước Street in Gò Công (Võ Văn Nhơn, 2007).

Nữ lưu thơ quán was the first publishing house in French Indochina to focus mainly on women's literature (or literature for women)[16]. The publishing house became associated with both female and male writers from across French Indochina, including Đạm Phương from Huế, Nguyễn Thị Đan Tâm from Phủ Quảng, Tùng Viên from Phủ Quảng, Vũ Xuân Đệ from Hà Nội, Quốc Anh (a teacher) from Phú Thọ and Á Nam Trần Tuấn Khải from Hà Nội (Cao Tự Thanh, 2012, pp. 140–144). Phan Thị Bạch Vân and her associates published translations of foreign novels and wrote their own books, textbooks, and articles on various topics; these were mostly concerned with women's issues, women's rights and family issues such as the recommended way to raise children or appropriate education for the husband and wife (Nguyễn Ngọc Phan, 2015; Võ Văn Nhơn, 2011).

Biographies of great women from the history of Vietnam, and even France, were very popular among women, but caught the attention of the Sûreté, the French secret service, because of the books' emphasis on pre-colonial leaders and their patriotic character[17]. According to Marr, a brief biography of a Korean woman who fought Japanese colonial rule was the first specifically women-oriented book to be banned in Annam. Five other books of this type were banned in 1929. Later the Nữ lưu thơ quán (Women's Press) had to be shut down and Phan Thị Bạch Vân was fined for 'subversive activities and disturbance of peace by literature and ideas' (Hoàng Quốc Trị, 2013).

Vần quốc ngữ is a miniature volume, 22 centimetres long, comprising just 16 pages. On the first page, the space meant for the publishing house's advertisement and the publisher's introduction, it says that books from Nữ lưu thơ quán are designated for 'unmarried young girls (*thiếu nữ*) [...] are very useful for the young. They are written in an easy-to-understand style and are easy to identify with. The knowledge will deepen and progress as it is read [...] The novels tell stories about morality.' As a sales strategy, the publishing house Nữ lưu thơ quán offered its readers three different modes of subscription: for one year, 36 books for 10 piastres; for six months, 18 books for five piastres; or for four months, 12 books for 3.50 piastres.

Vần quốc ngữ starts with an alphabet in minuscule and majuscule letters for both block letters and handwriting, and on the next page it shows Latin and Arabic numbers. The following three pages (pp. 4–6) focus on practising reading, *vần xuôi*, the same rhyme syllables for future reading in following chapters, and the next two pages (pp. 7–8) practise the opposite; different rhyme syllables, *vần ngược*. Next, the five different tones and their usage with vowels are displayed on page 9. Page 10 starts with a set of reading practice parts.

The book comprises seven reading texts, each focusing on a different topic, namely: 'Local proverbs' (*Phương ngôn tục ngữ*); 'Text for a girl who is still a little girl' (*Con gái còn nhỏ*); 'Text for a girl who can already read' (*Con gái biết đọc*); 'Women's skills' (*Nữ công*); 'A girl also has to love her country' (*Con giá cũng phải thương nước*); and two texts meant to be learnt by heart, '*Bài học thuộc lòng*'. The very first reading, called 'First text', (*Bài đọc thứ nhứt*), afforded the reader only words to practise instead of a coherent text. The rest of the texts afford a better insight into what the girls were supposed to read and why: 'when the girl can read and write she should ask her parents to buy some interesting books to get to know precious stories from the past'. The girls should read because 'The history of our country has many stories that girls nowadays should know' – about how girls were supposed to be educated and well mannered.

The main objective of text number four was to highlight the importance of education and behaviour. It chiefly says that a girl should please her parents by the way she behaves and by her ability to write in *chữ quốc-ngữ*, which is a sign of a well-educated girl.

'Text Number Four

The girl that is still very young

The girl that is still very young has to study chữ quốc-ngữ [Latinised form]. She should read perfectly and write interestingly. She should play and go to bed at the appropriate time. She should not tease and shout, laugh and cry inappropriately. Her face must be clean and her gait and posture must be mannered. Parents will be pleased and the others will praise.'

(Translated by Marta Lopatkova)

The sixth text focuses on women's skills, *Nữ-công*, one of the four virtues which, according to Confucianism, every girl and woman should possess.

'Text Number Six

Women's skills

Once a girl can read, she should learn women's skills. What are the women's skills? Women's skills are: to stitch, to patch, to embroider and to cook.

At first you learn to stitch and patch, later you will learn how to embroider. You will learn how to cook at the age of fifteen or sixteen. A girl who knows well women's skills helps her parents a lot.

A girl who is not keen on learning, and does not know the women's skills, is often considered as being thoughtless by others.'

(Translated by Marta Lopatkova)

All the texts presented in *Vần quốc ngữ* were interlaced with Confucian concepts of filial piety and women's virtue, but also with the modern Western obsession with cleanliness. Another interesting feature which fits into the scheme sketched in the preceding paragraphs is the presence of patriotism in text number seven, entitled *Con gái cũng phải thương nước* [A girl also has to love her country]. Although it might seem surprising, calls for patriotism and emphasis on the importance of national history and the idea of their 'own' country are often present in books published in the 1920s. We cannot be sure in what specific context the books were published. We can only assume that sometimes books containing such content escaped the strict eyes of censors; sometimes they were published and later banned. At short periods of time when censorship was loosened – which happened, for example, throughout the Popular Front's reign between 1936 and 1939 – it was possible to publish books with contentious content that would otherwise be barred (Zinoman, 2001). Also, censorship was less strict in Cochinchina, where the publishing house Nữ lưu thơ quán (Women's Press) was located, than in Annam and Tonkin (Taylor, 2013, p. 503, Nguyen-Marschall, 2008, p. 59).

Text number seven presents a combination of two, at first sight very different concepts, providing a clear example of how the symbiosis of Confucianism and French modernity looked like. It could serve as a summary of all the ideas presented in previous texts. In the first three paragraphs, the author emphasises a woman's pure love for her husband, children and other relatives. She should love the whole of society, *cultivate her virtuousness* (a Confucian concept) and be aware of her heavy responsibility towards her country and nation (a modern concept).

'Text Number Seven

A girl also has to love her country
The girl that is still very young has to love her parents, brother
And sisters,
Her aunts, uncles and other relatives.

When she grows up and has not yet a husband, she has to Cultivate her virtuousness.
When she has a husband she has to love him and
when she has children, she has to love her children.

A girl has to love the whole of society,
She has to love her country. To be a girl means
A heavy responsibility towards the nation.
(Translated by Marta Lopatkova)

Later in the text, this symbiosis is enforced further by an inclusion of the classical Chinese text 'The Qishi Woman of Lu', from the Warring States period (475–221 BCE) which was apparently popular among Vietnamese intellectuals.

'During the time of Duke Mục-công, of the state of Lỗ, in the village of Tất-thất, there was one
girl that was not married, often leaned against a pillar and groaned.

Her voice was as bright as the song of a crane.
All the passersby who heard her felt sorry for her.
One day a woman from the neighborhood passed by and asked:

"Why are you moaning so pitifully? Is it because you want to marry? I will be your matchmaker."
The girl answered: "No ... you do not understand what bothers me ..."

"I am not distressful because I am not married. I worry that the Duke of Lỗ is old and the crown prince is still very young."

Old woman laughed and said: "This is the concern of high mandarins. What does a woman have to do with it?"'

In the next two paragraphs the girl explains how unpredictable events create and influence the reality and lives of other people. Using simple life events – or the micro context – she explains the wider impact these situations have on the whole community – the macro perspective.

'It is not like that. You don't understand.
There are many things that are not connected but
they relate to the happiness or misfortune of all the people.
One day a guest from Tấn stayed in our house. He tied up his horse in our garden.
But the horse got loose, and tramped on the vegetables
And that year we had no vegetables to eat.

Then there was a girl from the neighboring village. People said
that she eloped with someone. Her parents asked my brother to search for her.
But he encountered a flood and drowned.
This is how I lost my brother.

Now the Duke of Lỗ is old and weak. The Crown Prince is too young.
Cruel and dishonourable men are wicked.

When misfortune strikes the state Lỗ not only the Duke but also the mandarins will have problems.
Ordinary people will suffer.

Where should all the women go to find peace?

I am deeply concerned.

Three years later, the state of Lỗ was thrown into chaos.
The State of Tề together with the state of Sở assaulted the state of Lỗ.
The men fought in battles.
The women had to supply food.
There was none who would sit in tranquility.
Since then noble men praised the girl from Tất-thất:
"Far reaching were the thoughts of the girl of Tất-thất".'

(Translated by Marta Lopatkova)

We can also find the classical text 'The Qishi Woman of Lu', for example, in another book designed for girls and women – *Đài gương Kinh* from 1925, edited by the famous Vietnamese poet Nguyễn Khắc Hiếu, also known by the pen name of Tản Đà (Nguyễn Khắc Hiếu, 1925). The Chinese original is presented in 'Biographies of the Benign and Wise' in *Biographies of Eminent Women* (Leeand Stefanowska, 2007) which traditionally served as a study material for girls and women, not only in China but also in Vietnam.

The last two texts were meant to be learnt by heart; they were written in rhyme, and referred to two national heroines: one of the famous Trung Sisters, Bà Trưng Trắc, and Lady Trieu, Bà Triệu Ẩu. Both had been female warriors who had fought Chinese invaders. In 40 CE Bà Trưng Trắc led a movement against the Chinese for three years, and Lady Trieu, who has been called the Vietnamese Joan of Arc, fought the Chinese in the third century. These two heroines, and a number of others, were extremely popular during the colonial period among anti-colonial Vietnamese nationalists, and their popularity was again a thorn in the colonial administration's side. Their appearance in what ostensibly appears a conservative book with modest aims testifies to the convergence of modern and potentially revolutionary nationalist thought, Confucianist reaction and the earliest efforts at Vietnamese female education.

Conclusion

Although the cultural shock Vietnam experienced in the middle of the nineteenth century was massive, and Vietnamese society faced the challenge of new Western concepts and the process of modernisation, Confucianism's deep roots within that society were not completely eradicated. This was because of several reasons. First it was simply not possible to uproot such deeply held beliefs and practices in such a short period of time. Secondly, the French benefited from the strong sense of loyalty and obedience created by the hundreds of years of the privileged position held by Confucianism in Vietnam. This tendency to lean towards certain classical Confucian ideas is visible not only in the curriculum at schools and in the discourse created by the French, but also in the conservative textbooks produced by the Vietnamese, subject to French approval but disseminated widely in the 1920s and 1930s. The textbook *Vần quốc ngữ* is an illustration of a symbiosis of resistance towards the French and reactive conservatism. The sense of patriotism and an acceptance, and attempt to take ownership, of the externally driven modernity is evident in its propagation of *chữ quốc-ngữ* and idea of women's education combined with the Confucian concepts of filial piety and the four virtues. Vietnamese society underwent significant and fundamental change due to the introduction of the new education system by the French in the first decade of the twentieth century. This was most obvious in the creation of the hybrid Franco-Annamite system, which involved both boys and girls. As a result of these educational reforms, girls were, for the first time, integrated into formal institutional education. Although there are a number of different views as to the effectiveness of the French-designed education system, it is evident that it was this new Franco-Annamite system which went on to produce many of the important female personalities of the following decades and served to completely change Vietnam both culturally and socially.

Notes

1 Đông Dương tạp chí, No 16, (1913). p. 7.
2 For example, a manual of family rituals, *Thọ Mai Gia Lễ* - one of only a few preserved hard copies of which, published in 1866, can be found in the library of The Institute of Hán-Nôm Studies (Viện nghiên cứu Hán nôm) in Hanoi.
3 'Địa vị người đàn bà trong xã hội nước ta'('Women's position in our society'), April 1924.
4 Chữ Nôm is the ancient ideographic vernacular script of the Vietnamese language.
5 For further reading on female scholars in Vietnam I recommend a publication of the Hán Nôm Institute Đỗ Thị Hảo (ed.), 2012. Các nữ tác gia Hán Nôm Việt Nam (Khảo cứu, phiên âm, dịch chú văn bản tác phẩm, Nhà xuất bản khoa học xã hội, Hà Nôi).
6 http://saigon-vietnam.fr/chasseloup-laubat_fr.php.
7 The term 'Annamite' refers to Annam (the French protectorate encompassing central Vietnam) and its people. During the colonial era this term was widely used instead of Vietnam or Vietnamese for all inhabitants of Tonkin, Annam and Cochinchina.
8 Gustave Dumoutier, Les Débuts de l'Enseignement Français au Tonkin (1887), 1. in Vu, 2012.
9 INDO GGI 7707 rapports de M. Gourdon (Ha, 2014, p. 185).
10 From 1930, a baccalaureate from a Franco-Annamite school had the same validity as one from a lycée in France.
11 During the school year 1922–23, 178 students attended (Đàn bà mới, special issue, 1942). The number of students during the first year at the elementary school level was 129 (Văn Thảo Trịnh, 2009).
12 Đông Dương tạp chí, (1914). p. 2.
13 Règlement Général de l'Instruction Publique en Indochine, adopted by A. Sarraut, 21 December 1917 in Saigon. p. 38, quoted in (Tran, 2010, p. 10).
14 'French is optional in village and communal schools, facultative in infant course [sic] and compulsory in preparatory and elementary courses of schools de *plein exercice*.' (Tran, 2009, p. 13).
15 In 1935 Nhị Linh criticized in an article entitled 'Sạch sẽ là văn minh'– [Cleanliness is Civilization] – the Chinese and their cultural heritage and impact on Vietnamese society, because they insisted on purifying the soul and spirit of a man instead of cleaning the body, clothes and home. 'Sạch sẽ là văn minh' [Cleanliness is Civilization], Phong hóa, No. 146, 26 April 1935, 1 (in Tran, 2015, p. 6).
16 Nowadays Phan Bội Châu Street.
17 La Sûreté générale indochinoise, usually abbreviated to Sûreté –the French colonial secret police, whose main task was to oppose forms of anti-colonial or nationalist activities.

References

Cao Ta Thanh. 2012. *Ph1 nn Việt Nam trong llon ss, tâp 2, Ph, nn Vii Nam tham Pháp thuu (1862–1945)*. Hà Nôi: Nhà xuất bản Phụ nữ.
Dang Thi Van Chi. 2016. 'Vietnamese Women In the First Half of the 20th Century'. 1st ed. [online]. *Journal of Mekong Societies*. 11:1. Available at: https://mekong journal.kku.ac.th/Vol11/Issue01/02.pdf. Accessed on 29 March 2016.

Đỗ Thị Hảo ed. 2012. *Các nữ tác gia Hán Nôm Việt Nam*. [Khảo cứu, phiên âm, dịch chú văn bản tác phẩm]. Hà Nôi: Nhà xuất bản khoa học xã hội.
Dumoutier, M. G. 1887. *Les Debuts de l'enseignement Français au Tonkin*. Hanoi: F.-H Schneider.
Elliott, D. 1999. *The Sacred Willow: Four Generations in the Life of a Vietnamese Family*. New York: Oxford University Press.
Gouvernement Général de l'Indochine. 1942. *Annuaire Statistique de l'Indochine*. Neuvième Volume 1939–1940. Direction des Affaires Économiques et Administratives, Service de la Statistique Générale. Hanoi: Imprimerie d'Extrême-Orient.
Ha, M. 2014. *French Women and the Empire*. Oxford: Oxford University Press.
Hoàng Quốc Trị. 2013. *Sự hình thành các tổ chức đầu tiên của phụ nữ Việt Nam*. [online] Liên hiệp các hội khoa học và kỹ thuật Việt Nam, in press 7.6.2013. Available at: www.vusta.vn/vi/news/Thong-tin-Su-kien-Thanh-tuu-KH-CN/Su-hinh-thanh-cac-to-chuc-dau-tien-cua-phu-nu-Viet-Nam-48741.html. Accessed on 26 March 2016.
Lee, L. X. H. and Stefanowska, A. D. 2007. *Biographical dictionary of Chinese women: Antiquity through Sui, 1600 B.C.E.-618 C.E*. Armonk, NY: M.E. Sharpe.
Li, T. 2007. 'Considering Book Trade – the Material Foundation of Confucian Learning in the 17th and 18th centuries in Vietnam'. *Vietnam Social Sciences*, 124. pp. 4–17.
Marr, D. 1981. *Vietnamese Tradition on Trial, 1920–1945*. Berkeley, CA: University of California Press.
Nguyễn Khắc Hiếu. 1925. *Đài gương Kinh, 1925 Ấn bản In lần thứ 2*. Hà Nội: Nghiêm Hàm.
Nguyễn Ngọc Phan. 2015. *Phan Thị Bạch Vân: Nữ lưu đất Gò Công*. [online] Báo Áp Bắc, in press, 16.4.2015. Available at: http://baoapbac.vn/dat-nuoc-con-nguoi/201504/phan-thi-bach-van-nu-luu-dat-go-cong-601593/. Accessed 26 March 2016.
Nguyen-Marschall, V. 2008. *In Search of Moral Authority: The Discourse on Poverty, Poor Relief, and Charity in French Colonial Vietnam*. New York: Peter Lang Publishing.
Phan Thị Bạch Vân. 1929. *Vần quốc ngữ*. Gò Công: Nữ lưu thơ quán.
Quartararo, A. T. 1995. *Women Teachers and Popular Education in Nineteenth-century France: Social Values and Corporate Identity at the Normal School Institution*. Delaware: University of Delaware Press.
Tai, H.-T. H. 1996. *Radicalism and the Origins of the Vietnamese Revolution*, Revised ed., Cambridge, MA: Harvard University Press.
Taylor, K. and Whitmore, J. 1995. *Essays into Vietnamese Pasts*. Ithaca, NY: Southeast Asia Program, Cornell University.
Taylor, K. 2013. *History of the Vietnamese*. Cambridge: Cambridge University Press.
Tran, Thi Phuong Hoa. 2009. *Franco-Vietnamese schools and the transition from Confucian to a new kind of intellectuals in the colonial context of Tonkin*. [Online]. In: Harvard-Yenching Institute Working Paper Series. Available from: https://harvard-yenching.org/sites/harvard-yenching.org/files/featurefiles/TRAN%20Thi%20Phuong%20Hoa_Franco%20Vietnamese%20schools2.pdf. Accessed 26 March 2016.
Tran, Thi Phuong Hoa. 2010. *Franco-Vietnamese schools for girls in Tonkin at the beginning of the 20th century*. [Online]. In: Harvard-Yenching Institute Working Paper Series. Available at: www.harvard-yenching.org/sites/harvard-yenching.org/files/Tran_Thi_Phuong_Hoa_Franco_Vietnamese_schools_for_girls_in_Tonkin.pdf. Accessed on 26 March 2016.

Tran, Thi Phuong Hoa. 2015. *Urban Women: education, hygiene, feminine hygiene products and the Emerging Commodity Market in Early Twentieth-Century Tonkin.* [Online]. In: Harvard-Yenching Institute Working Paper Series. Available from: www.harvard-yenching.org/sites/harvard-yenching.org/files/featurefiles/Tran%20Thi%20Phuong%20Hoa_Urban%20Women.pdf. Accessed 29 March 2016.

Văn Thảo Trịnh. 1993. *L'idéologie de l'école en Indochine (1890–1938)*. Tiers-Monde, 133. 169–186.

Văn Thảo Trịnh. 2009. *Nhà trường Pháp ở Đông Dương*. Hà Nôi: Nhà xuất bản thế giới.

Vietnam National Archives Centre No. 1 (VNAC I). RHD-3754. 1918. *Programme de l'enseignement elementaire franco-indigene des écoles elementaires au Tonkin.*

Võ Văn Nhơn. 2007. *Một nhà văn nữ tranh đấu cho nữ quyền vào đầu thế kỷ XX.* [Online] Tuổi Trẻ Online, 8 March. Available from: http://tuoitre.vn/mot-nha-van-nu-tranh-dau-cho-nu-quyen-vao-dau-the-ky-xx-190045.htm. Accessed 13 March 2016.

Võ Văn Nhơn. 2011. 'Tiểu thuyết hành động vào đầu thế kỷ XX ở Nam Bộ'. *Tậ p chí khoa học xã hội*, 6(154). pp. 28–32.

Vu, M. 2012. 'Examining the Social Impacts of French Education Reforms in Tonkin, Indochina (1906–1938)'. *Student Pulse*. 4(04).

Vu, T.P. 2011. *Luc Xi: Prostitution and Venereal Disease in Colonial Hanoi*. Honolulu: University of Hawai'i Press.

Zinoman, P. 2001. *The Colonial Bastille, A History of Imprisonment in Vietnam, 1862–1940*. Berkeley, CA: University of California Press.

Zinoman, P. 2014. *Vietnamese Colonial Republican: The Political Vision of Vu Trong Phung*, Berkeley, CA: University of California Press.

8 Tinkering your way to prosperity

Technical education, auto-mechanics and entrepreneurship in late-colonial Vietnam

Erich DeWald

LEEDS BECKETT UNIVERSITY

In his study of technology in the colonial Netherlands East Indies, Rudolf Mrázek observed that colonial training for engineers and mechanics produced in them a deep sense of alienation and anxiety. While their mastery of these new trades enabled them to find and establish themselves in a new, modern world, their daily work with machines meant that they were increasingly distanced from the society and culture around them. They could embrace technological modernity, but at a cost. Put another way, 'while the people handled, or were handled by, the new technologies [...] their culture, identity and nation came to feel awry' (Mrázek, 2002, p. xvi). The native and colonial elites Mrázek examined, such as Pramoedya, found it difficult to live comfortably in their colonised homeland while also embracing the civilising mission of a colonial modernity set on reforming and even remaking that homeland. Their very professional existences were part and parcel of the unrelenting change to the Indies that a colonising modernity precipitated.

It is certainly true that European imperialism in the nineteenth and twentieth centuries in Southeast Asia was predicated on the seemingly contradictory goals of rapidly occupying and transforming indigenous societies while simultaneously maintaining political-economic stability. It is not, however, clear that these contradictions necessarily led to anomie, alienation and anxiety. In Mrázek's study of prominent figures in Indies life, the sense of a whole old world lost and a whole new world gained is palpable (pp. 56, 192). Yet, in the present study of students and entrepreneurs in the mechanics' trade of Saigon, this absolutist sense of technology and modernity does not hold. They do not appear to have thought their training closed an old world to them; nor did they conceive a whole new world opening to them as a result of their studies and acquired skills. Being a technician or mechanic was not a wholesale embrace of the new and a corresponding rejection of the old. They did not seek to acquire complete knowledge or complete expertise. As historians of the automobile in Japan and the United States have observed, early converts to mechanical technology were 'tinkerers', not 'scientists' (see *inter alia* Takahashi, 2000; Franz, 2005).

This study shows that many mechanics and former graduates of colonial technical schools in southern Vietnam thought of their occupations in similar terms[1]. They had good reason, too. To succeed in business, 'common sense' dictated that mechanics had general technological know-how. The marketplace simply could not provide for specialised mechanics' enterprises. By examining the records of the technical schools of Cochinchina (southern Vietnam) alongside contemporary newspaper accounts of the mechanics' trades and commerce, this article sheds light on the development of 'street-level' Vietnamese knowledge of technology and commerce that developed under the eye of colonial authorities, who paid scant attention. This exploration of the technical schools of French Indochina forms part of a larger book-length study of the history of everyday technology in Vietnamese society during the late colonial period.

Background of the schools

This street-level view of technical training and expertise was not, it goes without saying, the view expressed in the colonial administration and the colonial educational services. The technical schools of French Indochina had been set up to create francophone and francophile technical specialists able to serve the colonial administration.

The first western-style schools in Indochina were established in the early years of French occupation. These schools, the Collège d'Adran (founded in 1861), Collège Indigène later Chasseloup-Laubat (1864) and the Institut Taberd (1874) – all endeavoured to train expatriate French and elite Vietnamese, the former to continue their studies post-baccalaureate in France, the latter to serve in the administrative corps as native informants (Woodside, 1976, p. 46). While clearly useful in securing and maintaining French rule in the early years of the colonies in Indochina, this limited cadre of functionaries soon proved inadequate to the demands of economically and socially transforming ('*mise en valeur*') the colony[2]. As the French-controlled territory expanded, the needs for particularly skilled labour expanded, too. At the same time, education reform in France in the 1880s intoned the need for state-run comprehensive education. Extending the reach of state education would, it was thought, also extend the reach and influence of the state.[3]

It was partly with this goal in mind of extending and advancing the colonial state's 'civilising' mission that discussions for a technical school in Saigon began in the late 1880s. In part, though, these discussions emerged out of a dire need for trained workers able to operate and repair the machinery of the colonial state and colonial enterprises. The naval services and the artillery divisions of the colonial forces in particular needed labourers. So it was that in 1891 a small ad hoc annex to the Collège Chasseloup-Laubat was created to offer supplementary training in technical arts for students already enrolled at the college. By 1897 this annex had become the *Ecole Pratique d'Industrie*, the Technical Industrial School (EPI). Very much in keeping with the thinking of the then Governor-General of Indochina Paul Doumer, the school had two objectives, perceived by many at the time as being complementary goals:

to 'develop in students the basic rudiments of French language and civilisation', while also 'training indigenous craftsmen to use and maintain the machinery and engines of the colonial service and fledgling colonial enterprises' (Costeau, 1922).

By 1906 the labour pool created by the EPI was deemed insufficient in the light of the technical work to be done. To remedy this situation, a new school was created in 1906, the *Ecole Pratique de Mécaniciens Asiatiques*, the Technical School for Asian Mechanics (EPMA). The mission of this school was to 'train a mechanical cadre knowledgeable with the use of machinery in use on the vessels and the grounds of the military and merchant navies, the colonial administration and local industry' (Costeau, 1922). While the EPMA was distinct from the EPI, the two schools bore a number of similarities. Both were run by one head, stipulated to be an engineer retired from the French Navy. Both were housed in the shadow of the Collège Chasseloup-Laubat. Both offered students full tuition and boarding, alongside classes conducted in quite well equipped laboratories. Both offered entry by examination and, once accepted, generous bursaries for most students. After a three-year course of study and successful completion of final examinations, both schools offered students qualifications: a *certificat d'études pratiques industrielles* (certificate of practical industrial studies) from the EPI and a *brevet d'études techniques de deuxième degré* (second-grade diploma for technical studies) from EPMA. After their formal studies had finished, all students were offered – and required – to complete an apprenticeship working for the colonial administration. Graduates of EPI were seconded to the Flotilla Service of Cochinchina (*Service de la Flotille de la Cochinchine*) for three years, those of EPMA to the State Navy (*Marine d'Etat*) for two years. Their qualifications were inferior to those awarded to students in France. At the same time their training was shorter in length and the curriculum quite different. They were unable to compete with French-trained peers but, according to this paradigm for technical education, the young men would finish their studies and apprenticeships with skills, a career path nurtured by the colonial administration and at least a modicum of French 'civilisation'.[4] At the end of their studies and apprenticeships, they were to be granted 'all the privileges' established in 1892 for the indigenous government service members of Cochinchina (Arrêté of the Governor General of Indochina, 1906).

Perhaps the most significant difference between the two schools was the pedagogy. Both were intended to teach students 'practical' technical know-how as well as 'theoretical subjects' such as the French language, (French) history, geography, maths, geometry and industrial design (Conseil d'administration et de perfectionnement, 1923). While the students of EPMA were all meant to have completed primary school before entry, it was still deemed necessary to continue 'theoretical' education to produce 'well rounded' ('*équilibrés*') graduates. As students at EPI did not require a primary-school certificate to enrol at the school, it was deemed all the more important to inculcate 'theoretical' materials on civics, French literacy and numeracy into their studies. Over the course of their studies students were also channelled into particular specialisms: steam engineering, gas engineering, internal-combustion engineering, forging, fitting and finishing, draughtsmanship. In this way expertise would be available for the workplaces and marketplaces of Indochina (Conseil d'administration et de perfectionnement, 1923).

This model of colonial technical training – smuggling cultural 'improvement' into technical pedagogy intended to produce skilled specialist mechanics – remained a constant in the *écoles pratiques* of Saigon until their final closure during World War II. Numerous problems with this model arose, almost from its very inception, and several efforts were made to reform parts of the curriculum and mission of the school. Yet the basic model remained. On the one hand, local employers needed skilled labour. On the other hand, the need to foster social 'progress' through colonial education was a driving imperative of the colonial and imperial states. Despite repeated concerns over the failure of schools, very little changed. At the very least, this appears to have been the way that many students wanted it.

Problems with the schools

For teachers, administrators and employers, the official archives detail little other than problems with the schools. Too few students completed their studies. Too few students completed their apprenticeships. Those who did work for government and private enterprises were found to be wanting in aptitude, enthusiasm and 'civilised comportment' ('*conduite évoluée*'), according to the Chief Inspector of the Educational Service, a Mr Rosel (Conseil d'administration et de perfectionnement, 1924). Finally, very few graduates appeared to undertake careers in their chosen occupations, thereby undermining the purpose of the schools to produce technological know-how for an expanding modern colonial economy.

There was certainly a problem with retaining and graduating students at the *écoles pratiques*. Between 1897 and 1907, 124 students finished the school with certificates. Between 1911 and 1921, the school had graduated another 177 students. Between 1921 and 1943, 598 students graduated from three years of study from both schools. This is a substantial figure, though it pales compared to the nearly 5,000 students enrolled in that time (see Table 8.1).

Once graduates began their apprenticeships with the naval forces or with the artillery company in Cochinchina, there was little guarantee they would finish their placements. It is difficult to know how many apprentices abandoned their posts, but the tendency was affirmed by regular letters to the schools' directors and the office of the governor of Cochinchina from the officers in charge of these apprentices deemed military labourers ('*ouvriers militaires*'). In 1916 the Company of Indigenous Artillery wrote to report that within two weeks of starting at their apprenticeships, only two of 15 were still on the job (Dupuy, 1916). Another example from 1922 showed that three of 14 stayed in post more than a month (Maspin, 1922).

Table 8.1 Enrolment and graduates of the Écoles Pratiques 1897–1943

	EPMA	EPI	Graduates
1897–1907	—	193	124
1911–1921	297	316	177
1922	140	66	24
1923	148	69	28
1924	143	64	26
1925	157	67	24
1926	162	72	19
1927	124	81	18
1928	144	86	22
1929	162	84	27
1930	175	75	31
1931	160	73	33
1932	158	76	28
1933	154	71	29
1934	160	77	33
1935	161	75	34
1936	172	79	34
1937	159	74	32
1938	147	68	29
1939	163	76	31
1940	171	68	28
1941	143	63	26
1942	128	64	23
1943	109	59	19

Source: The schools' annual reports (École Pratique d'Industrie and École Pratique de Mécaniciens Asiatiques, 1907–1943).

With such an unpredictable supply of technically apt labour went an inconsistent skill set. Even those students who stayed on the job were, as the schools' examiners concluded in 1921, not valuable as qualified workers but merely as assistants ('*petits mains*') (Conseil d'administration et de perfectionnement, 1922, p. 4). As another lieutenant of the Cochinchinese fleet opined, to work as skilled craftsmen graduates of the *écoles pratiques* required intensive supervised instruction in 'the basics' ('*l'essentiel*') of 'working in a civil manner in a modern industrial workplace' (Conseil d'administration et de perfectionnement, 1922, p. 4).[5]

Finally, few graduates of the school appeared to take up work in the mechanical specialisms for which they had received training. On the one hand, administrators and school directors fretted over the steady trickle of letters from industrialists and entrepreneurs who demanded more mechanics able to work independently and to high quality in specialised workshops[6]. On the other hand, the governing committee of the school was aware that despite these demands for more technologically skilled labour, the truth was that the demand for such workers was not great. It was also not growing. While some employers clearly had a need for graduates of schools such as the *écoles pratiques*, these potential employers could not offer enough positions for the potential output of the schools. To attract and retain students on technical career paths, there had to be more well-paid work. If enough was not done to ensure good positions for these graduates, the committee opined, then 'they would have no option but to find work with Chinese employers[!]' (Conseil d'administration et de perfectionnement, 1922, p. 4).

Ensuring the supply of technological know-how

With the new emphasis on technical education in France after 1919 and the newfound vigour of the 'civilising mission' under Minister for Colonies Albert Sarraut, the schools' administrators began to take seriously the need effectively to improve the technical education of Indochina in line with the needs of colonial policy and of colonial industry[7]. To ensure greater retention and graduation in mechanical occupations, the schools' directors suggested a stick-and-carrot approach – measures which were put into practice by successive colonial administrations from 1922 onwards.

First, the stick. Entry into both schools was by examination. While some students did pay their fees, the majority of students who passed the entrance examinations were offered full or partial bursaries comprising the cost of fees and boarding. The rate for full fees including board stood at US $20 (twenty piastres) per month, or $220 annually. Over the course of three years, then, a student's education cost $660[8]. To compel students to stay in school and take their studies seriously, the schools' governing committee recommended that students' parents be obliged to repay the Government for the students' full fees should they abscond from their studies, should they not serve their two or three years in the colonial military and civil services and should they not then pursue a career for at least twelve years in the occupations they studied at the *écoles*[9]. (The committee also recommended that students of the school no longer be exempted from military service, which had previously been the situation with graduates of this school. This arrangement led to students entering the *école pratique* rather than the Collège Chasseloup-Laubat or the Ecole Normale d'Instituteurs in order to avoid military service[10].) Additionally, a decree was sent to all government agencies forbidding the hiring of graduates of the *écoles pratiques*, unless they had been contracted to employ these candidates (Conseil d'administration et de perfectionnement, 1922, p. 8).

Second, the carrot. The truth was, as the schools' governing committee soberly realised, that the wages offered to graduates on apprenticeships and in their first years in the labour market were low. The practice of taking in students from poorer backgrounds and giving them technical educations and upwardly mobile trajectories was scuppered by the economic realities of the marketplace (Règlement Général d'Instruction Professionnel, 1921). It was little use providing extensive, state-funded education when graduates could not expect wages higher than those of unskilled and untrained workers. Thus the committee recommended – and the government promptly enacted – supplementary wages for graduates of the schools to 'top up' their wages to make employment more attractive. Where they would have earned US $8 monthly without training, their subsidised wages as military labourers were increased to $10. This did increase the effective cost of each student's education to $360, but this was seen as a necessary burden to bear in order to fulfil the schools' mission (Conseil d'administration et de perfectionnement, 1922, p. 5).

Beginning in 1922 and continuing until the schools' wartime closure, governing committees also deliberated on the need to reform the curricula of the schools. Based on advice and recommendations gleaned from employers, functionaries and French residents more generally, a proportion of the committees' members thought the 'theoretical' aspect of students' tuition should be minimised in order to ensure the technical skill and technological know-how of graduates. As Eugène Tholance asserted in 1922, 'the insistence on complementing students' studies with theoretical subjects improved their intellectual development and their ease in French society but did not perfect their on-the-job skills. If anything, this general education appears to open career paths for students beyond their training' (quoted in Conseil d'administration et de perfectionnement, 1922, p. 6). All instruction should, the report concluded, keep to a minimum the content of courses that is not strictly applicable to their chosen trades.

Such efforts to make the education of the technical schools purely practical and remove the theoretical content were ineffective and desultory. After student protests in 1907, 1911, 1926 and 1931, colonial administrators perceived the dangers of providing young Vietnamese with a broad liberal education (Varenne, 1926). Despite repeated (and sporadic) efforts to reduce this dangerous 'liberal' pedagogy, theoretical elements remained in all Indochinese schools, precisely because it was critical to the *modus operandi* of a 'civilising' French imperialism. Perhaps most curiously of all, it was this general, liberal education that students of the *écoles pratiques* wanted.

Absconders

School and government authorities did not merely discuss these problems at the schools in cloistered committee rooms. There were efforts not only to track down truants and deserters but also, clearly, to reclaim monies for their aborted studies and apprenticeships. School and government authorities proved astonishingly inept at collecting students' debts. The discussions with former students and their families, however, reveal intriguing evidence of students' rationale for study, or not, whichever the case may have been.

It is somewhat surprising how singularly bad at collecting debts the schools' and the government's agents were. They were not given the resources of the *Sûreté Générale*, to be sure, but their ineffectiveness at finding former students and reclaiming money was remarkable. Three examples will suffice. One, a young man aged fifteen named Nguyễn Hữu Đinh, whose father was a nurse at the indigenous hospital (*hôpital indigène*), had absconded from his studies at the EPMA after four months. His location was unknown to the school's staff. When gendarmes were sent to his parents' address, they claimed no knowledge of his whereabouts, a claim officials did not believe. Further efforts to locate him were not made (Administrator of Cholon, 1924). Another young truant was Willy Ngô, a sixteen year-old whose French mother was a washerwoman at the teacher training college and whose Vietnamese father had died during World War I. His mother wrote to the school's director, who forwarded the request to the Governor, Maurice Cognacq. In the letter she begged the director to offer the boy a place so that 'at least one of my sons has a trade and a livelihood'. The request was granted even though the boy had yet to receive any formal education. Within five months he had left the school, whereabouts unknown. Again, efforts to locate him and return him to the school were fruitless, as were efforts to reclaim the fees for five months of tuition from his mother (see Naudon, et al., 1923–1924). Finally, in 1934 five boys in receipt of full scholarships for their studies absconded: Henri Berlioz, Dang-Vu-That, Luu-Van-Tho, Nguyen-Van-Rot and Ly-Van-Ky. Each student left his studies before the completion of his final year of studies. Repeated efforts to recover the money for their tuition from their families failed. The school was, however, able to locate each former student. They were all working as supervisors or foremen in mechanics' shops in Saigon, Cần Thợ or Bến Tre. The parents pleaded poverty; the boys appear to have successfully claimed that the agreement for returning the scholarships was between the parents and the administration. Further actions to retrieve the money were not taken (Report of the Headmaster, 1934).

Occasionally more systematic efforts were made to enquire about the activities and occupations of former students, graduates or otherwise. In 1919 an inspector of the Navy complained about the tendency of the schools' graduates to desert their posts. In the previous five years, he asserted, all but one of their mechanics from the school had deserted his post. Efforts to track these young men down were largely successful. Of thirty-nine men, thirty-two were located. Of these, nineteen were working as patrons or supervisors of mechanics' workshops. The rest were working in more junior positions in similar firms. The majority – twenty-six – were working in shops that specialised in automobile repair and maintenance. Only four were working in French-owned enterprises. In interviews with authorities, several of these men made two revealing claims repeatedly. First, they had been surprised by how little of their specialised training had been useful on the job, either at their apprenticeships or subsequently. Second, what they had found most useful about their training was the 'general education' they had received in literacy, maths and manners that had been most useful in finding work and succeeding at it (Boyer, 1919). Similarly, an inquiry conducted by the schools' governing committee in the summer of 1933 found that of the 49 graduates the committee contacted as part of a general inquiry among alumni, only one was practising the trade they had trained for. Upon further questioning these graduates plainly stated that they had never intended to pursue the profession their training had provided. They saw their preparation as 'general education'. As one 28-year-old, Trinh Van Chieu, baldly declared: 'Someone who can fix a lot of things and get along with many different kinds of people is a useful person everyone wants around. Nobody wants someone who can only fix one thing' (Conseil d'adminstration et de perfectionnement, 1922, p. 3).

In 1926, at a time when the students of the *École Pratique d'Industrie* of Hải Phòng had walked out of their classes in national remembrance of the death of Phan Chu Trinh, thirty-seven students at Saigon's *écoles pratiques* had officially protested in an open public letter about a number of concerns they had about the school, including a recent reduction of the theoretical element of their studies. Their objections to this change, clearly stated by one of the students, Nguyễn văn Bình, were practical and perceptive: they argued that the general education students had received at the EPMA was one aspect of their qualifications that most appealed to employers. They finished as quite well-rounded artisans who could adapt and work well in most industrial settings. Removing this general element of their tuition hampered their chances of employment and success. Fearing further student rebellion, the school decided to expel all thirty-seven students (reducing the school's total student body by one-third). Efforts to reclaim their fees were unsuccessful (Conseil d'administration et de perfectionnement, 1926). Efforts to alter the curriculum were equally ineffectual.

Practical education, technological know-how and the market in automobiles

School and government authorities failed to grasp the realities of the actually existing Vietnamese marketplace for machines and machinery. Students and graduates of the school seem to have understood better what they could hope to achieve with technical training and technological know-how[11]. The future lay in consumer goods, particularly in automobiles (Lan, 1936).[12]

From their inception the French colonies and protectorates of Indochina were run, at least in part, by machines. In the early days this machinery was limited to steam engines used in large-scale industrial projects such as irrigation, roadworks, port works and fledgling industrial enterprises. Only slowly did machine-powered goods expand in number and in prevalence. With the emergence and import of internal combustion engines, electrical engines and machine-powered automobiles in the first decade of the twentieth century, the skills of the mechanic became more and more desirable. It was really in the years after 1918 that the automobile became a common, though still

Technical education in colonial Vietnam 131

rare, site on the roads of Indochina. Some were in private service, especially for European residents and a small number of Vietnamese elites. Many of the automobiles on the roads were, however, in public service or government service. Added to this was the growing number of other industrially produced, engine-powered machines made of metal, goods such as the motorcycle, rice-mill, motor-powered boat, radio and phonograph. Automobiles were, however, the most numerous engine-driven machine good on the market. There were many of them; at least 18,000 registered automobiles of all classes by 1940 (see Table 8.2).

Even with the great number of automobiles, most observers of the market for machines and mechanics realised that there was not enough work on any one type of good or for any one type of occupation to support an entrepreneur, much less a larger enterprise. What the market offered was work for someone with the ability to fix many things well enough, not someone able to fix one type of good incredibly well. It was a marketplace offering success to tinkerers[13].

This lesson of the market is borne out not only in the testimony of delinquent students and apprentices. It is also clear from several success stories

Table 8.2 Registered automobiles in Indochina

1921	*319*
1922	*477*
1923	*504*
1924	*588*
1925	*607*
1926	*766*
1927	*1,019*
1928	*1,627*
1929	*1,143*
1930	*749*
1931	*628*
1932	*774*
1933	*842*
1934	*997*
1935	*1,105*
1936	*1,387*
1937	*1,288*
1938	*1,502*
1939	*1,713*
Total	*18,035*

Source: Office of the Governor-General of Indochina (1932 and 1940). Robequain gives a slightly smaller number of 17,800 registered automobiles in Indochina by 1938 (Robequain, 1938, p. 119).

among former students of the *écoles pratiques*, as well as advice and guidance offered to compatriots by successful businessmen in the mechanical trades. As a contemporary newspaper article about business and commerce by none other than Đào Duy Anh asserted, being a business person in our society is hard: 'it is well known among our people that trade is scornful but politics is important.' Furthermore, he declared, traders and businesspeople have to have the 'confidence to try things that are risky' and the 'ability to work at things until they figure them out' (Đào, 1932)[14].

Two former students of EPMA made a similar point when they were visited by authorities seeking to return them to their government-approved occupations. Vo-van-Duc and Bui-van-Thu had both left school after eighteen months' study and had, within three years, established their own mechanics' shop in Saigon with capital of US $3,000. They begrudgingly repaid their fees ($160 each) and reported that an acquaintance had encouraged them during their final month of study to find work as assistants in mechanics' shops in Saigon. They were able to make more than on their pre-arranged apprenticeships. Furthermore, they were able to acquire, in Duc's words, a knowledge of 'what people actually need you to fix', which was 'all sorts of things, very few of which were in the schools' workshops.' Thu, likewise, said that he learned how to 'give things a go' after leaving school, a 'necessity for anyone who wants to stay alive as a mechanic' (Varrechia, 1927).

Other successful former students of the *écoles pratiques* proudly proclaimed their ability to fix just about anything. Four advertisements in the *Annuaire Economique de l'Indochine* for auto-mechanics in Cochinchina during the 1930s all included names of owners, followed by qualifications awarded by the *écoles pratiques*, followed once again by marketing material declaring they could 'fix anything', 'solve problems with any machine big or small' or 'find an answer to all your mechanical needs'[15]. Another former student, a graduate named Nguyen Van Chuc, was a successful businessman who later exhibited his goods at the Hanoi Fair in 1934, using the advertising motto, 'a real jack-of-all-trades' ('*un vrai touche-à-tout*') (Office for Economic and Administrative Affairs, 1934). Another, Hoàng Văn Luân, became the second-in-command (and later the owner) of one of Indochina's most successful indigenous automobile sellers and operators, Phạm Văn Phi et Cie. In an article in *Khoa Học Phổ Thông* (*Popular Science*) he asserted that the secret to his success was the 'curiosity I learned during my studies ... and the confidence for being able to solve any problem eventually which I learned in my first years on the job at Phạm Văn Phi' (Annuaire économique de l'Indochine: Tonkin et Nord-Annam, 1926, p. 312.).[16]

This view of the demands and needs of the marketplace expressed by students of the *écoles pratiques* was also expressed elsewhere by other enterprising mechanics and technologically-minded entrepreneurs. Nguyễn Văn Cửa, the owner and manager of the Etablissement Bainier de l'Indochine, Indochina's largest automobile seller and repair shop, also wrote articles in *Khoa Học Phổ Thông* about the realities and prospects of the automobile and mechanics trades. Not only did he claim few could hope to succeed as well as he had (no doubt due to his uncanny ability to generate income from generous state contracts for automobile services); he also encouraged aspiring mechanic-entrepreneurs to take any work that comes their way. This would mean that they could 'get any work that comes your way and start to make connections with people beyond your family circle'. It would also mean that they acquired more and more skills, able to expand their network even further (Nguyễn, 1935). It was a virtuous cycle where tinkerers could most easily prosper.

Further articles in the Vietnamese and French languages spanning the period from the early 1920s to the early 1940s make similar points about both the career of the entrepreneur and the auto-mechanics trade in particular. Two articles about auto mechanics in *Le Progrès Annamite* from 1924 and 1926 asserted that the country did in fact need more competent mechanics 'to deal with the ever growing number of machines being run by technological idiots'. It also expressed some sympathy (and frustration) with 'the difficulty of staying in business when you have to be able to fix anything that comes through the shop door'. That said, if entrepreneurs had a 'can-do spirit' and were 'able to sweet-talk high fees out of customers', they would 'become rich in no time' (Truong, 1924; Bich, 1926)[17].

Conclusion

In many ways the evidence presented here is nothing more than circumstantial testimony of a 'common sense' view of the marketplace expressed by working and aspiring Vietnamese artisans and businesspeople. Theirs was a common-sense view that a willingness to tinker plus a modicum of general civil colonial knowledge was enough technological know-how to pursue such a career. They seem to have been aware of the needs of the marketplace; there was too little work to specialise in any one type of machinery or craftwork. Working in the few establishments that offered this specialised work, such as in the service of the colonial administration or larger industrial concerns, did not pay well enough, compared with the possible money to be made as a generally skilled tinkerer with broad familiarity with machinery and enough social grace and French language to be able to solicit trade from well-to-do Vietnamese, Chinese and French families. While it is clear that many of the absconders and school-leavers did not set out to manage or even start businesses, it is equally clear that a number of such men did work in professional and management roles in trades, working as general mechanics who would take work on automobiles when they could. Otherwise, they would build their customer bases by doing what business came their way. In the febrile and unequal economy of colonial Vietnam, Saigon was perhaps the best place for such young men to conduct business and for that business to take root and thrive. Despite failing at their studies, some of the former pupils of the *École Pratique des Mécaniciens Asiatiques et d'Industrie* did just that.

Notes

1. Throughout this study, the term 'Vietnam' is used to refer to the three majority Vietnamese (kinh) provinces of French Indochina that comprise today's Vietnam: Cochinchina, Annam and Tonkin. All Vietnamese names have been transcribed in the form in which they originally appeared in the originals: thus Nguyen Van Chuc without diacritics but also Hoàng Văn Luân with diacritics.
2. On education in French Indochina, see: Kelly (1975, 1984); Van (1995); and, one surprisingly lucid colonial text, *Le service d'instruction en Indochine* (1931). On the policy of developing Indochina's economy (*mise en valeur*), see, *inter alia*, Thomas (2005). For a comparison with other European colonies in East and Southeast Asia, see: de Jong and Ravesteijn (2008); Goh (2013); and, Kargon (2010).
3. On education in France, see Belhoste (2003), Weber (1976).
4. On the inspiration for technical schools in colonial Southeast Asia, see Knight (2007).
5. The deficiency of students was also surely the result of the admission to the school of many students through back channels. Vietnamese and French elites often enquired with the schools' directors—sometimes through local colonial *résidents* or *administrateurs*—about their child or relative taking up a place in the schools. See, for example, the case of Vo-van-Thom of Hà Tiên (Third Section of the First Office of the Government of Cochinchina, 1923), or the case of Nguyễn Văn Giàu's youngest son (Nguyễn Văn Giàu and Cognacq, 1924).
6. See the more than eighty letters from local business people and government contractors spanning the period 1909 to 1941: (Letters, 1909–1941).
7. The Astier law of 1919 created a comprehensive scheme of technical schools and education in France: see Outrey (1921).
8. For comparison, the monthly pay of an indigenous soldier in the colonial forces was $8, and that of a skilled machinist between $12 and $15.
9. This fee amounted to $20 per month of study, or $220 per year of study. Thus parents might be obliged to pay as much as $660 twelve years after their child's studies finished (Conseil d'administration et de perfectionnement, 1922, p. 5).
10. This stipulation had been passed into law by Governor-General Klubowski on 4 October 1910: (Arrêté of the Governor General of Indochina, (Klubowski), 1910). These regulations were changed in line with the recommendations of Lieutenant-Governor Lehalle (1922).
11. On the widespread dilemma of those with formal education having difficulties obtaining qualifications and good employment, see, *inter alia*, Pham (1985, pp. 116–133).
12. On the automobile industry and auto repairs around the globe, see: McIntyre (2000); Kline and Pinch (1996); Coopey et al. (2010); and, Laird (1996). On the automobile in France, see Loubet (2001)and Loubet (1996). On the automobile and technical labour in Indochina, see Del Testa (2005).
13. On the economics and commerce of the period, see Brocheux (1976), Cao (1979, pp. 44–72), Murray (1980, pp. 216–233) and Booth (1991).
14. On entrepreneurship in Vietnam, see: Tạ (2006, 2007) and Malarney (1997).
15. The students were Hop Long, Bui van Ngo, Nguyen The Cong and Phan Thiêu Van. See Annuaire Economique de l'Indochine (Economic Yearbook of Indochina) (1932, 1934, 1937, 1938). Also see advertisements for mechanics in Vade Mecum Annamite, administratif, commercial, agricole et littéraire, 1931).
16. See, Hoàng (1936, p. 37).
17. A similar point is made, too, in the prognosis of the ills of Vietnam's regional economies in the study written by the editorial staff of the Institute for Far Eastern Industry and Commerce (Viễn Đông Kỹ Nghệ Thương Mại) (1931).

References

Archival materials

Administrator of Cholon. 1924. *Note Postale to the office of the Governor of Cochinchina.* 24 August. Archives of the Government of Cochinchina. VI A/8/316 (2.1). Ho Chi Minh City: Vietnam National Archives Centre II.

Annuaire Economique de l'Indochine [Economic Yearbook of Indochina]. 1932, 1934, 1937 and 1938. Hanoi: Imprimerie d'Extrême-Orient.

Annuaire économique de l'Indochine: Tonkin et Nord-Annam. 1926. Hanoi: Imprimerie d'Extrême-Orient.

Arrêté of the Governor General of Indochina. 1906, 19 April. Archives of the Government of Cochinchina. VIA.8/287(1). Ho Chi Minh City: Vietnam National Archives Centre II.

Arrêté of the Governor General of Indochina (Klubowski). 1910. 4 October. Archives of the Government of Cochinchina. VIA.8/287(1). Ho Chi Minh City: Vietnam National Archives Centre II.

Bich, D. N. 1926. 'Commerce et l'avenir' [Trade and the Future]. *Le Progrès Annamite (Annamite Progress)*, 11 November.

Boyer, H. 1919. *Report to the director of the school and the first office of the Government of Cochinchina.* 26 November. Archives of the Government of Cochinchina. VIA.8/287(1). Ho Chi Minh City: Vietnam National Archives Centre II.

Conseil d'administration et de perfectionnement. 1922. *Report.* 4 October. Archives of the Government of Cochinchina. VI A/8/316 (2.1). Ho Chi Minh City: Vietnam National Archives Centre II.

Conseil d'administration et de perfectionnement. 1923. *Rapport Annuel* [annual report]. Archives of the Government of Cochinchina. VI A/8/316(2.3). Ho Chi Minh City: Vietnam National Archives Centre II.

Conseil d'administration et de perfectionnement. 1924. *Procès-verbal* [Minutes]. 18 March. Archives of the Government of Cochinchina. VI A/8/316(2.4). Ho Chi Minh City: Vietnam National Archives Centre II.

Conseil d'administration et de perfectionnement. 1926. *Procès-verbal* [Minutes]. 20 May. Archives of the Government of Cochinchina. VI A/8/316 (2.5). Ho Chi Minh City: Vietnam National Archives Centre II.

Costeau, P. 1922. *Briève histoire des écoles pratiques de Saïgon* [report]. Archives of the Government of Cochinchina. VI-A/8/316 (2.1). Ho Chi Minh City: Vietnam National Archives Centre II.

Đào, D. A. 1932. Kinh-tế với cải-cách (Economics and reform). *Kim Lai tạp chí (Present and Future magazine)*, 10 March, pp. 79–80.

Direction Générale d'Instruction Publique. 1931a. *Le service d'instruction en Indochine.* Hanoi: Imprimerie d'Extrême-Orient.

Direction Générale de l'Instruction Publique. 1931b. *La Cochinchine scolaire.* Hanoi: Imprimerie d'Extrême-Orient.

Dupuy. 1916. *Note Postale to the Director of the Ecole Pratique and the Governor's office.* 7 October. Archives of the Government of Cochinchina. VI A/8/316 (2.2), Ho Chi Minh City: Vietnam National Archives Centre II.

Ecole Pratique d'Industrie and Ecole Pratique de Mécaniciens Asiatiques. 1907–1943. *Annual Reports.* Saigon: Imprimerie d'Extrême-Orient.

Hoàng V. L. 1936. 'Kỹ nghệ có làm giàu không?' [Does technology make you rich?]. *Khoa Học Phổ Thông (Popular Science)*, 1 January.

Institute for Far Eastern Industry and Commerce (Viễn Đông Kỹ Nghệ Thương Mại). 1931. *Kỹ Nghệ và Thương Mại Hai Sức Mạnh (Strong and Mighty Industry and Commerce)*. Saigon: Imprimerie Duc Than.

Lan, K. 1936. 'Cơ khí là tương lai' [The future is mechanical]. *Nghề Mới (New Occupations)*, 10 April.

Lehalle. 1922. *Report*. 20 February. Archives of the Government of Cochinchina. VI A/8/316 (2.1). Ho Chi Minh City: Vietnam National Archives Centre II.

Letters. 1909–1941. *Correspondence between local business people and government contractors*. Archives of the Government of Cochinchina. VI A/8/316 (2.11). Ho Chi Minh City: Vietnam National Archives Centre II.

Maspin. 1922. *Note Postale to Director Tholance*. 18 November. Archives of the Government of Cochinchina. VI A/8/316 (2.2), Ho Chi Minh City: Vietnam National Archives Centre II.

Naudon, et al. 1923. *Letters*. 3, 13 and 19 December. Archives of the Government of Cochinchina. VI A/8/316 (2.1). Ho Chi Minh City: Vietnam National Archives Centre II.

Nguyễn, V. C. 1935. 'Làm nghề máy xe hơi' [Being an auto-mechanic], *Khoa Học Phổ Thông (Popular Science)*, 16 June, pp. 23–24.

Nguyễn Văn Giàu and Cognacq, M. 1924. Letters. 8 and 16 May. Archives of the Government of Cochinchina. VI A/8/316 (2.1). Ho Chi Minh City: Vietnam National Archives Centre II.

Office for Economic and Administrative Affairs. 1934. *Note Postale to the office of the Governor General of Indochina*. 4 October. Archives of the Government-General of Indochina. 4726. Aix-en-Provence: Archives Nationales d'Outre-Mer.

Office of the Governor General of Indochina. 1932 and 1940. *Letters to the Chamber of Commerce of Paris*. 7 March 1932 and 4 January 1940. Archives of the Agence de la France d'Outre-Mer. 230, d.102. Aix-en-Provence: Archives Nationales d'Outre-Mer.

Outrey, E. 1921. *Letter to the Governor of Cochinchina*. 17 May. Archives of the Government of Cochinchina. VI A/8/316(2.4). Ho Chi Minh City: Vietnam National Archives Centre II.

Règlement Général d'Instruction Professionnel. 1921. Archives of the Government of Cochinchina. VI A/8/316 (2.1). Ho Chi Minh City: Vietnam National Archives Centre II.

Report of the Headmaster. 1934. *To the Governor*. 23 May. Archives of the Government of Cochinchina. VI A/8/316 (2.1). Ho Chi Minh City: Vietnam National Archives Centre II.

Robequain, C. 1938. *L'Evolution économique de l'Indochine française*. Paris: Hartmann.

Third Section of the First Office of the Government of Cochinchina. 1923. *Letter to the headmaster of the Ecole Pratique d'Industrie*. 16 October. Archives of the Government of Cochinchina. VI A/8/316 (2.1). Ho Chi Minh City: Vietnam National Archives Centre II.

Tholance, A. 1922. *Note sur l'enseignement technique en Indochine française*. 12 September. Archives of the Government of Cochinchina. VIA.8/289(4). Ho Chi Minh City: Vietnam National Archives Centre II.

Truong, V. L. 1924. 'Le progrès économique' [Economic Progress]. *Le Progrès Annamite (Annamite Progress)*, 24 April.
Vade Mecum Annamite, administratif, commercial, agricole et littéraire. Thời sự cẩm nang tuế thứ canh ngũ niên [Annamite Administrative, Commercial, Agricultural and Literary Handbook]. 1931. Saigon: Imprimerie de Bui Van.
Varenne, A. 1926. Note Postale. 4 April. Archives of the Government-General of Indochina. 17472. Hanoi: Vietnam National Archives Centre I.
Varrechia. 1927. *Note Postale to the headmaster of the Ecole Pratique*. 6 June. Archives of the Government of Cochinchina. VI A/8/316(2.7). Ho Chi Minh City: Vietnam National Archives Centre II.

Secondary works

Belhoste, B. 2003. *La formation d'une technocratie. L'Ecole polytechnique et ses élèves de la révolution au second empire*. Paris: Belin.
Booth, A. 1991. 'The Economic development of Southeast Asia: 1870–1985'. *Australian Economic History Review*, 31(1), pp. 20–52.
Brocheux, P. 1976. 'Crise économique et société en Indochine française'. *Revue Française d'Histoire d'Outre-Mer*, 63(3), pp. 655–667.
Cao, V. B. 1979. *Giai cấp công nhân việt nam, thời kỳ 1936–1939*. Hanoi: NXB Khoa Học Xã Hội.
Coopey, R. et al. 2010. 'Power without knowledge? Foucault and Fordism, c.1900–1950'. *Labor History*, 51(1), pp. 107–125.
Franz, K. 2005. *Tinkering: consumers reinvent the early automobile*. Philadelphia: University of Pennsylvania Press.
Goh, C. B. 2013. *Technology and entrepot colonialism in Singapore, 1819–1940*. Singapore: Institute of Southeast Asian Studies.
de Jong, F., and Ravesteijn, W. 2008. Technology and administration: the rise and development of public works in the East Indies. In: Ravesteijn, W., and Kop, J. (eds.) *For profit and prosperity: the contribution made by Dutch engineers to public works in Indonesia, 1800–2000*. Leiden: KITLV Press, pp. 47–66.
Kargon, R. 2010. 'Making Manila modern: science, technology and American colonialism, 1898–1915'. *Historia Scientiarum*, 19(4), pp. 209–224.
Kelly, G. P. 1975. *Franco-Vietnamese schools in Indochina, 1918–1938*. PhD thesis. University of Wisconsin at Madison.
Kelly, G. P. 1984. 'The presentation of indigenous society in the schools of French West Africa and Indochina, 1918 to 1938'. *Comparative Studies in Society and History*, 26(2), pp. 523–542.
Kline, R. and Pinch, T. 1996. 'Users as agents of technological change: the social construction of the automobile in the rural United States'. *Technology and Culture*, 37(2), pp. 763–795.
Knight, G. R. 2007. Technology, technicians and bourgeoisie: Thomas Jeoffries Edwards and the industrial project in sugar in mid-nineteenth-century Java. In: Bosma, U., Giusti-Cordero, J. A. and Knight, G. R. (eds.) *Sugarlandia revisited: sugar and colonialism in Asia and the Americas, 1800–1940*. London: Berghahn Books, pp. 31–51.
Laird, P. W. 1996. '"The Car without a Single Weakness": Early Automobile Advertising'. *Technology and Culture*, 37(4), pp. 796–812.

Loubet, J.-L. 1996. 'L'industrie automobile française d'une crise à l'autre'. *Vingtième Siècle*, 92(1), pp. 66–78.
Loubet, J.-L. 2001. *Histoire de l'automobile française*. Paris: Seuil.
Malarney, S. 1997. State stigma, family prestige and the development of commerce in the Red River delta of Vietnam. In: Hefner, R. ed. *Market cultures: society and morality in the new Asian capitalisms*. Boulder, CO: Westview Press, pp. 268–289.
McIntyre, S. L. 2000. 'The Failure of Fordism: reform of the automobile repair industry, 1913–1940'. *Technology and Culture*, 41(2), pp. 269–299.
Mrázek, R. 2002. *Engineers of happy land: technology and nationalism in a colony*. Princeton, NJ: Princeton University Press.
Murray, M. J. 1980. *The development of capitalism in colonial Indochina, 1870–1940*. Berkeley, CA: University of California Press.
Pham, C. D. 1985. *Vietnamese peasants under French domination, 1861–1945*. Berkeley: Center for South and Southeast Asia Studies, University of California.
Tạ, T. T. 2006. 'Thương Nghiệp Việt Nam Trong Những Năm 20 Thế Kỷ XX' [Vietnamese Commerce in the 1920s]. *Nghiên Cứu Lịch Sử* (*Historical Research*), 357. pp. 46–52.
Tạ, T. T. 2007. 'Sự Phát Triển Của Ngành Dịch vụ Vận Tải Trong Những Năm 20 Của Thế Kỷ XX' [The development of transportation services during the 1920s]. *Nghiên Cứu Lịch Sử* (*Historical Research*), 364. pp. 39–44.
Takahashi, Y. 2000. 'A Network of tinkerers: the advent of the radio and television receiver industry in Japan'. *Technology and Culture*, 41(3), pp. 460–484.
Tang, J. P. 2011. 'Technological Leadership and Late Development: Evidence from Meiji Japan, 1868–1912'. *Economic History Review*, 64(3), pp. 99–116.
Del Testa, D. 2005. Automobiles and anomie in French Colonial Indochina. In: Robson, K. and Yee, J. *France and 'Indochina': cultural representations*. Lanham, MD: Lexington Books, pp. 63–77.
Thomas, M. 2005. 'Albert Sarraut, French colonial development, and the communist threat, 1919–1930'. *Journal of Modern History*, 77(1), pp. 917–955.
Van, T. T. 1995. *L'Ecole française en Indochine*. Paris: Karthala.
Weber, E. 1976. *Peasants into Frenchmen: the modernization of rural France, 1870–1914*. Stanford, CA: Stanford University Press.
Woodside, A. 1976. *Community and revolution in modern Vietnam*. Boston, MA: Houghton Mifflin.

9 Despite Education
Malaysian Nationhood and Economic Development 1874–1970[1]

Elsa Lafaye de Micheaux

CENTRE ASIE DU SUD-EST, PARIS AND UNIVERSITY OF RENNES

Having been exceptionally strong from the 1970s to the Asian crisis of 1997, Malaysian growth has remained generally intense and robust since then: the country can contend for the rank of developed country in 2020. Poverty has in the meantime considerably decreased, and social mobility between the 1970s and the present has been significant. But in contrast, the education of Malaysians seems mediocre, the result of a system regarded as weak, relatively perverse and largely blocked. Moreover – and this was still noticeable during the ceremonies celebrating the sixtieth anniversary of independence on 31 August 2017 – while the country purports to share a collective sentiment of national pride, its educational system has been marked by three decades of massive discrimination in favour of the *bumiputra* ('sons of the soil'), to support and benefit the Malay majority population to the detriment of the other communities that make up this plural Southeast Asian society.

Typically, we attribute to education functions of ideological and cultural transmission, as well as of national construction (Hobsbawm and Ranger, 1983), training of elites and social reproduction (Bourdieu and Passeron, 1964; Bourdieu and Passeron, 1971), management of inequalities and, last but not least, economic development. The investment in human capital is indeed supposedly a key to the labour productivity (Becker, 1962), to growth (Lucas, 1988; Fontvieille, 1990), and competitiveness associated with the capacity for innovation of the national workforce (Romer, 1990). In Malaysia, at least up until independence in 1957, few if any of these noble objectives had been achieved by the education system. The brief history of education in Malaysia presented in this chapter demonstrates that Malaysian education is much more divisive than constructive: the separation, segmentation and preservation of ethnic divisions are the end result of an initial century of educational development in Malaysia (1874–1970). The economic side of the issue, which was less prominent during this historical interval, had not yet become the knot of contradictions it is now, but many of the ingredients of the paradox were set in motion during these first evolutionary decades.

This chapter uses a simple periodisation of the history of Malaysian education from Aziz et al. (1987), retaining two phases: the colonial period, which begins with the Pangkor Treaty, when British control was imposed in the Malay States (part 1), and the post-independence period (part 2), characterised by the foundation of a genuine education system worthy of the name. It would indeed be premature to speak of an education system in a colonial situation in which coexisted four school systems, all of which were unequally developed and sometimes very incomplete. It was only once independence occurred that an effort towards coherence was made in the wake of the Razak Committee report (Malaysia, 1956), then of the Rahman Talib Committee report (Malaysia, 1960). The structure of the system then became more intelligible, and we can then speak of the development of education. The analysis ends in 1970, when the broad autonomy of educational development in relation to economic development was suspended.

The slow implementation of a segmented and coerced educational system under British Malaya (1874–1957)

Although the number of enrolled pupils and the average number of years of study of Malaysians increased during the colonial period, the discrepancies in the paths followed by the different actors (British Government, local administrators, ethnic communities) resulted in the creation of a nebula of very small schools reflecting the diversity of Malaysian society and the colonised-society/colonial-society dichotomy, rather than an actualcohesive system. For several decades, Chinese children were taught Chinese history and geography, as well as Confucian principles; Malays studied the Koran, and Tamil schoolchildren used textbooks imported from India and Ceylon. Pupils in English schools learned about European wars and the coal basins of the English Midlands (Chang, 1971).

During the colonisation years, no one clear orientation gained the upper hand, be it in terms of power or in intensity of investment efforts, leading to educational fragmentation: 'there was no overall educational policy to foster a national education system' (Aziz et al., 1987, p. 75). The general argument of the main research on the origins of the Malaysian education system is that the seeds of social division were sown during the colonial period, by the choices made in favour of a splintered education system (Loh, 1975).

The contradictory principles that presided over the education of the population in British Malaya

During the colonial period, only a small local elite had the privilege of receiving an English-language education, a requisite preparation for future positions in the colonial bureaucracy and in European-managed trading or manufacturing companies[2]. At the turn of the twentieth century, the then Resident General of the Federated Malay States, Frank Swettenham, commented on the ethnic division of labour, deeming it sufficient for the vast majority to read and write in their mother tongue and to learn the role assigned them by the colonial administration: 'Put crudely, the European was

Education in Colonial Malaysia 141

to govern and administer, the immigrant Chinese and Indian to labour in the extractive industries and commerce, and the Malay to till the fields' (Andaya and Andaya, 1982, p. 222).

Over time, the education system reinforced the division of labour put in place by the British, aiming to reproduce perfectly assimilated work roles. In 1920 R. J. Wilkinson, the Education Director, affirmed:

> 'The government's goal is not to produce a few well-educated young people, nor a large number of less well-trained boys, but rather to improve the masses, and to make the son of a fisherman or peasant just a more intelligent fisherman or peasant than his father – to make a man whose education will allow him to understand how much his place in life is in keeping with his environment'.
> (Annual Report on the FMS [FederatedMalayStates] for 1920: 3, quoted in Roff, 1967, p. 127)

The principles at the basis of the development of education in the colony were contradictory. They were inspired by European ideas on education that were popular in Europe at the end of the nineteenth century, a progressive philosophy according to which instruction was fundamental for the individual: in the United Kingdom, the Elementary Education Act of 1870 (commonly known as Forster's Education Act) recognised that it was the State's duty to educate every child. Education had to be free of charge, as did books and slates. But these educational principles were at the same time extremely conservative socially. Indeed, the main concern of administrators was that, above all, all citizens knew their social status and never sought to improve it. In addition, it seemed there was a considerable danger of seeing a spread of subversive ideas (and especially critiques of English political economy) throughout Southeast Asia.

Two schools of thought were in conflict in the 1830s with regard to the language of schooling in British colonies. Long debates pitted the Liberals – 'diffusionists' who advocated one single language, English, the language of intellectual emancipation – against the Orientalists – conservatives who wished to protect the cultural and linguistic diversity of the country (Loh, 1975). This debate was acted out in Malaysia over a half century later, when the decision to establish separate schools in vernacular languages (the three tongues of the three ethnic categories) in the country prevailed over the desire to have a heterogeneous population sharing a common language (Rabindra, 1981). Mastery of English was thereby limited to the local elite, who, sharing the financial interests – and to a certain extent the class interests – of the British, desired to be educated in that language (Barlow, 1995).

The stated desire to expand education widely among the indigenous population met another obstacle: above all, the colonial authorities wanted to avoid reproducing the Indian situation, where part of the population had become educated and then found itself overqualified in relation to local skilled-employment opportunities as early as the 1850s. Unemployment among Indian university graduates fuelled political discontent in India as individual aspirations, out of sync with assigned social and work positions, generated frustrations and eventually demands that threatened the colony's stability. In fact, a 1904 report noted that, out of almost 3,000 boys coming out of the vernacular schools in the Malaysian state of Perak in the previous years, only one had secured employment as an office clerk (Orr, 1972).

It seems that Swettenham explicitly preferred that Malays remain undereducated and, in particular, that they not learn English:

> 'The one danger to be guarded against is an attempt to teach English indiscriminately. It could not be well taught, except in a very few schools, and I do not think it is desirable to give the children of an agricultural population an indifferent knowledge of a language that to all but the very few would only unfit them for the duties of life, and make them discontented with everything like manual labour'.
>
> (Swettenham [1890] *Perak Annual Report*, quoted in Barlow, 1995, p. 374)

We can thus get a sense of the contradictory auspices under which the Malaysian educational system was 'cobbled together' during the colonial period, from 1874 to 1957. For Malaysian commentators, there is no doubt that here lies one of the main mechanisms of the segmentation of Malaysian society, along the ethnic lines that have manifested themselves in every walk of life and in every era since then:

> 'the motives of British domination in Peninsular Malaysia, which was essentially economic imperialism, governed the British attitudes towards the provision of education. It became the principal mechanism to ensure the compartmentalisation of the various ethnic groups and of insuring Socialisation into the respective racial groups.'
>
> (Santhiram, 1996, p. 22)

Towards a fragmented and incoherent system fraught with contradictory tensions

This section presents the different types of school, which were distinguished on the basis of ethnic categories (vernacular schools for the vast majority and English-language schools for a minority) and gender. It also must be noted that the British administration gave the different Federal States the prerogative to create schools; there was no centralised management of the educational system. Consequently, each designed its own system, particularly for language teaching; the education policy at this time could be defined as 'polarisation.' (Alis Puteh, 2006, pp. 63–75).

The Malays[3]

In the Malay tradition, the centrality of Islam had long before led to the creation of Koranic schools. Traditional Koranic education consisted of reading and reciting the Koran without necessarily understanding it; in the countryside, this remained the sole form of education for generations. The British created the first vernacular Malay schools just after the 1874 Pangkor Treaty; the first school, constructed in Klang, dates from 1875, followed by one in Kampung Glam (1876) and another in Perak (1878). These basic primary schools offered only a six-year curriculum. However, their educational goals focused less on reading, writing or arithmetic than on instilling modern social values, such as obedience and punctuality, to prepare Malay students to accept their place in colonial society. Nonetheless, beginning in 1885, Johor state enacted the first compulsory education code, dedicating a state office and a high official to education. Teaching in *Bahasa Melayu* (Malay language), Johor State's Islamic schools, known as *madrasas*, combined general with religious studies. Facilities and faculties were often of good quality; some *madrasas*, famous for their teaching, attracted students from other parts of the region (Koh, 1991, pp. 125–156).

Within the Malay community, the distinction between the ruling class and the *rakyat* (people) became accentuated, with the former benefiting from English instruction in the cities while the latter found it hard to gain access to good-quality vernacular schooling. Since schooling was not compulsory in all states, the mostlyrural Malay children did not attend for very long, even when they had access to school; poor families preferred that children work at home or in the fields. Thus Malaysian social stratification grew stronger (Hirschman, 1974, pp. 18–58) as the colonial administration made material and symbolic differences more rigid by conferring more power to the nobles – authority, tax collection, government positions, and education, particularly in English.

The Indians

Christian missionaries built several Tamil-language schools in Penang, Malacca and Singapore in the first half of the nineteenth century, but none came into operation until 1870. Funding for the missionary schools depended on an annual aid allocation from the British Parliament (Barlow, 1995). In the agricultural regions of Perak and Negri Sembilan, the colonial government opened Tamil-vernacular schools in 1900. However, the government clearly expected that missionaries and rubber and coffee plantation-owning companies would take responsibility for educating the Indians. Since the colonial administrators did not offer subsidies or programmes for teaching, the quality of primaryeducation varied greatly across plantations and farming areas. It was not until 1923 that the Labour Code obliged every plantation housing more than ten resident or working children to provide formal primary education. Often, teachers in these plantation schools were only *kangani* (local Tamil 'headmen' who recruited bonded Indian immigrant workers) and office workers, or simply farm labourers who knew how to read. Classes were most often taught in Tamil, or, depending on the location, in Hindi, Punjabi or Telugu. Schoolbooks were imported from India, so pupils learned more about Indian culture, history and geography than about the country where they were growing up. Only after World War II did the government, in anticipation of independence, put any effort into Tamil school programmes, orienting them a little toward local, Malaya-related subjects (Andaya and Andaya, 1982, p. 223).

Attendance at the plantation schools was not compulsory and, as in the Malay vernacular schools, the curriculum officially lasted six years. However, plantations offered work to 10- and 12-year olds, so few young ethnic Indians felt motivated to pursue their studies (Rabindra, 1981), most dropping out after the first three years (for a definitive work on this subject, see Loh, 1975, p. 101).

In 1937, 548 Indian schools educated 23,350 children. Teaching quality remained poor due to mediocre teacher skills – most often limited to knowing how to read and write (Rabindra, 1981). No Tamil-vernacular school provided secondary education. This once again created a deep language division between poor ethnic Indians living on plantations or in cities and the ethnic Indian middle class and bourgeoisie – city-dwelling shopkeepers, traders and office workers – who studied English at British schools in the cities. From 1919 to 1936, ethnic Indians accounted for 30 per cent of the students attending private English schools in the cities (Andaya and Andaya, 1982, p. 229). At the end of the 1940s, one could distinguish four types of Indian schools, each determined by its source of funding: (1) the government's 36 (mostly urban) Tamil schools, (2) plantation schools, accounting for three-fifths of all students taught in Tamil, (3) missionary schools, and (4) schools run by local community councils.

It is likely that, in addition to its mediocrity, Tamil-vernacular instruction constituted a major obstacle to ethnic Indian social mobility, since no teacher-training programme existed until 1937. Speaking only the minority language, ethnic Indians could hardly leave the plantations and climb the social ladder, despite having attended school for a few years. Since ethnic Indian plantation workers had no option besides sending their children to Tamil-vernacular plantation schools, the educational system prevented social advancement; in fact, one of the children's (very narrow) means of rising above their parent's farm-worker status was to become a Tamil-language teacher in a plantation school (Rabindra, 1981).

The Chinese

For many years, the education of ethnic Chinese in British Malaya remained the exclusive province of the Chinese community. Prior to the twentieth century, the Chinese education programme remained traditional, founded on knowledge of the classics and Confucianism. Scholars and high-level graduates proved rare, as most ethnic Chinese were economic migrants. Once again, the teachers' only qualifications were being able to read and write fluently. The teaching method emphasised reciting texts, without necessarily expecting the student to master the meaning. Three types of Chinese schools co-existed in British Malaya: (1) schools created by a district, clan, or family council, (2) schools founded by businessmen who paid for teachers, and (3) schools where individual tuition fees paid for teachers. Here again, teaching quality varied widely, but British authorities tolerated it, since the community's desire to create its own schools relieved them from having to do so themselves for quite some time.

Nevertheless, China's influence on school curricula began to pose problems for British leaders around 1920, when Communist Party ideas began to appear. The increasing politicisation of educational programmes intensified, with a conflict between the Kuomintang, the dominant Chinese party, and China's Communist Party, obliging the British to intervene. In 1920, colonial authorities took legal control of the schools through the Registration of School Ordinance; this met with protests from ethnic Chinese community leaders (Ang, 2014). From 1929 the authorities also tried to take control of educational programmes by financing some of the schools. In 1935, Mandarin became the language of instruction in Chinese schools, and a teacher-training programme was introduced to orient the curriculum toward British Malaya-related subjects. However, many Chinese schools refused government subsidies in a bid to maintain their independence. That said, half of all students in the English-language British schools attended by the urban bourgeoisie were ethnic Chinese (Tan, 1981).

The education of girls

The extreme fragmentation of this educational system increases when analysed by gender (see Figures 9.1 and 9.2, below). Education aimed at girls fell ten years behind that for boys; the first government-run girls' school, conducted in the Malay vernacular, was established in Singapore in 1884, followed by another in Penang five years later (1889). Prior to the establishment of these girls-only schools, girls could attend with their brothers, since the first schools were not exclusively for boys. The number of girls' schools increased very slowly up to the 1930s, not least because the government – as was often the case – focused on educating boys. Pedagogic ambitions for girls differed, as well; a shortage of general-education teachers occurred in the 1930s, resulting in an emphasis on traditional manual skills: sewing, basket-weaving, and so forth. In addition, young Malay girls did not have equal educational opportunities because much depended on where they lived. In 1909, British Malaya counted 42 girls' schools, 37 of which were located in Perak. By 1930, the total number of girls' schools had doubled, but remained unevenly distributed, with 60 of 82 in Perak. However, very few young Malay girls continued their studies into secondary school (Tan, 1981), as the enrolment data attests.

The results of colonial-era education efforts

The result of the implementation of the elements of an educational system during the colonial period can be assessed on the basis of dispersed data. Those from the Ministry of Education (quoted by Aziz et al., 1986, Table 4.1), illustrate the progress, all students combined, of enrolment between 1938 and 1957: in primary education, enrolment rose from 211,000 in 1938 to 453,000 in 1947, and reached one million pupils in 1957. Meanwhile, enrolment in secondary education also registered progress: from 23,500 in 1938 to 105,000 children in 1957 (most of the improvement having taken place from 1947 to 1957). The census, which provides the average number of years of study of Malaysians, can also be used to measure the evolution of the level of education reached by the adult population, for the different age ranges, while distinguishing both ethnic categories and gender (Hirschman, 1974, p. 16; Lafaye de Micheaux, 2017, p. 71).

We can thus draw out a few broad trends regarding the compared accomplishments of the different branches of the system that had been implemented: first of all, there was a tendency towards an increase in the average number of years of study in Malaysia. Therefore, in collating this result with the number of enrolled schoolchildren, we observe that, over time, the educational system managed to reach more and more children at the primary level. Furthermore, although this movement played a lesser role, more people had access to secondary education. In addition, the gap between men and women was extremely wide, since even the youngest women were not even half as well educated as men of the same age. However, they had better access to primary education than at the beginning of the century, because at that time the gap between girls and boys amounted to a factor of ten for the Malays and the Chinese, and a factor of five and a half for the Indians. For about fifteen years, the gap increased significantly between Malay girls and boys, because the education of Malay girls did not progress. For the children of the Chinese and Indian communities in Malaysia, this progress moved more in parallel, although boys' education still progressed more rapidly.

These two major tendencies of education's evolution during the colonial period (growth and gender difference) are clearly shown in the figures representing the successive cohorts that went through the educational system during the first half of the twentieth century (Figures 9.1 and 9.2).

An exponential-type growth can be observed for the education of women, who nonetheless did not, by the end of the period, reach even half the educational level of the men (on average two years for those who were enrolled in 1950, as opposed to close to five years for men). The 1920s seem to evidence

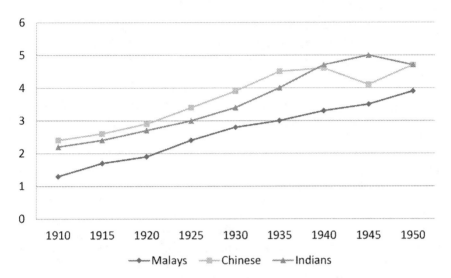

Figure 9.1 Average number of years of study for males who entered into the Malaysian educational system between 1910 and 1950
Source: Author's calculation.

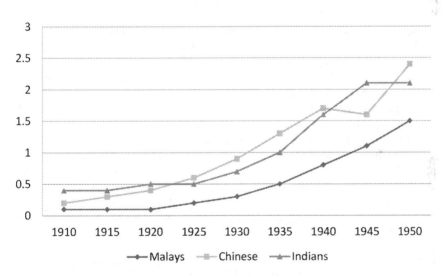

Figure 9.2 Average number of years of study for females who entered into the Malaysian educational system between 1910 and 1950
Source: Created by the author from data sourced from Hirschman, 1974.

an acceleration in the participation of girls in the educational system. The years 1935–45 show a slowing in progress for men.

Finally, the gap between the ethnic categories was also very high, opposing the Malays, who were less educated on average, to the Indians and Chinese. This gap is explained not by higher dropout rates among the Malays – Hirschman (1972) has shown that the rate of completion at the primary and secondary levels was the same for the different ethnic groups – but rather by an unequal access to institutions. Since schools were established in cities first, while in rural areas they were established with greater difficulty, the non-Malays, often more urban-based, consequently had easier access to the educational system. This gap scarcely varied during the first half of the twentieth century, oscillating between 0.9 and 1.1 years less for the Malays than for the Chinese. The initial gap of 0.2 years between average Chinese and Indian education levels was completely absorbed because, starting in 1923, the plantations became obliged to establish schools; as soon as this occurred, the education of Indians increased more rapidly. In some years, the average level of education among Indians even rose above that of the Chinese. From 1935 to 1950 in the Chinese community, there was a marked downturn in the progression of education for both genders. This tendency can be interpreted as the effect of a restriction on education spending in the Chinese community as a result of the 1929 crisis, but more directly for the 1945 figures as an effect of the Japanese occupation (1942–1945). Indeed, Chinese education had specificity in relation to the other two in that its funds rested entirely on the Sino-Malaysian community.

Thus, the conservative policy of the colonial administration did not give itself the means to achieve its official objectives (educate the administered population) because, among other things, mandatory schooling was only established very slowly. It missed the opportunity to use education to forge a plural society on foundations other than the ethnic ones engendered by the British activities in the Peninsula. In thus failing to combine the different ethnic groups through a generalised and homogenous educational policy, the government participated in maintaining a plural economy in which the Malays occupied the least privileged positions. We shall see that, while the Malaysian educational policy that was initiated at the time of independence explicitly sought to forge a unified nation through a common language and common educational programs, the results were admittedly visible but the ambiguities in the face of the plural society remained.[4]

The first national educational policies and the perpetuation of income inequalities through education, 1957–1970

The first post-colonial educational policy was implemented following two reports: that of the committee led by then Minister of Education Tun Abdul Razak (1956), which resulted in the Education Ordinance of, 1957; and that of the committee led by his successor Abdul Rahman Talib (1960), which was favourable to the imposition of *Bahasa Melayu* as the main language of instruction and the source of the Education Act of 1961. Both were texts which successively endeavoured to identify the educational foundations of a national unity and to implement a consistent system satisfying the needs of the nation, and promote its development.

The report of the Razak Committee (Malaysia, 1956) made recommendations to create a national educational system that would be acceptable to the entire population:'having regard to the intention to make Malay the national language of the country whilst preserving and sustaining the growth of the language and culture of other communities living in the country'. This report recommended the implementation of a national educational system based on the use of a common language as instructional medium, a common teaching programme, teaching staff with a unified status and an independent inspection system (Chang, 1971). The Sino-Malaysian activists of the social-educational movement consider this text to be 'a rare official document that favoured the interests of non-bumiputra' (Ang, 2014, p. 48).

The development of secondary education and the question of the teaching medium

The problem of the language of instruction was approached in an ambiguous manner during the first years of independence. As we have seen, the intention to promote *Bahasa Melayu* as a common language, while preserving the languages and cultures of the other communities, was a position advocated by the Razak Committee report of 1956. The guarantees provided for maintaining teaching in the different maternal languages for the Chinese and Indian communities had the trade-off of imposing a common programme and schedule for the three types of schools, and the obligation to learn *Bahasa Melayu* or English. The subsidised schools, henceforth called National Schools, were always of three types at the primary level (Malay, Chinese, Indian). Primary education was to last 6 years. Then, secondary education was to be no longer available in vernacular languages (Chinese secondary schools were no longer subsidised) but only in *Bahasa Melayu* and English. Temporary 'Remove Classes' were created on the sidelines of the curriculum to teach English to children from Tamil and Chinese schools, in order to help them integrate into the national system at the secondary level. For the Indian children, this reform finally offered a real opportunity to pursue their studies beyond primary school (Santhiram, 1996, p. 33). At the end of the six-year primary level, approximately 35 percent of the pupils were sent on to secondary school. Entrance selection was determined on the basis of an exam created in 1958, but then abolished in 1964. It was the secondary sector that most significantly progressed in the years after independence.

In 1960, primary schools (with a six-year curriculum) comprised over one million pupils, the first cycle of secondary school (three years) 89,000 pupils, and the second cycle (two years) 25,000 pupils. Thus, approximately 90

150   *Elsa Lafaye de Micheaux*

percent of Malaysian pupils were in primary school, which was a sign that only this basic level of education was really developed at that time. But these reforms signalled the start of secondary-school development. Indeed, the Rahman Talib Committee report (Malaysia, 1960) endorsed many of the decisions made in the previous report and introduced free primary education, as well as professionalising the secondary school system for pupils who did not manage entry into the academic secondary system. Henceforth, there was to be only one single medium of instruction for secondary school (English or *Bahasa Melayu*). Public primary education became free in 1962. In 1964 the Government changed its secondary education policy again and abolished the entrance exam at the end of primary school, delaying it until the end of the second year of secondary school. Secondary-level education became free for the first cycle (lower secondary) in 1965. Thus, if one includes the 'Remove Class', there were nine years of schooling without an enrolment barrier. In 1970 secondary education and the upper levels accounted for one-quarter of the enrolled population, compared to less than one-tenth a decade earlier (Aziz, 1986, Table 4.3). The same trend is observed in the enrolment data: remaining stable for the primary level with 88 percent of the relevant age group, the enrolment rate dramatically improved between 1960 and 1970 at secondary level, increasing from 9.4 to 52.2 percent at lower secondary and from three to 20 percent at upper secondary (Mingat and Tan, 1992).

The problem of language remained a key issue, because English was designated the secondary-level language of instruction, despite the anger of the Chinese community, which no longer received subsidies for the secondary schools that taught in Mandarin and in other Chinese dialects, and to the dissatisfaction of the nationalist Malays, who had been waiting since 1957 for an effective *Malayanisation* process to be implemented in the schools, in the programmes and through teaching in *Bahasa Melayu*. But the National Language Act of 1967, which affirmed that the Malay language is the only national language, did not find any direct and immediate application in the schools. English-language primary schools, for example, only taught minor subjects in the national language (morals, music, PE, health, etc.); secondary schools did not all teach in the Malay language. It was only after the events of 1969 that the policy aiming at imposing *Bahasa Melayu* came to impose itself forcefully and without ambiguity as a crucial means to construct the Malaysian nation (Santhiram, 1996, p. 34).

The embryonic state of higher education

After regular secondary education, the course of study carried on with Form VI' or post-secondary, which lasted two years (with 1,557 students of 17 and 18 years old in 1960) and granted the diploma necessary for access to higher education. If one counts only the students in teacher-training colleges, there were 8,071 students in higher education in 1960, that is, less than one percent of the enrolled population; put another way, enrolment in higher education represented four per cent of the relevant age group in 1960 (Mingat and Tan, 1992). It reflects a very embryonic stage of a highly elitist higher education at that time. The Malaysian academic university system's roots are found in British institutions, and it retained the dominant traits of those institutions until well after independence, like a 'transplant of the British system'. As in most developing countries that were former colonies, the academic and administrative university tradition of the 'mother' country was transmitted beyond the period of foreign administration. In Malaysia, it was the British approach which predominated, based on strict disciplinary division and the affirmation of the autonomy of the institution *vis-à-vis* the state (Altbach and Selvaratnam, 1989).

Tertiary level education was born with the construction, at the beginning of the twentieth century, of the first Medical School: the King Edward VII College of Medicine, founded in Singapore in 1905. In 1929, Raffles College was created, also in Singapore. Although funded by the British Government, this institution was managed by an independent counsel. It provided a traditional curriculum in the main fields (mathematics, English, history, biology, chemistry, physics and geography). These two institutions merged in 1949 to become the University of Malaya, of Singapore, an autonomous body that built its programmes along the lines of the academic model of the University of Cambridge in three fields –arts, science and medicine – and delivered a degree. Over succeeding years, schools of education, engineering, law and agriculture were created. This sole Singapore university counted 2,684 students in 1957 (Aziz et al., 1986). It has been accused of being elitist by analysts of the Malaysian educational system, and higher education would continue to follow this logic of reproduction of social elites up into the 1970s. Indeed, until the end of the 1960s, access to higher education would remain very limited, despite the creation of a satellite of the university at Kuala Lumpur in 1959 with 323 students, which would then become the autonomous University of Malaya (UM) in 1962, by which time it comprised 1,341 students. It should be pointed out that, since the Education Act of 1961, private institutions of higher education were only allowed the status of college, and not that of university, that is, they did not have the right to deliver a degree (equivalent to a Bachelor's, which, in the labour market, then bestowed the title of engineer, officer or executive), but only certificates and diplomas (one and two years after the *Sijil Tinggi Persekolahan Malaysia* (STPM – High School Certificate of Malaysia, the diploma which provided access to higher education). Thus, private institutions did not have the right to propose the coursework and the diplomas required to access the professional categories equivalent to that of manager. This measure categorically blocked the creation of a Chinese university in Malaysia, which the Chinese community had requested.

In 1965, because of the separation from Singapore, UM became the only university in the country, with 2,835 students. In 1967, a committee on higher education was appointed under the direction of the incumbent Minister of

Education, to 'revisit the state of higher education in the Federation of Malaya in order to make suggestions towards its development and improvement in light of foreseeable needs and the country's financial resources' (Selvaratnam, 1989, p. 191). The recommendations were numerous and ambitious, and would come into effect only during the following period. For instance, the committee recommended that 20 percent of the age group had access, whilst, at that time, only 4,570 students were registered at UM (Selvaratnam, 1989, p. 189), representing 0.6 percent of the relevant age group (Mingat and Tan, 1992).

As can be clearly discerned, in 1969 the university system was merely embryonic. During the following years, new 'traditional' universities were created as a result of the report produced by the 1967 higher education committee, which had recommended that new public higher education institutions be created. In this early post-independence period, these were: Universiti Sains Malaysia, Penang (University of Science Malaysia, established in 1969) and Universiti Kebangsaan Malaysia, Serdang, Selangor (National University of Malaysia, 1970). The total population in higher education grew from 8,000 students in 1960 to 14,000 in 1970 (Aziz et al., 1986: Table 4.2).

It was only at the end of the 1970s that the system broadened out and diversified, thanks to the establishment of technical and professional institutions of higher education and of colleges (which deliver inferior diplomas to a degree) (Lee, 1997a, p. 197). Finally, English remained the university language of instruction for quite some time after the British had departed, even more so as, without a local university tradition, the vast majority of professors were expatriates, who contributed to perpetuating British modes of operating the university.

Public education spending

Analysed from the angle of public education spending, the post-independence period is quite easy to describe. Spending was characterised by relatively marked growth, with a tailing-off, however, in the second half of the period. The growth rate was around 12.1 percent per year on average over the decade. The initial years show strong growth: 23 percent per year between 1960 and 1962 when, after the publication of the Rahman Talib Committee report in 1960, the Education Review Act of 1961 implemented the reforms;and 13 percent thereafter, from 1962–66. Finally, the last four years of the decade show a slight drop (to between 4 and 7 percent per year). From 1960 to 1970, the overall figure of the education budget increased from 180 to 520 million Malaysian ringgits; while this fluctuated slightly as a proportion both of the budget and of gross domestic product (GDP), it remained close to 18–19 percent of the budget and to four percent of GDP (Aziz et al., 1986).

In Malaysia, the material conditions of production were not so much determined by the level of training possessed by employees as by the decisions to valorise capital within the given natural resource sector made by the holders of European capital, primarily London-based operators. As for the increase in the level of education of Malaysians, it did not then depend on a state budget more or less proportionate to the country's GDP, but on European principles relative to education and on votes in the British Parliament. Thus, the reciprocal coherence and constraints that these two phenomena exerted on one another within a national economy are not identifiable in Malaysia, at least not up until independence. During the following decade, the two magnitudes increased together, but the growth rate of education spending seems from the start to have been lower than that of GDP, and its rhythm is less volatile: the disjunction between the two dynamics remains clear-cut.

Coherencies within the system and the reproduction of a highly inegalitarian post-colonial society

Although the education system was more coherent at the end of the 1960s than it was during the colonial period, at the primary level – to which not all had access – it remained separated along linguistic lines that overlapped with ethnic differences, with Malay-, Chinese- and Indian-type national schools. The effect of the education system on social reproduction will never be as marked in the history of Malaysia as in these years preceding the introduction, in 1971, of the New Economic Policy (NEP): this system reproduced an inegalitarian society by making mass education really possible only at the primary level, which pooled three-quarters of Malaysian pupils (and where 88 percent of the age category was enrolled) and by ensuring elites were reproduced through a limited number of English language-based schools requiring tuition fees – a situation that continued on into higher education according to the erstwhile British model, to which very few students had access. Even more subtly, and to attract the support of the local Malay aristocracy, only commoners were required to pay tuition fees for the English schools; the pupils belonging to the families of the Sultans and the Malay nobility were able to study there free of charge. Thus, except for these high-society Malays, only the children of the urban bourgeoisie could afford to study there (Andaya and Andaya, 1982, p. 229).

For some, the reform of the education system, in order to lay the foundations of a more unified society, was an urgent matter:

'[...] it is clear the interactions between the plural structure of Malaysian society and its plural educational system, reinforced by an economic specialization of the different ethnic communities, has engendered the absence of a national conscience, social fragmentation and economic imbalances. We can say on this subject that the present obstacles to the construction of the Nation and the development of the country can be found in the problems inherited from the past [...] under the colonial regime'.

(Chang, 1971)

This critical analysis of colonialism was justified, as it placed the education system at the heart of the construction and reproduction of income inequality. This system therefore also contributed to the social crisis that finally erupted in 1969. In 1970, the multicultural Malaysian society was indeed still a largely traditional, rural, and relatively poor society, despite the fact that the territory was one of the most profitable British possessions. Less than a third of the population worked in the modern capitalist economic sector set up by the British. Finally, only a social fringe that had fully benefited from the advantages of colonisation lived at the level of, and according to the rhythm of, Western consumerism.

The precise statistics provided by the socio-demographic West Malaysian Family Survey (WMFS, 1966–1967), while not covering the entire active population, make it possible to give a solid overview of the gaps between ethnic groups and the link between ethnic categories, education level and income earned (the sample included 5,312 married men; the survey was longitudinal, renewed every ten years, and was careful to follow the same individuals). For example, the average monthly income of Malays belonging to the upper-level categories was 280 ringgits: a far lower income than that earned among the other ethnic categories with a similar social status (Chinese: 459 ringgits; Indian: 491 ringgits).

This gap can be partially explained by the lower educational level of Malays, both in general, and at an equivalent professional status (on average, the Malay workers completed 3.9 years at school, as against 5.6 and five years, respectively, for the Chinese and the Indians). In the case of managerial and professional status, the Malays showed an average of 7.3 years of schooling, compared with 9.2 years for the Chinese and 10.5 years of schooling for their Indian counterparts (WMFS, quotedin Hirschman, 1974, p. 18). What emerges from these statistics is the very wellestablished economic link between income and educational level;the inequality in access to education depending on ethnic category seems to be the source of these income inequalities. In the previous section, it was shown how the education system inherited from the British colonial administration was itself ethnically structured, that is, strongly differentiated according to the ethnic category to which the pupils belonged. Most of the Malays received a few years of very low-quality primary education and followed in their parents' footsteps, remaining in the *kampongs* (villages) as farmers or fishermen. The 1967 sample indicated that for a national average of 4.4 years, the Malays had on average received one and a half years of education less than the Chinese and Indians.

Therefore, the probability of being at the bottom of the social ladder or, for a given social status, to earn the lowest incomes, was greater for the Malays, and correlatively in the dominated sectors, it was the probability of being Malay rather than Chinese or Indian that was the highest. Similarly, when one earned a high income, there was a higher probability of belonging to the Chinese community, and statistically, being Chinese meant having a lower probability of being poor. Also, we can assert that social structure and ethnic structure had a tendency to overlap in Malaysia. As far as the desire to determine whether it was a class society (Jomo, 1988) or if the major social opposition was between races, it would seem that these were two quite satisfactory and not incompatible ways of describing reality, since the two dimensions overlapped in Malaysia, in large part because of the segmented and restrained organisation of education.

Conclusion

The principles that express and contradict themselves in the creation of the schools of British Malaya gave rise to a narrow and fragmented school system, as it appeared at the end of the colonial period. The main accomplishments of the 1960s, in the wake of the Razak Committee's report (Malaysia, 1956), led to an initial coherent structuring of the educational system, and to its quantitative development. But, detached from economic developments, it directly contributed to the reproduction of inequalities, significantly maintaining the link between inter-ethnic inequalities and class rifts. Despite the first national educational policies, the fabrication of income inequalities through schooling therefore continued after independence. This dynamic lasted until, as a result of the race riots of May 1969, the emergency government led by Tun Abdul Razak tackled this acute social issue as part of the NEP (Faaland et al., 1990).

With the NEP (1971–1990), the Government broke with the *laisser-faire* approach inherited from the British and placed discrimination at the heart of the Malaysian educational system: the logic of ethnic division was, as a result, enduringly strengthened (Lee, 1997b). Indeed, a positive discrimination policy introducing quotas into higher education suddenly placed educational policy at the service of the double aim of reducing poverty and restructuring society. The Government announced from the very beginning that education would play a determinant role in the objectives of the NEP:

> 'The development of education affects the nation in many of its vital characteristics. It is a means to modernize society and to reach its social aims: equality of opportunity and national unity.'
> (Malaysia, 1970)

From that moment on, education in Malaysia, for the first time in its history, was written into the same political design as the question of economic development and nation-building via the reduction of inequalities. Later, in the 1990s, attempts were made to integrate the concern for congruence between the educational programmes offered and the needs of the economy, and the liberalisation of higher education that resulted (by means of the Higher Education Bill, 1995), opened the door to new contradictions, *inter alia*: inflation of education costs; braindrain; lowering of the general level in English; and a plethora of diplomas and programmes in Islamic education, resulting in a persistent shortage of qualified manpower.

Notes

1 This chapter has been translated from French into English by Mrs Francie Crebbs, Translator, CNRS, Centre Asie du Sud-Est (CASE), Paris.
2 For more extensive writings on the Malaysian educational system and the differences between ethnic communities, see Tan (1988), Tan and Santhiram (2010), Lafaye de Micheaux (2000), Santhiram (1999).
3 This depiction of the scattered educational system among the three main Malaysian communities and between boys and girls is directly borrowed from (Lafaye de Micheaux, 2017, pp. 67–70), with the kind approval of the Malaysian Publisher, SIRD, Kuala Lumpur.
4 For a recent survey of the current state of the nation-building and language issues and of the higher education controversial achievements, readers could refer to Lee, H. G., 2017.

References

Alis Puteh. 2006. *Language and Nation Building: A Study of the Language Medium Policy in Malaysia.* Petaling Jaya: SIRD.
Altbach, H. and Selvaratnam, V. (eds.), 1989. *From Development to Autonomy.* Dordrecht: Kluwer, pp. 187–205.
Andaya, B. W. and Andaya, L. Y. 1982. *A History of Malaysia.* London: Macmillan.
Ang, M. C. 2014. *Institutions and Social Mobilization: The Chinese Education Movement in Malaysia, 1951–2011.* Singapore: ISEAS Publishing.
Aziz, A., Chew, S. B., Lee, K. H., and Sanyal, B. C. 1986. *University Education and Employment in Malaysia.* Paris: UNESCO.
Barlow, H. 1995. *Swettenham.* Kuala Lumpur: Southdene.
Becker, G. 1962. 'Investment in Human Capital: a theoretical analysis'. *Journal of Political Economy*, LXX, pp. 9–49.
Bourdieu, P. and Passeron, J.-C. 1964. *Les Héritiers.* Paris: Minuit.
Bourdieu, P. and Passeron, J.-C. 1971. *La Reproduction.* Paris: Minuit.
Chang, P. 1971. 'Headteacher's responsibilities in Nation-building: the Malaysian Case'. *Malaysian Journal of Education.*
Faaland, J., Parkinson, J. R., and Saniman, R. 1990. *Growth and Ethnic Inequality: Malaysia's New Economic Policy.* Kuala Lumpur: Dewan Bahasa dan Pustaka.
Fontvieille, L. 1990. 'La croissance de la dépense publique d'éducation en France (1815–1987)'. *Formation-Emploi* 31. pp. 61–71.
Hirschman, C. 1972. 'Education in colonial Malaysia'. *Comparative Education Review,* 16. pp. 486–502.
Hirschman, C. 1974. *Ethnic and Social Stratification in Peninsular Malaysia.* Monograph Series of the American Sociological Association. Washington, DC: American Sociological Association.
Hobsbawm, E. and Ranger, T. (eds.), 1983. *The Invention of Tradition.* Cambridge: Cambridge University Press.
Jomo, K. S. 1988. *A Question of Class: Capitalism, the State and Uneven Development in Malaysia.* Singapore: Oxford University Press.

Koh, K. K. 1991. *Malay Society, Transformation and Democratisation.* Subang Jaya: Pelanduk.
Lafaye de Micheaux, E. 2000. *Education et croissance en Malaisie, étude d'un lien fragile.* PhD thesis. Dijon (unpublished).
Lafaye de Micheaux, E. 2017. *The Development of Malaysian Capitalism: from British Rule to the Present Day.* Petaling Jaya: SIRD.
Lee, M. N. 1997a. Reforms in Higher Education in Malaysia. In Watson, K., Modgil, C, and Modgil, S. *Education Dilemmas: Debate and Diversity.* London: Cassell, pp. 195–204.
Lee, M. N. 1997b. 'Education and the State: Malaysia after the NEP'. *Asia Pacific Economic Review,* 17(1), pp. 27–40.
Lee, H. G. 2017. *Education and Globalization in Southeast Asia, Issues and Challenges.* Singapore: ISEAS Publishing.
Loh, F. S. 1975. *Seeds of Separatism: Educational policy in Malaya, 1874–1940.* East Asian Social Sciences Monographs. Oxford: Oxford University Press.
Lucas, R. E. 1988. 'On the Mechanics of Economic Development'. *Journal of Monetary Economics* 22. pp. 3–42.
Malaysia. 1956. *Report of the Education Committee 1956.* Kuala Lumpur: Government Press.
Malaysia. 1960. *Report of the Education Review Committee 1960.* Kuala Lumpur: Government Press.
Malaysia. 1970. *New Economic Policy, 1971–1975.* Economic Planning Unit. Kuala Lumpur: Government Press.
Mingat, A. and Tan, J. P. 1992. *Education in Asia: A Comparative Study of Cost and Financing.* Washington: World Bank, Regional and Sectoral Studies.
Orr, K. 1972. 'The Benefit of Schooling in a Malay Kampong'. *Malaysian Journal of Education,* 9(1). pp. 76–81.
Rabindra, D. 1981. 'A general survey on education amongst the Malaysian Indian plantation community'. *Malaysia in History,* 24. pp. 77–94.
Roff, M. 1967. '*The politics of language in Malaya*'. *Asian Survey,* 7(5). pp. 316–328.
Romer, P. M. 1990. 'Endogenous Technological Change'. *Journal of Political Economy.* 98:1. pp. 71–102.
Santhiram, R. 1996. 'Malaysia's educational development: A study of inter-ethnic relations'. *Journal of the Institute of Asian Studies,* 13(2), pp. 17–48.
Santhiram, R. 1999. *Education of Minorities: the case of Indians in Malaysia.* Petaling Jaya: Child Information, Learning and Development Centre.
Selvaratnam, V. 1988. Ethnicity, inequality, and higher education in Malaysia. *Comparative Education Review,* 32(2), pp. 173–196.
Selvaratnam, V. 1989. Change amidst continuity: University development in Malaysia. In: Altbach, H. and Selvaratnam, V. (eds.), *From Development to Autonomy.* Dordrecht: Kluwer, pp. 187–205.
Tan, L. E. 1988. *The Politics of Chinese Education in Malaya, 1945–1961.* Kuala Lumpur: Oxford University Press.
Tan, S. A. J. 1981. 'The Education of Malay girls: a Brief History'. *Malaysia in History,* 24. pp. 117–123.
Tan, Y. S. and Santhiram, R. 2010. *The Education of Ethnic Minorities: the case of the Malaysian Chinese.* Petaling Jaya: SIRD.

10 Full colour illustrations

Presentations of race in Singapore's history textbooks, 1965–2000

Theophilus Kwek

Introduction

A nation, argued Ernest Renan (1882), requires the 'possession in common of a rich legacy of memories': the shared narrative of a national past, on which to build an identity and common purpose. Following in the footsteps of Eric Hobsbawm (1983) and Benedict Anderson (1983), various historians have come to examine the shaping of this narrative as a political project, in particular through the construction of a national history curriculum and its implementation in the classroom. Specifically, Laura Hein and Mark Selden argue (1998) that 'stories [...] about the national past' included in history textbooks are 'invariably prescriptive', while Norman Vasu et al. (2014) describe the broader narratives presented as 'powerful and necessary tools in shaping national identity'. These dynamics are present in Southeast Asia, where Anthony Milner (2005) and Helen Ting (2009) have identified nationalist agendas in Malaysia's history textbooks before and after independence, while Agus Suwignyo (2014) has shown the extent of state manipulation in Indonesian textbooks under Suharto's dictatorship.

Since its separation from Malaysia in 1965, Singapore's education system has been seen as essential for nation-building and economic progress (Cheng, 2016). Even before independence, Education Minister Ong Pang Boon declared educating loyal citizens with a 'national consciousness' to be an objective of the common syllabus (Straits Times, 1964). Subsequently, education's role in 'inculcating habits and attitudes' suitable for national development was officially espoused by the Ministry of Education (MOE) (Tan, 1970). To these ends, the newly independent state regulated many aspects of the education system through the late 1960s and early 1970s (Barr and Skrbis, 2008), from the content of textbooks to the number of hours spent on each subject weekly (see for example Tan, 1970). In particular, as Goh Chor Boon and S. Gopinathan have pointed out (2005), planning of the history curriculum was progressively centralised – from the standardisation of history as a taught subject to the publication of the first state-authored textbook in 1984, and later the creation of National Education (NE) – reflecting an increasing awareness of the potential for history education to shape national identity. By the late 1990s, the history curriculum was seen by Singapore's leaders as integral to education's nation-building objectives, or, in Prime Minister Goh Chok Tong's words, as nothing less than 'education for citizenship' (MITA, 1996).

The connection between history and nation-building suggests that Singapore's history textbooks provide an important window to how the state constructs and entrenches its official narrative. One important aspect of this narrative is the textbooks' presentation of race, widely taken as the primary basis of division in Singaporean society (Benjamin, 1976). Throughout its independent history, Singapore has promoted an official ideology of meritocracy and multiculturalism (Tan, 1999), so much so that the birth of a multiracial society has been called a 'defining gesture' of nationhood (Poon, 2009). As early as 1967, Singapore's identity as a 'multi-racial and multi-religious community' was presented as a key characteristic of the country in official publications (see for example Aaron, 1967), while the image of a multi-ethnic utopia was promoted in the media (Vasil, 1995). In later decades, scholars have documented the deliberate visual construction of multiculturalism in Singapore's public media (Lee et al., 2004), including choreographed dances at annual National Day Parades to signify the country's harmonious multiracial composition (Rajah, 1999). Official rhetoric has also been matched by state policy, with major elements of social provision (including housing and education) being mediated through racial categories, or implemented by state-sponsored ethnic 'self-help' groups (Stimpfl, 2006). In the early 1990s, following a leadership transition within the ruling People's Action Party (PAP), Prime Minister Goh maintained that Singapore's multiracialism was a 'fundamental policy [that would] never change' (MITA, 1993).

Before considering how this official multiracialism is presented in history textbooks across the period, it is essential to understand its inner workings. Singapore's policy of multiracialism is mediated through four official ethnic categories – 'Chinese', 'Malay', 'Indian', and 'Other' (CMIO) – with religions and cultures seen as composites, and extensions, of these labels (Poon, 2009). Originating in colonial policy (Benjamin, 1976), these categories were considered 'founding races' of Singapore after independence (Hill and Lian, 2013). They have since been preserved and naturalised in government policy, referring to essentialised notions of ethnic and cultural characteristics even as markers of 'racial' identity have fallen into disuse elsewhere (Ang and Stratton, 1995).

Syed Aljunied argues (2012), for instance, that although 'Malays' have different class, educational, gender, and linguistic affiliations (Ooi, 2005), they are officially portrayed as a homogenous group based on assumed similarities. Likewise, Vineeta Sinha shows (Sinha, 2006) that diverse cultural symbols of the Indian community in Singapore have been subsumed under a label privileging the symbols and practices of Hinduism; while class, language, and religious differences in the Chinese community have also been homogenised in state policy (Cushman and Wang, 1988).

In a system where multiracialism and multiculturalism are conflated or taken as synonymous, culture and religion are officially treated as essentialised aspects of ethnicity. In turn, an essentialised notion of ethnicity lends itself to the propagation of official and popular stereotypes. From government ministers exhorting Malays to be 'less interested in agricultural matters', based on a perception that they hold 'rural world views' (cited in Benjamin, 1976), to Prime Minister Lee Kuan Yew's suggestion that Indians possess 'benign leisure values' as opposed to the 'intense and exacting civic culture' of the Chinese (cited in Moore, 2000), political leaders have popularised various assumed characteristics underpinning each racial group's role in the national project. At the same time, rather than containing ethnic loyalties within an overarching national identity, Singapore's pervasive system of ethnic classification has re-emphasised ethnicity in public life. As Michael Barr and Zlatko Skrbis have observed (2008), Singaporeans frequently associate their national identity with their racial category, while Lian Kwen Fee contends (2006) that being Singaporean is 'necessarily a hyphenated identity'. It is precisely because Singapore's official multiracialism is so firmly entrenched that many adopt a racialised view of their own place in state and society.

This chapter draws on the analysis of Singapore's history textbooks to observe how the principles and paradoxes of state multiracialism, so central to its society and self-image, find expression in official narrative. Its most original contribution is a critical discourse analysis of (both official and non-official) textbooks and teaching resources used in Singapore schools from 1965 to 2000[1]. Textual constructions are analysed alongside pedagogical aids such as caricatures, photographic captions, and mnemonics to understand how students were prompted to engage with, and internalise, a particular narrative of race in the nation's history. These findings are contextualised against the progressive consolidation of history curriculum planning under state control across three periods – 1965–1980, 1980–1990, and 1990–2000 – driven by an increasing appreciation for the relevance of history education to nation-building. A final section considers some continuities that underpin conceptions of race in the national narrative, as well as possible trajectories for history education in the present.

Separation and anxiety: 1965–1980

When Singapore unexpectedly attained independence in 1965, policymakers had yet to fully grasp the relevance of history education to nation-building. Accordingly, refashioning the curriculum was not among the new state's immediate priorities. Pre-independence textbooks by Joginder Jessy (1961) and Kennedy Tregonning (1964) – which presented Singapore's history as part of a Malayan trajectory – were used till the early 1980s (Blackburn, 2012), and the port-city's narrative was not their central concern (Goh and Gopinathan, 2005). Although both authors expanded their texts in the 1970s to include events leading up to Singapore's independence, both accounts still focused on Malaysian nationalism. For example, against the triumphalist mood in independent Singapore, Jessy (1974) presented its departure from Malaysia as 'secession', while Tregonning (1972) called it a 'courageous' choice – on the part of Malaysia's, not Singapore's, leaders. As Blackburn argues (2012), endorsement of these textbooks suggests that independence 'was slow in making its impact felt' on the curriculum, and little official effort was made to rewrite Singapore's history in these early years.

Such apparent disinterest can be seen as part of political leaders' efforts to signal that, for pragmatic reasons, a 'collective amnesia' was most appropriate for Singapore's development (Lian, 1999). As the Education Minister Ong Pang Boon later reflected:

> 'History has no immediate practical use. It does not help us compute our way through life. Thus [...] it is pushed out of the curriculum to make room for more immediately attractive and useful studies.'
> (cited in Afandi and Baildon, 2010)

Such a view was evident in the structure of the common syllabus. At lower secondary level, combined history and geography were given 2.5 of 28 school-hours in a week, half of that allocated to 'first language' (Tan, 1970). From 1972, history was axed altogether from the Primary School Leaving Examinations (Lau, 2004). In Nicole Tarulevicz's analysis (2009), the state had chosen to deprioritise history teaching in the name of survival – a stance expressed in then-Foreign Minister S. Rajaratnam's pithy injunction that 'knowing where you are going is more important than knowing where you came from' (cited in Lau, 2004).

Other political motives lay behind the de-emphasis of national history. First, Singapore had scarcely been imagined as an autonomous nation when jointly ruled with Malaya under the British, and it was difficult to craft a narrative of independent Singapore that suggested anything other than a shared future with Malaysia (Kwa, 1999). Indeed, the contemporary historian John Gullick (1969) found it difficult to craft an acceptable, separate chronology of Singapore: the island had not only been 'as much a part of Malaysia as any other', but 'expelled for unruly behaviour'. Any attempt to retrace the recent past thus threatened Singapore's nascent self-perception as a new sovereign nation. Second, Singapore's leaders saw recent outbreaks of internal conflict through the prism of ethnicity, and sought to avoid what they saw as inevitable repercussions of teaching different racial groups about their histories. Specifically, following what were perceived as violent 'race riots' in 1964, the government feared that any emphasis on cultural identity would exacerbate inter-ethnic strife among Singaporeans (Goh and Gopinathan, 2005). In Foreign Minister Rajaratnam's words (1984), a 'collective lobotomy' of national history at this stage was necessary to avoid 'turning Singapore into a bloody battleground' for communal infighting (see 'Continuities', below).

The painful politics of independence thus contributed to a low degree of central oversight for textbooks of this period. Nevertheless, they exhibited three key trends in the presentation of race that can be understood in light of this context. First, textbooks of the late 1960s included extensive accounts of pre-colonial history which depicted Chinese, Malays, and Indians as sharing a long-established presence in Malaya. Tregonning's History (1964) began with a chapter on the 'Non-Islamic Background' of Southeast Asia, implicitly challenging the idea of a pre-existing 'Malay' race with a discussion of 'aboriginal-Malays or proto-Malays'. Not only did 'Indians [begin] coming to the Malay peninsula [...] centuries before the Christian era', it argued; the Chinese also arrived 'as early as the Indians'. Another textbook published in the same year (Dance et al., 1964) narrated how Gujerati merchants collaborated with the Malay Sultans, and included a 'Chinese account of Malacca' as one of its main sources. Even volumes from the late 1970s stressed the importance of a Hindu administrative system along with China's 'friendship and protection' for successful polities like Malacca, thus entrenching all three main racial groups in Malaya's pre-colonial history (Kok, 1978).

On one hand, the textbooks' portrayal of these three groups as established presences in Malaya's pre-colonial history can be seen as a response to the *bumiputera* discourse of postwar Malay nationalism (see Siddique and Suryadinata, 1981). At the same time, as a 1964 textbook explained, a multiracial pre-colonial history was intended to discourage ethnic 'insularity' – instead, students should appreciate the 'influence [...] of so many different peoples' on the region (Dance et al., 1964). This admonishment echoed contemporary rhetoric that Singaporeans should 'learn to be tolerant and appreciative of one another's traditions' in the name of political cohesion (Social Affairs Minister Othman Wok, cited in Benjamin, 1976). In 1969, drawing on existing tensions, celebrations for the anniversary of Sir Stamford Raffles' arrival had been criticised by a Chinese broadsheet for commemorating the 'historical accident' of colonialism over contributions of rank-and-file Chinese (Sin Chew Jit Poh, 1969), and by the Singapore Malay National Organisation for 'not portraying the existence of Malays' in Singapore (Utusan Melayu, 1969). Criticisms like these heightened sensitivities around the presentations of different races in official media, including textbooks: an MOE publication the following year took pains to stress the 'principle of parity of treatment' across the races (Tan, 1970). Special efforts to emphasise intra-racial diversity in the period's textbooks suggest that their authors saw history teaching as a potential counterweight against interracial tension.

Second, textbooks from the period acknowledged a remarkable level of intra-ethnic diversity in pre-colonial and colonial Southeast Asia. Although Chinese, Malays, and Indians were portrayed as entrenched in the region, these labels did not reflect the essentialised CMIO framework of later texts; rather, there was relatively nuanced discussion of each community. One textbook discussed ancient Srivijaya as a cross-cultural centre for Buddhism, and explained how the uptake and practice of the faith varied by class (Dance et al., 1964). Another included an extensive section on the 'Origin of the Malay states' with specific references to interactions between Bugis, Achinese, Minangkabau, Sakai, and others (Tan, 1975). Malay anti-colonialists were not portrayed as a homogenous ethnic lobby, but a cause with various subdivisions: Arab-educated, Malay-educated, and English-educated nationalists were presented as coming from different backgrounds, and having distinct demands (Kok, 1978). Jessy (1974) specifically described Chinese immigrants in Singapore as a mixture of 'Cantonese, Hokkiens, Teochew, Hylam, Kheks, and others', accurately reflecting the presence of distinct linguistic communities, and contrasted this to the relatively homogenous population of Hong Kong. In embracing the cultural diversity of Southeast Asia, and not type-casting its population by ethnicity, these textbooks suggest that a state-led process of ethnic essentialisation had not yet been consolidated during this period.

A third feature was the consistent portrayal of both the colonial and self-governing state as a successful mediator between ethnic interests. Tregonning's chapter (1972) about the 'Creation of a Plural Society' began by claiming that this was the 'most important event' in colonial Malaya. The facing page featured the first textbook illustration of state-directed multiracialism: a 1902 photograph of Agent Sir Hugh Clifford with Sultan Idris and Raja Chulan of Perak in London for the coronation of King Edward VII, intended to represent the British administrators' successful efforts at 'co-ordination' with Malay leaders. Other textbooks from the period listed 'peace and stable government' over Malaya's races as the main draw for Chinese and Indian immigrants (Kok, 1978), and argued that the post-war Government's first success was in 'resolving racial conflicts' and achieving 'inter-communal co-operation' (Tan, 1975).

In the same vein, an early state-authored resource on Singapore's independence framed the post-separation PAP Government as the champion of 'a truly multi-racial society [...] without regard to race or religion' (Tan, 1972). By contrast, the wartime Japanese state was presented in terms of its unfair ethnic policies, particularly for being 'especially cruel to the Chinese' (ibid.). Such portrayals positioned Singapore's colonial and independent rulers alike as peacemakers among ethnic groups, warned implicitly of the dangers of bad governance for a volatile, multi-ethnic community, and harmonised with the PAP's interests in presenting itself as a bulwark against societal collapse (Tarulevicz, 2009). Given the politics of the island's separation from the Federation of Malaysia, such portrayals also accorded with the PAP's attempt to define itself against Malaysia's leaders through an 'ideology of multiculturalism', which, according to official rhetoric at the time, made merger 'untenable' (Pereira, 2006).

Rehabilitating history: 1980–1990

By the 1980s, Singapore's leaders were increasingly conscious of the role that history education could play in nation-building. Speaking to the Historical

164   *Theophilus Kwek*

Society of Nanyang University in 1978, Prime Minister Lee Kuan Yew encouraged students to 'retain a keen sense of our inheritance', which would 'inoculate' them against foreign 'attitudes to life' (Ministry of Culture, 1978a). Later that year, he declared on national television that Singaporeans should 'know something of [their] past [...] to identify [themselves]' (Ministry of Culture, 1978b). As Blackburn and Hack argue (2012), it was at this juncture that national history returned to the official curriculum: in 1980, the MOE established the Curriculum Development Institute of Singapore (CDIS), which released the two-volume *Social and Economic History of Modern Singapore* in 1984. Echoing Lee, the new textbook suggested that a 'basic knowledge of national history' was necessary to foster an 'identity with, and loyalty to, our Republic' (CDIS, 1984a). This was not only the first full, state-authored presentation of Singapore's past, but also the most comprehensive resource to be printed in colour up till this point. As such, it was instrumental in developing the use of caricatures and illustrations to cement presentations of Singapore's ethnic groups and their cultural traits. Independently-written textbooks, such as Kok Koun Chin's *Malaya and Singapore 1400–1963* (Kok, 1988), were still published during this period, but were mostly earlier texts updated to match the new syllabus (cf. Kok, 1978).

Textbooks from this period began to adopt an essentialised conception of ethnicity, ascribing fixed cultural and religious characteristics to each of the official racial groups. The ethnic communities themselves were seen as responsible for remaining so distinct from each other: authors like Kok (1988) asserted that 'each race wanted to preserve its own customs', and supported this with anecdotal evidence. In one text, the story of a businessman who sent his impressionable son to China was used to demonstrate that the Chinese 'clung to Chinese customs' (CDIS, 1984a). Moreover, authors took many contextual factors shaping each ethnic community for granted as racial traits. The Europeans, for instance, were presented as a civic-conscious group who 'took part in public meetings [for] the well-being of Singapore', and who were responsible for its 'system of law and order' (ibid). There was no suggestion that these contributions could be better attributed to European administrators' positions of dominance.

In the resulting matrix of racial characteristics, there was a clear moral hierarchy led by Chinese traits, followed by Indian and Malay ones. While Chinese and Indian immigrants were presented as enterprising, Malays were typified as local or rural, thus treating indigeneity itself as a character trait. In Kok's description (1988), Chinese 'easily found employment' upon arrival in Malaya, but Malays 'preferred planting *padi* or fishing' and were 'not interested in working in plantations'. Malay parents, he claimed, 'did not realise the need for education', and kept their children at home despite being offered free schooling. Similarly, the CDIS textbook of 1984 recorded that Malays 'lived a simple life' and relied on 'selling foodstuffs and other goods' to others. Its chapter on 'The Malays' includes an illustration of 'A Horse-Carriage with a Malay Driver', whose caption ('Which person do you think was a

European?') directly linked the ethnic and economic differences between the fashionably-dressed man boarding the carriage and the one in traditional attire holding the door. In contrast, the Chinese were presented as 'hardworking, enterprising, and resourceful' (Kok, 1988). While rich Chinese like Seah Eu Chin and Tan Kim Seng were named as having set up schools, hospitals and clan associations, no contributions by Indians or Malays were listed (CDIS, 1984a).

Likewise, discussions of housing associated the Chinese with 'urban areas' and Indians with 'estates and plantations', but Malays with 'rural areas' – signalling associations with commerce, industry and agriculture respectively (Kok, 1988). Moreover, while Indians 'helped with the construction of roads and railways', and Chinese were 'responsible for the growth of new towns', Malays were entirely unmentioned in the same textbook's section on 'Economic Development' (ibid.). Another text dwelled briefly on social problems among the Chinese, but rather than presenting these as communal traits (as in its discussion of the Malays), attributed them to general poverty and an imbalanced gender ratio (CDIS, 1984a). Overall, the Chinese were portrayed as models of more desirable characteristics than the other races.

Second, the period's textbooks presented a retrospective reading of the CMIO categories as they were understood in independent Singapore into the island's past. The *Social and Economic History* (CDIS, 1984a) painted pre-colonial Singapore as a *tabula rasa* where multiracial society could later flourish: after the Portuguese burned the last indigenous 'outpost' in 1613, 'jungle [...] spread over the whole island'. Distinctions were made among the Javanese, Orang Laut, and various Malay sultanates before this point, but those who settled afterwards were described monolithically as 'Malays' and 'Chinese'. The British landing in 1819 was accompanied by a caricature of 'a Sepoy holding a Musket', with the explanation that 'an Indian soldier' went ashore with Raffles and his assistant, Major William Farquhar (ibid.). Despite evidence of distinct settlements on the island prior to the arrival of the British, each having separate spheres of regional influence, the textbook narrative presented the simplified conclusion that a new colony was founded with Chinese, Malays, Indians and Europeans[2].

The model of four distinct races was further developed in the texts' discussion of colonial rule. In *Malaya and Singapore* (1988), Kok updated the ethno-neutral description of Singapore's colonial population in his 1978 textbook to stress that society included 'Malays, Chinese, Bugis, Indian, and Europeans'[3]. (Kok, 1988). Subsequently, sections on education policy in colonial Singapore featured separate analyses of Malay, Chinese, Tamil, and English developments (ibid.). Similarly, the *Social and Economic History* described how Raffles planned separate housing for 'Chinese, Indians, Malays, and Others', and had individual sections for 'Archipelago Traders' (referring to the Malays), 'Chinese Traders', and 'European Ships' (CDIS, 1984a). By the end of the nineteenth century, Singapore was presented as a 'multi-racial society [...] three-quarters Chinese, with Malays, Indians, and people of other races': essentially the same terms used to describe the CMIO framework of the 1980s (ibid). Three chapters in the same text ('The Malays and Other Muslims', 'Europeans, Indians, and Other Minority Groups', and 'The Chinese') were devoted to delineating these categories. According to the authors, the umbrella term 'Malays' included those from 'Malaya, Sumatra, and the Riau-Lingga Archipelago' as well as 'others [...] of similar race', grouped together with 'other Muslims'. On the other hand, 'Other Minority Groups' was an all-encompassing term for Europeans, Eurasians, Armenians, Jews, and others (ibid.). As Brenda Yeoh and others have shown, not only was colonial Singapore far more diverse than these pages suggest; contemporary residents also opposed colonial policies administered along such racial lines (Yeoh, 2003; Pereira, 2006). Through those rigid categories, however, the textbooks consistently subsumed Singapore's colonial society into four official racial groups.

Personalising the narrative: 1990–2000

Despite these efforts to rehabilitate the history curriculum during the 1980s, the 1990s saw a renewed concern among Singapore's political leaders that history was 'not a deeply felt, vital part of [students'] collective memory' (MITA, 1996). This can be seen as a product of the ruling PAP's contemporary fears of shifting political loyalties. In 1996, Prime Minister Goh attributed younger Singaporeans' desire for parliamentary opposition to their 'lack of knowledge of Singapore's history' (ibid.). While their parents had 'voted solidly' for the PAP, the young had 'no personal experience of Singapore's struggle', and hence undervalued his party's 'strong leadership'. To remedy this, he argued, history teaching should emphasise 'the constraints we face, how we have overcome them, and what we must do to thrive' – a narrative he referred to as 'national education' (NE). The following year, NE was duly prepared as a curricular campaign by the MOE and launched by Deputy PM Lee Hsien Loong, with an accompanying 'NE Exhibition' in the city centre in 1998, which all students (and many other Singaporeans) attended (MOE, 1997).

In a parallel development, the CDIS was brought under the MOE's central Curriculum Planning Division (CPD) to form the Curriculum Planning and Development Division (CPDD), reflecting greater centralisation of syllabus planning (MOE, 1996). The CPDD and other government agencies began releasing a comprehensive range of NE resources, including tours to historic locations and teachers' guides to raise classroom engagement. State efforts were mirrored by privately-written textbooks like Diana Chua's *Singapore History Come Alive!* (1997), or quiz-books like *The Singapore Story* (Rajamanikam, 1999), all of which were intended to prepare students for the new curriculum. Many echoed Goh's desire for pupils to form personal connections with official history. As one *National Heritage Tour* (CPD, 1996) put it, Singapore's young 'did not have memories [...] to bind them to their homeland', and could only 'develop strong bonds' by studying its past. As a contemporary publication of the Singapore Heritage Society put it (Kwok et al., 1999), these moves could be seen as a concerted effort to 'construct national myths and, by extension, national loyalties'.

Presentations of race in the educational resources of this period saw three key developments: expansions and modifications to racial essentialisation, positive portrayals of European colonialism, and arguments for a paternal state. The first involved entrenching the CMIO categories as essentialised compounds of 'culture, rituals, traditions, and values' (CPD, 1996). To this end, the CPD prepared *National Heritage Tours* to three 'special ethnic areas': Chinatown, Kampong Glam, and Little India. The Little India tour framed the area as a 'microcosm of India' and aimed to uncover an 'imprint of Indian identity' comprising 'Indian costumes', 'Indian cooking and spices', and 'Indian art' (ibid.). Though acknowledging that Indians came from Bangladesh, Malaysia, Ceylon, and Pakistan, the guidebook privileged Tamil elements: pupils were taught the Tamil practice of joining palms and saying 'Vanakkam' as a 'traditional Indian greeting', and Tamil was the default 'Indian language' while other languages were labelled 'dialects'. The guidebook also promoted certain stereotypes, presenting illustrations of a snake charmer, guard, and washerwoman as typical 'Indian occupations' (ibid.). Notably, a textbook published the following year departed from a Tamil-dominant presentation of Indians only to promote yet another occupational stereotype. According to this text, 'Indians' (specifically Sikhs) made 'good policemen' because they were 'large in build', and their 'beards and turbans frightened thieves' (Chua, 1997).

In addition to reinforcing racial essentialisation, textbooks began to treat groups outside the CMIO model as new, essentialised categories of their own. For example, while 'other Muslims' were previously grouped with Malays, textbooks from the 1990s actively distinguished Arabs from Malays. However, they were also uniformly presented as having come to Singapore 'to trade', a stark economic contrast from Malays who came to 'escape war-torn homelands' or 'find work' (Chua, 1997 and CPDD, 1998). Little else was written about them, except that they were Muslims. In one quiz-book, *The Singapore Story,* pupils were given four options for the question 'The Arabs came to Singapore to _____'. The choices were to 'trade', 'teach', 'preach Islam', or 'settle down', and the only correct answer was 'trade' (Rajamanikam, 1999). The Peranakans – who, being descended from older immigrant families, had higher levels of ethnic intermarriage – formed another community that did not fall neatly within the CMIO model. One textbook noted that they observed a 'mixture of traditions', but did not treat this as evidence of cultural heterogeneity. Instead, pupils were instructed to identify something Western (a clock), something Chinese (a spittoon), and something Malay (clothing) in a picture of a Peranakan woman, thus reconciling her to the established categorisation and promoting, ironically, a fixed idea of cultural diversity (CPDD, 1998).

168 *Theophilus Kwek*

Another trend was the positive portrayal of European colonialism, and correspondingly, an emphasis on the paternal state's role in preserving Singapore's racial configuration. In *Malaya and Southeast Asia* (CDIS, 1996), the 'Founding of Singapore and its Development up to 1823' was presented entirely in terms of what the British authorities achieved. Students were taught to remember terms of the 1819 Treaty (such as 'Factory for the British', 'Respect for the Sultan', and so on) using the mnemonic 'FRIENDS', and an accompanying caricature depicted a traditionally-attired Malay man (the Sultan) welcoming a formally-dressed white man (Raffles) to Singapore (ibid.). Other caricatures highlighted the effectiveness of colonial policies, with Chinese thieves apprehended by white policemen. While no explicit statements about ethnicity were made, the only portraits featured in the text were of Europeans, and both first-hand sources at the end of the chapter were by British Resident, John Crawfurd, reflecting the prominence accorded to a white colonial perspective (ibid.). Similarly, though equal curriculum time was given to discussing Chinese, Malays, Indians, and Europeans in the *Social Studies Teachers' Guide* (CDIS, 1994), the last section – 'Review the Big Picture' – instructed pupils were asked to see 'Singapore through the eyes of a European Artist'. Yet another text described Raffles' town plan as a successful move to organise the 'disorderly shops and houses' of the Chinese, Malays, and Indians, making it 'easier for each race [...] to have their own leaders look after them' (Lim, 1999). In all these portrayals, British colonialism was depicted as a benevolent force exercising enlightened stewardship over a multiracial colony.

This portrayal of colonialism is significant because it was linked rhetorically, in the textbooks, to the paternalist policies of the post-Separation PAP Government. General parallels were drawn between Raffles and PAP leaders: the cover of *Singapore History Come Alive!* (1997), for example, showed portraits of Stamford Raffles, Lee Kuan Yew, and Goh Chok Tong above a banner proclaiming 'From 1819 TOWARDS 2000'. The text itself presented a developmental arc led by these figures. Just as colonial rulers 'maintained law and order' and implemented housing and education policies, the PAP was 'well-organised', and 'worked hard [...] to solve problems of unemployment, housing and education' (ibid.). Crucially, PAP leaders were seen to inherit the duty of ethnic management in contemporary policymaking. From the late 1980s, ethnic quotas (such as limiting Malay occupation of a block of flats to 20 per cent) had replaced a first-come-first-serve system previously used for public housing allocation (Chua, 1991). In textbook discussions of Raffles' town plan, teachers were encouraged to 'ask pupils where they would have lived if they had lived in Singapore during that time', and whether they 'lived along communal lines [...] in present-day Singapore' (CDIS, 1994). Rather than eliciting open-ended responses, teachers were then to 'bring to pupils' attention that for purposes of racial harmony, we no longer do so' – thus justifying the post-independent government's ethnic housing policies (ibid.). Singapore's stability and social cohesion were, as such, presented in highly relatable terms as a result of 'strong leadership, far-sighted policies, hard work and sacrifice', of the PAP (CPD, 1996).

Continuities

In examining history textbooks from each of the three time frames (1965–1980, 1980–1990 and 1990–2000), the preceding sections present several trends in how ethnicity has been portrayed: the consolidation of an essentialised conception of race, the development and modification of CMIO racial categorisation, and the strengthening of the PAP Government's portrayal as an indispensable broker of race relations. Across the period, these trends ran parallel to the gradual centralisation of history curriculum planning. This section considers, however, that these changes were underpinned throughout the period by the consistent presentation of racial diversity as a threat to Singapore's sovereignty and stability.

First, history textbooks presented race as an alternative source of loyalty, and hence a threat to national sovereignty. The *History of Malaya* (Kok, 1978) described how 'immigrant races [...] pledged allegiance to their mother country', an attitude 'dangerous to the unity and solidarity of Malaya'. Not only were immigrants seen immediately as 'races', they were also portrayed as mercenary, having come to Malaya 'solely to earn as much money as possible [...] and then return home'. In its discussion of specific races, the *Social and Economic History* (CDIS, 1984a) described Indians as not having 'the feeling of belonging to this country', seeing themselves as 'foreigners living in a foreign land', while the Chinese allegedly 'never forgot their links to China', and 'thought of China as their homeland'. *Malaya and Singapore* (Kok, 1988) described the tendency to 'form associations based on race' as a key issue in colonial Singapore, and subsequently stated that various groups did not develop 'feelings of belonging'. Towards the end of the period, *Singapore History Come Alive!* (Chua, 1997) stated that 'Malay, Chinese, Indian, Arab, and European' immigrants 'did not intend to stay' in Singapore, but planned to leave 'once they had made enough money'. By associating races with other homelands, the textbooks presented race itself as a marker of competing loyalties.

Conversely, in discussions of post-Separation exigencies, the textbooks set racial loyalties in contrast to national loyalties. The first text to focus on Separation, *The Struggle for Freedom* (Tan, 1972), quoted the Government, reminding people to be 'united without regard to race'. Likewise, the *Social and Economic History* (CDIS, 1984b) stated that a people 'divided by race [...] had to owe their loyalty to only one country'. Under its section on 'Singapore as an Independent Country', *Singapore History Come Alive!* (Chua, 1997) featured a caricature of four children intended to represent the CMIO races, with text emphasising that Singaporeans 'must realise they [...] belonged only to one nation'. Such presentations implied that racially-defined loyalties were in active competition with national allegiance. Many texts also portrayed the post-independence government as an active player in society's transition from communal to national allegiances. The *History of Modern Singapore* (CPDD, 1998), for example, described how PAP leaders 'took steps to build a nation' by 'opening [jobs] to all races', placing 'children of different races' in the same schools, and creating multi-racial housing estates. The post-independence project of creating a 'state-instituted plural society', in Joseph Stimpfl's words (Stimpfl, 2006), was thus seen as the solution to competing racial allegiances.

Second, history textbooks presented racial differences as latent sources of communal tension, and hence threats to social stability. This could be seen in consistent portrayals of the 1964 riots as a predominantly racial affair, national in scale, and fundamentally antagonistic, while popular accounts suggest a more nuanced historical reality. Tregonning's revised textbook (1972) claimed that the riots reflected 'appalling depths of communal ill-will', and a state of 'volatile explosiveness'. Though the *Struggle for Freedom* (Tan, 1972) acknowledged that 'many [...] protected their friends of other races', it described the 'serious racial riots' in vivid detail, with 'bands of roaming youths [...] attacking innocent people in the streets'. The *Social and Economic History* (CDIS, 1984a; CDIS, 1984b) stated that these were the 'worst riots in Singapore' since 1900, and recorded casualties in racialised terms as 'almost all Malays and Chinese', while *Singapore History Come Alive!* (Chua, 1997) presented the riots as a racial disagreement so serious that 'the whole island was put on curfew'. A brief account in the *History of Modern Singapore* (CPDD, 1998) was accompanied by a caricature of a Malay and a Chinese man reacting to the news in shock, and a photograph of 'soldiers guarding the roads to prevent fighting'. All depicted the riots as widespread, hostile, and essentially racial, in line with what Prime Minister Goh presented as 'basic facts [of] nationhood': that the riots had involved a 'basic disagreement' over 'race relations' in which 'many people were killed' (MITA, 1996).

Presentations of the 1964 riots were important in illustrating continuities in the textbooks' treatments of ethnicity because of their recurrence in official explanations of Singapore's racial policies. The riots appeared in state-endorsed television programmes and museum exhibitions as manifestations of 'racial divisions', and as evidence that the alternative to 'interracial harmony' was 'rioting and chaos' (cited in Low, 2001). Both implicitly and explicitly, they became instrumental in defining Singapore's multiculturalism. However, the perception that they were a predominantly racial matter is not shared by many eyewitnesses, who saw them instead as 'a Muslim religious matter'. Others blamed Indonesian agents, or political controversy, some going so far as to say there was 'nothing racial about the riots' (cited in Jasmin, 2013). Moreover, the alleged scale of the riots obscured the fact that for many, the conflict was 'far removed from everyday life': both Chinese and Malay informants reported that their estates were 'peaceful', and that they were 'not frightened' (cited in Low, 2001). Finally, official presentations of the riots as fundamentally antagonistic served to entrench a narrative of racial difference as a source of threat. Popular memories of the riots, however, privilege accounts of families of different races 'bringing food [for those] afraid to go out', or 'forming a vigil [...] to last through the nights' (Low, 2001). These memories challenge the ideas that race was the central issue in the conflict, and that the state was indispensable in restoring order. Situating textbook presentations against popular accounts reveals the extent to which the former supported a narrative of race as a threat to social stability.

As such, race is presented in history textbooks throughout the period as being, in Lian's words (2006), 'dangerous to social stability' and 'subversive of national loyalty'. These continuities do not only reflect the views of those who shaped the history curricula, but further explain various changes described in the previous sections. As Philip Holden observes (2009), 'racial governmentality' in Singapore has 'sought to mould and indeed manufacture ethnicities for pragmatically expressed reasons of state', including the perceptions of threat explored in this section. The spectre of competing racial loyalties can be seen as an impetus for the development of an essentialised discourse of race over the period, which extends the state's homogenising power over elements of racial identity. Instead of symbols and traditions which may serve as stronger sources of allegiance, racial groups are distinguished by elements which fall within the state's control, such as official languages, residential districts, and festivals (Chua, 1998). The textbooks assign each community a function within the national project, such that – to borrow one of the 'NE Messages' promoted in the 1990s – 'many races, religions, languages, and cultures [can] pursue one destiny' (see for example Lim, 1999). Race itself, as a compound of cultural elements, is used to reinforce a 'sense of pride in our nation' by capturing, for students, the 'rich diversity of our heritage' (CPD, 1996).

Likewise, the consolidation of a CMIO model in textbooks reflects the narrative of race as a threat to stability because it presents the four races as partners in nation-building, but also as distinct groups in perpetual tension. David Birch suggests (Birch, 1993) that policymakers have adopted 'discourses of crisis' to keep Singaporeans 'constantly aware' of national identity. Textbook presentations of fixed racial divisions thus keep the question of Singapore's multiculturalism perpetually in focus. Statements highlighting the contributions of each racial group, or descriptions of societal progress organised into sections corresponding with the four races, serve to present the national project as a sum of distinct group. Using the history curriculum in this way to stress 'the threat of racial tension' emphasises, at the same time, the 'shared experience of building the nation' as a part of citizenship (Tarulevicz, 2009).

Conclusion

This chapter has considered how the idea of ethnicity, and specific racial groups, are presented in Singapore's history textbooks from 1965 to 2000. Throughout the period, presentations of ethnicity are marked by a sense of threat to Singapore's sovereignty, from competing racial loyalties; and to its stability, from centrifugal racial dynamics. These continuities, which accord with perspectives articulated by Singapore's policy elite, serve to explain several key changes over time, including: the development of an essentialised conception of race, the application of a progressively modified CMIO framework to the past, and the entrenchment of the paternal state as a defender of multiracialism in Singapore. At the same time, individual sections have demonstrated how particular iterations of these trends can be attributed to features of their time.

While Singapore's textbooks have served an important educational purpose in simplifying and presenting history, they have also wielded significant power to entrench a dominant narrative through simplification and presentation. In addition to the centralisation of curriculum planning, accounts from the National Institute of Education (NIE) suggest that efforts to train history teachers in the official narrative have become more rigorous, especially after the introduction of NE (see for example NIE News, April 1997 and NIE News, July 1997). As a result, the classroom experience of the official narrative has become 'hegemonic and totalising', and rendered 'alternative memories [...] irrelevant, inaccurate, and even illegitimate', as seen in comparisons between presentations of the 1964 riots and eyewitness accounts (Low, 2001). With regard to other areas of the curriculum, Kevin Blackburn suggests that such alternative memories, transmitted by family networks, can provide Singapore's students with a means to challenge official narratives (Blackburn, 2013). But he also acknowledges, unfortunately, that many families have 'absorbed [...] the official narrative of history', or adopted it as 'part of their identity as Singaporeans', thus internalising rather than challenging official memory (ibid.).

The implications of this chapter are that the findings above – an essentialised notion of race, an established CMIO framework, and an entrenched view of the state's indispensability – are taught, experienced, and absorbed as part of the official narrative, thus shaping popular conceptions of race and national identity. While it is difficult to isolate the curriculum's effects from those of wider racial policies, many have noted how these policies affect identity formation in Singapore (Aljunied, 2010). In particular, the propagation of racial essentialisation in the classroom has been shown to distort individual identification: in one study, a child who initially identified as Malay later 'clarified that he was Indian-Muslim', having considered Islam, at first, as distinctive to Malays (Lee et al., 2004). More recently, others have documented the absorption of particular elements of the NE syllabus into popular discourse (Loo, 2013). Across 35 years of policymaking, narratives of race in earlier textbooks have arguably shaped the views of curriculum planners and their peers who have gone through the system, contributing to the strengthening of particular trends in later years.

Given the entrenchment of the official narrative, then, any successful challenge to the dominant position must come from within the curriculum. Goh and Gopinathan argue that the MOE began to introduce some level of debate to the history curriculum in the 2000s, stating in its official guidelines that 'students should be taught [...] that there can be multiple and conflicting interpretations' of some historical events (Goh and Gopinathan, 2005). However, the centrality of racial categorisation to the official conception of Singaporean society, as well as the close association between racial division and political legitimacy, suggests that presentations of race are less amenable to re-evaluation or questioning. One resource from 2007, created by the National Museum for educational use, purports to engage with 'personal historical knowledge' and shifts the focus of its illustrations from official figures like Raffles or Lee Kuan Yew to household objects such as laundry-poles and family photographs (cited in Tarulevicz, 2009). But it continues to reflect elements of racial essentialisation (depictions include a stereotypical Chinese shop-house and a young Chinese girl), while Tarulevicz notes the 'obvious absence of Malays and Indians' and a 'privileging of the colonial image' in its presentation. While some flexibility has thus been admitted, at the time of writing this chapter, recent portrayals of race continued to reflect the trends evident in textbooks from 1965 to 2000.

In sum, presentations of ethnicity in Singapore's history curriculum have been shaped by, and used to support, an official narrative that sees race as the primary basis of division in Singaporean society, and hence adopts racial management as the primary basis of political legitimacy. In turn, the narrative of race presented in the history curriculum has formed part of policymakers' efforts to shift popular conceptions of race in Singapore's society and history. Shifts in political imperatives across three broad time frames have prompted variations in how race is portrayed, but continuities over the whole period reflect more fundamental perspectives which anchor the narrative of race as threat, and the gradual effects of centralised curricular planning. Through this process, the state has entrenched some insecurities and downplayed others, and future shifts in the curriculum must account for the effects of this period's developments on the views and identities of a generation of Singaporean students.

Notes

1 A list of the primary sources surveyed is available in the References section.
2 Contrasting accounts place the pre-colonial population between 500 and 1,000; all agree that it comprised Orang Kallang, Orang Seletar, and Orang Laut among other culturally distinct groups. See Rahmat, 2008.
3 Kok's 1978 textbook notes that Chinese outnumbered Malays, but does not list races and emphasises the total number of people. Compare Kok, 1978, p. 47, with Kok, 1988, p. 56.

References

Primary sources

Aaron, J. 1967. Some Facts about Singapore. In: *Development and Commemoration of National Day*. Singapore: Usaha Enterprises. (Text note: the Government 'supplied all material for the booklet').
Chua, D. 1997. *Singapore History Come Alive! For Young Singaporeans*. Singapore: Preston.
Curricular Development Institute of Singapore (CDIS). 1984a. *Social and Economic History of Modern Singapore*, Book I. Singapore: Longman.
Curricular Development Institute of Singapore (CDIS). 1984b. *Social and Economic History of Modern Singapore*, Book II. Singapore: Longman.
Curricular Development Institute of Singapore (CDIS). 1994. *Social Studies Secondary 1, Teachers' Guide*. Singapore: Longman.
Curricular Development Institute of Singapore (CDIS). 1996. *Malaya and Southeast Asia*. Singapore: Manhattan Press.
Curricular Planning Division (CPD). 1996. *National Heritage Tour: Little India*. Singapore: Ministry of Education.
Curriculum Planning and Development Division (CPDD). 1998. *History of Modern Singapore*. Singapore: Longman.
Dance, E. et al. 1964. *History for Singapore Secondary Schools*, Vol. 2. Singapore: Longman.
Gullick, J. 1969. *Malaysia*. London: Benn.
Jessy, J. 1974. *Malaysia, Singapore, and Brunei, 1400–1965*, 2nd edition. Singapore: Longman.
Kok, K. C. 1978. *History of Malaya*. Singapore: Oxford University Press.
Kok, K. C. 1988. *Malaya and Singapore 1400–1963: A Comprehensive History*. Singapore: Oxford University Press.
Lim, S. E. 1999. *Social Studies Resource Companion*. Singapore: Pan Pacific.
Ministry of Culture. 1978a. The PM's Address to the Historical Society, Nanyang University, February 10. In: *Bilingualism in Our Society*. Singapore: Singapore National Printers.
Ministry of Culture. 1978b. Text of a discussion on TV with Mr Lee Kuan Yew. In *Bilingualism in Our Society*. Singapore: Singapore National Printers.
Ministry of Education (MOE). 1996. *Press Release: Establishment of Educational Technology and Curriculum Planning and Development Divisions*. 25 November. Available at: www.moe.gov.sg/media/press/1996/pr03596.htm. Accessed: 1 March 2016.
Ministry of Education (MOE). 1997. *Speech by Brigadier-General Lee Hsien Loong, at the Launch of National Education on 17 May 1997*. Available at: www.moe.gov.sg/media/speeches/1997/170597.htm. Accessed: 1 March 2016.
Ministry of Information and the Arts (MITA). 1993. *National Day Rally 1993*. 15 August.
Ministry of Information and the Arts (MITA). 1996. *National Day Rally 1996*. 18 August.
NIE News. 1997. *The Future of History*. April.
NIE News. 1997. *Seminar on National Education*. July.
Rajamanikam, K. 1999. *The Singapore Story: A Quiz Book*, Singapore: Times Media.

Sin Chew Jit Poh. 1969. *What one should know when celebrating the anniversary of the founding of Singapore.* 8 July.
Straits Times. 1964. *Time to Rewrite our History: Minister.* 24 November. p. 13.
Tan, D. E. 1975. *A Portrait of Malaysia and Singapore.* Singapore: Oxford University Press.
Tan, P. B. (for Ministry of Education), 1970. *Education in Singapore.* Singapore: Educational Publications Bureau.
Tan, S. I., 1972. *The Struggle for Freedom.* Parts 1 and 2. Singapore: Educational Publications Bureau.
Tregonning, K. 1964. *A History of Modern Malaya.* London: Eastern Universities Press.
Tregonning, K. 1972. *A History of Modern Malaysia and Singapore,* Revised. Kuala Lumpur: Eastern Universities Press.
Utusan Melayu, 1969. *150th Anniversary celebrations 'do not portray the existence of Malays in the Republic' – PKM.* 28 August.

Secondary sources

Afandi, S. and Baildon, M. 2010. History Education in Singapore. In: Nakou, M. and Barca, I. ed(s.) *Contemporary Public Debates over History Education.* Charlotte, NC: Information Age Publishing. pp. 223–242.
Aljunied, S. M. K. 2010. 'Ethnic Resurgence, Minority Communities, and State Policies in a Network Society: The Dynamics of Malay Identity Formation'. *Identities: Global Studies in Culture and Power,* 17. pp. 304–326.
Aljunied, S. M. K. 2012. Malay Identity in Postcolonial Singapore. In: Mohamad, M. and Aljunied, S. M. K. ed(s). *Melayu: The Politics, Poetics, and Paradoxes of Malayness.* Singapore: National University of Singapore Press. pp. 145–167.
Anderson, B. 1983. *Imagined Communities: Reflections on the Origin and Spread of Nationalism.* London: Verso.
Ang, I. and Stratton, J. 1995. 'The Singapore Way of Multiculturalism: Western Concepts / Asian Cultures'. *Sojourn.* 10(1). pp. 65–89.
Barr, M. and Skrbis, Z. 2008. *Constructing Singapore: Elitism, Ethnicity and the Nation-Building Project.* Copenhagen: Nordic Institute of Asian Studies.
Benjamin, G. 1976. The Cultural Logic of Singapore's Multiculturalism. In: Hassan, R. ed. *Singapore: Society in Transition.* Singapore: Oxford University Press. pp. 115–133.
Birch, D. 1993. Staging Crises: Media and Citizenship. In: Rodan, G. ed. *Singapore Changes Guard.* Melbourne: Longman Cheshire. pp. 72–83.
Blackburn, K. 2012. Turnbull's History Textbook for the Singapore Nation. In: Tarling, N. ed. *Studying Singapore's Past: C. M. Turnbull and the History of Modern Singapore.* Singapore: National University of Singapore Press. pp. 65–86.
Blackburn, K. 2013. Family Memories as Alternative Narratives to the State's Construction of Singapore's National History. In: Loh, K. S. et al. ed(s). *Oral History in Southeast Asia: Memories and Fragments.* New York: Palgrave Macmillan. pp. 55–81.
Blackburn, K. and Hack, K. 2012. *War Memory and the Making of Modern Malaysia and Singapore.* Singapore: National University of Singapore Press.
Cheng, Y. 2016. 'Learning in Neoliberal Times'. *Environment and Planning A,* 48(2). pp. 292–308.

Chua, B. H. 1991. 'Race Relations and Public Housing Policy in Singapore'. *Journal of Architectural Planning Research*, 8(4). pp. 343–354.

Chua, B. H. 1998. 'Culture, multiracialism, and national identity in Singapore'. In: Chen, K. H. ed. *Trajectories: Inter-Asian Cultural Studies*. London: Routledge.

Cushman, J. and Wang, G. ed(s). 1988. *Changing Identities of the Southeast Asian Chinese since World War II*. Hong Kong: Hong Kong University Press.

Goh, C. B. and Gopinathan, S. 2005. History Education and the Construction of National Identity in Singapore, 1945–2000. In: Vickers, E. and Jones, A. ed(s). *History Education and National Identity in East Asia*. New York: Routledge. pp. 210–218.

Hein, L. and Selden, M. 1998. 'Learning Citizenship from the Past: Textbook Nationalism, Global Context, and Social Change'. *Bulletin of Concerned Asian Scholars*, 30(2). pp. 3–15.

Hill, M. and Lian, K. F. 2013. *The Politics of Nation-Building and Citizenship in Singapore*. Abingdon: Routledge.

Hobsbawm, E. 1983. Inventing Traditions. In: Hobsbawm, E. and Ranger, T. ed(s). *The Invention of Tradition*. Cambridge: Cambridge University Press. pp 1–14.

Holden, P. 2009. A Literary History of Race: Reading Singapore literature in English in an historical frame. In: Goh, D. et al. ed(s). *Race and Multiculturalism in Malaysia and Singapore*. Abingdon: Routledge. pp. 70–85.

Jasmin, F. Bte, 2013. *Analysing the Perceptions and Portrayals of the 1964 Racial Riot in Singapore*. Unpublished thesis. National University of Singapore.

Kwa, C. G. 1999. Remembering Ourselves: Remembering 'sireh' sets and 'riots'. In: Kwok, K. W. et al. ed(s). *Our Place in Time: Exploring Heritage and Memory in Singapore*. Singapore: Singapore Heritage Society. pp. 47–58.

Kwok, K. W. et al. 1999. Introduction. In: Kwok, K. W. et al. ed(s). *Our Place in Time: Exploring Heritage and Memory in Singapore*. Singapore: Singapore Heritage Society.

Lau, A. 2004. The National Past and the Writing of History in Singapore, in Ban, K. C. et al. ed(s). *Imagining Singapore*. Singapore: Marshall Cavendish International, pp. 46–65.

Lee, C. et al. 2004. Children's experiences of Multiracial Relationships in informal Primary School settings. In: Lai, A. E. ed. *Beyond Rituals and Riots: Ethnic pluralism and social cohesion in Singapore*. Singapore: Marshall Cavendish. pp. 114–145.

Lian, K. F. 1999. The Nation-State and the Sociology of Singapore. In: Chew, P. and Kramer-Dahl, A. ed(s). *Reading Culture: Textual Practices in Singapore*. Singapore: Times Academic Press. pp. 37–54.

Lian, K. F. 2006. Race and Racialisation in Malaysia and Singapore. In: Lian, K. F., ed. *Race, Ethnicity and the State in Malaysia and Singapore*. Leiden: Koninklijke Brill. pp. 219–233.

Loo, T. 2013. Historical Reconciliation in Southeast Asia. In: Kwak, J. H. and Nobles, M. ed(s). *Inherited Responsibility and Historical Reconciliation in East Asia*. Abingdon: Routledge. pp. 81–99.

Low, A. 2001. 'The Past in the Present: Memories of the 1964 'racial riots' in Singapore'. *Asian Journal of Social Sciences*, 23(3). pp. 431–455.

Milner, A. 2005. Historians Writing Nations: Malaysian Contests. In: Wang, G. ed. *Nation-Building: Five Southeast Asian Histories*. Singapore: Institute of Southeast Asian Studies. pp. 117–162.

Moore, R. Q. 2000. 'Multiculturalism and Meritocracy: Singapore's approach to race and inequality'. *Review of Social Economy*, 58(3). pp. 339–360.

Ooi, G. L. 2005. 'The Role of the Developmental State and Interethnic Relations in Singapore'. *Asian Ethnicity.* 6(2). pp. 109–120.

Pereira, A. 2006. No Longer 'Other': The Emergence of a Eurasian Community in Singapore. In: Lian, K. F. ed. *Race, Ethnicity and the State in Malaysia and Singapore*. Leiden: Koninklijke Brill. pp. 5–32.

Poon, A. 2009. Pick and Mix for a Global City: Race and cosmopolitanism in Singapore. In: Goh, D. et al. ed(s). *Race and Multiculturalism in Malaysia and Singapore*. Abingdon: Routledge. pp. 70–85.

Rahmat, H. 2008. 'Portraits of a Nation'. *Indonesia and the Malay World*. 36(106), pp. 359–374.

Rajah, A. 1999. Making and Managing Tradition in Singapore: The National Day Parade. In: Kwok, K. W. et al. ed(s). *Our Place in Time: Exploring Heritage and Memory in Singapore*. Singapore: Singapore Heritage Society. pp. 66–75.

Renan, E. 1882. What is a Nation? trans. M. Thom. In: Bhabha, H. ed. 2013. *Nation and Narration*. Abingdon: Routledge. pp. 8–23.

Siddique, S. and Suryadinata, L. 1981. 'Bumiputra and Pribumi: Economic Nationalism (Indiginism) in Malaysia and Indonesia'. *Pacific Affairs*, 54(4), Winter 1981–1982, 1981–1982. pp. 662–687.

Sinha, V. 2006. Constructing and Contesting 'Singapore Hinduism'. In: Lian, K. F. ed. *Race, Ethnicity and the State in Malaysia and Singapore*. Leiden: Koninklijke Brill. pp. 145–168.

Stimpfl, J. 2006. 'Growing Up Malay in Singapore'. *Asian Journal of Social Sciences*. 25(2). pp. 117–138.

Suwignyo, A. 2014. 'Indonesian National History Textbooks after the New Order'. *Bijdragen tot de Taal-, Land- en Volkenkunde*. 170. pp. 113–131.

Tan, A. 1999. Two Imaginings: The Past in Present Singapore. In: Kwok, K. W. et al. ed(s). *Our Place in Time: Exploring Heritage and Memory in Singapore*. Singapore: Singapore Heritage Society. pp. 111–128.

Tarulevicz, N. 2009. 'History making in Singapore: Who is producing the knowledge?' *New Zealand Journal of Asian Studies*, 11(1), June 2009. pp. 402–425.

Ting, H. 2009. Malaysian History Textbooks and the Discourse of Ketuanan Melayu. In: Goh, D. et al. ed(s). *Race and Multiculturalism in Malaysia and Singapore*. Abingdon: Routledge. pp. 36–52.

Vasil, R. 1995. *Asianising Singapore: The PAP's Management of Ethnicity*. Singapore: Heinemann.

Vasu, N., Chin, Y. and Law, K.-Y. 2014. Introduction: Un/settled narrations. In: Vasu, N., Chin, Y. and Law, K.-Y. ed(s), *Nation, National Narratives, and Communities in the Asia-Pacific*. Abingdon: Routledge. pp. 1–8.

Yeoh, B. 2003. *Contesting Space in Colonial Singapore*. Singapore: National University of Singapore Press.

11 State and Islamic Education Growing into Each Other in Indonesia

Kevin W. Fogg

OXFORD CENTRE FOR ISLAMIC STUDIES

Introduction

Since the 1950s, discussion of Indonesian society has incorporated the idea of *aliran* (streams), parallel communities living side-by-side but with different lifestyles, largely differentiated by religious devotion. The concept was first articulated by the anthropologist Clifford Geertz in his classic *The Religion of Java* (Geertz, 1960), where he identified three groups: *priyayi* (noble elites), *abangan* (syncretic or non-pious commoners), and *santri* (devout Muslims, a term drawn from the word for students at religious schools). The idea – especially the categories of *abangan* and *santri* dividing society along devotional lines – has since become ubiquitous from anthropology (R. Hefner, 2000), to religious studies (Woodward, 1989; Daniels, 2009), political science (Ufen, 2008; Liddle and Mujani, 2007), and history (Ricklefs, 2012), and even permeated popular discussion.

A key structure in society that facilitated parallel but non-mixed *aliran* was a completely divided educational system. One century ago, and even at the time when Geertz conducted fieldwork in the 1950s, the Islamic and state-backed educational systems were basically separate and distinct. Religious schools trained and socialised students from pious backgrounds to focus on religious life, and state schools (colonial or later Indonesian) trained and socialised students from non-pious backgrounds to serve the state, leading to the long-term entrenchment of social divisions. The idea of differentiated social education in Indonesia connects with the theoretical work of Pierre Bourdieu (2011), but in this case the division is not along class lines but rather devotional lines.

This social structure has radically changed over the last sixty years, as these two educational systems have grown into each other. This process is neither the radicalisation or Islamisation of Indonesian state education nor the watering-down of religious teachings, but rather the convergence of two previously separate and distinct educational traditions into one more thoroughly integrated system, aimed at creating 'good' (including properly pious) citizens. Traditional Islamic schools have adopted not only the form but also much of the content previously only found in government-sponsored education, and state schools have more seriously considered religious topics, as part of the standardisation of Indonesian education under an increasingly bureaucratised and influential state[1]. This has included not only increased secular content at religious schools and increased religious content at state schools, but importantly greater numbers of students moving back and forth between the Islamic and state education systems[2]. Simultaneously, Indonesia has seen a vast increase in the number of students attending schools and the average educational attainment levels for students, making the integration of the educational system that much more consequential.

Two separate systems

To understand this process, one must start with the system around 1900, when traditional Islamic education and colonial or state education were entirely separate and distinct[3]. These separate systems had different goals, different funders, and different methods. Whereas the Islamic educational system had evolved over several centuries in response to the needs and desires of local society, the state educational system was created in the nineteenth century because the Dutch did not recognise the value of the Islamic educational system and wanted to ensure that workers were trained for colonial needs (Graves, 2010). A small percentage of students would get exposed to both systems, but otherwise Islamic and state education did not mix.

Traditional Islamic education was based in local communities[4]. Schools would rise around a leading Islamic scholar, and often they would last for the duration of that scholar's career only, sometimes passed to a son or student, but often fading away as other scholars rose in prestige at their own centres (cf. Steenbrink, 1974, p. 113). The generic term for traditional Islamic schools in Indonesia is *pesantren*, the Javanese name meaning the place where *santri* or religious students reside, but similar kinds of arrangements were found all over the archipelago and onto the Malay peninsula, with a variety of names (*dayah, surau, langgar, pondok*, etc.) (Azra, Arianty and Hefner, 2010, p. 173). The basic feature of instruction from the nineteenth century was reading the Islamic scriptures, and at particularly good schools additional texts would be added (Ricklefs, 2007, p. 52). At the most prestigious centres of learning the students would be residential and earn certificates for their mastery of texts in the Islamic sciences, also contributing to the teacher's livelihood by working the fields or helping in business in exchange for their tuition. Students could also range in age, from 10 to 30 years old, and in competence, from government elementary school graduates to the illiterate (Hamka, 1974 quoted in Steenbrink, 1986, p. 46).

Even as late as the 1950s, Geertz described Islamic schools in Indonesia as a separate system, generally informal (without grades or set curriculum, for example) and quite different from the state schools (Geertz, 1960). These systems could function in isolation from one another in part because of strong cultural biases among Indonesian Muslims. A superstition in Aceh taught that those who learned to write in the Romanised script (a key skill at colonial schools) would lose their right hand in the afterlife (Reid, 2014, p. 26). More generally, there was a belief among Muslims that 'Those who get education [in the Westernised system] will become apostates', such that Islamic schools remained the key educational opportunity for many pious communities (Srimulyani and Buang, 2014, p. 91). Indeed, the goal of the Islamic schools was to create good Muslims, but Islamic education was at best ambivalent and at worst antagonistic to the state.

State education under the Dutch colonial system, on the other hand, was intended first and foremost to create useful colonial servants. Natives (as the Dutch called them) were taught to read and write and to do mathematics so as to work in bureaucratic offices or in Dutch firms. Around the turn of the twentieth century, opportunities widened as the Dutch shifted their colonial outlook towards a so-called 'Ethical Policy', hoping to uplift the people of the archipelago (Ricklefs, 2008, pp. 89–93).[5] In the first decades of the twentieth century, opportunities for Indonesians to reach higher achievements in this system, and even to sit alongside Dutch students, increased. The number of subjects available for study (including medicine, law, engineering, and architecture) also increased, and students at the highest levels of achievement could study in the Netherlands. Still, there was little attempt to educate the masses, leaving more than 90 per cent of Indonesians illiterate in 1942 (Supomo, 1955). Furthermore, there was no religious content in these Dutch colonial schools, although the Dutch did provide some financial support to independent Christian schools in several regions[6]. At the same time, the Dutch colonial government refused to give subsidies to Islamic schools. In 1888, the Governor-General argued it was unwise to help schools that would not have a positive reaction to Dutch influence in the archipelago (Steenbrink, 1986, pp. 6–7).

The two systems – Islamic and Dutch colonial – did overlap a little in the form of students at the Dutch colonial schools who would receive religious instruction after school hours. This category included many of the most prominent leaders of Indonesia after independence (Latif, 2008, pp. 203–209). Apart from the small number of students who sought Islamic education alongside their Dutch instruction (a distinct minority even among those privileged students who had access to the Dutch system), Islamic education and state education did not overlap.

Despite being entirely different systems, there were some commonalities between them. Both systems were designed for men and boys, and both largely ignored women. The few women's institutions that were established from the late nineteenth century focused on basic skills and handicrafts at first, and the few well-educated women in the archipelago had been instructed or tutored privately (Azra, Arianty and Hefner, 2010, p. 180). Only later did the idea of mass education for girls take root (see, for example, Rasyad, Salim, and Saleh, 1991)[7].

Additionally, both Islamic education and state education also functioned as a kind of liminal zone for young men. Benedict Anderson (1972, pp. 4–5) identified some of the features of traditional Islamic education that facilitated this temporary exit from society: the location of Islamic schools outside of major urban centres, the students' intense devotion to their teacher, and the spirit of initiation into special knowledge. Jeffrey Hadler (2008, chapter 4) has extended this to think about how the colonial school-bench was alienating in a different way: pulling a pupil away from the cultural practices of his family and encouraging connection with a distant land.

At the end of the Dutch colonial period in 1942, the Japanese estimated that there were roughly equal numbers of students in Java's 1,831 Islamic boarding schools and the Dutch-sponsored schools on the island (Federspiel, 2001, p. 70). The Islamic schools, though, were in the midst of sweeping changes in orientation.

Islamic schools adopt new forms and content

The first major transformation of education in Indonesia in the twentieth century involved Islamic schools adopting the structure and some content from their secular competitors. As early as 1905 there were Islamic schools adopting the structures of grades, pre-set curriculum, and classrooms inspired by the Dutch colonial schools (Wildan, 2013, p. 193), but this trend accelerated through the 1920s and 1930s. In part this was a response to teachers returning to Indonesia from studies in the Middle East and bringing back with them new educational patterns that they saw in Cairo and Mecca (Abdullah, 1971, p. 223; Nu'man, 1999, chapter 3). There were some cases where Islamic schools adapted to better compete with missionary schools (van Bruinessen, 2008, p. 218). At other times, Dutch colonial regulations pushed forward standardisation; when the Dutch tried to standardise and control all schools and all teachers, many Islamic schools responded by accommodating the colonial state in form if not in content (Abdullah, 1971, pp. 208–210). Although the obvious reforms were initially in the structures of Islamic education, gradually there were impacts in the content, too. Some of this new content was in keeping with the Islamic nature of schools, such as the impressive increase in Arabic competency among Indonesian students in this era (Fogg, 2012, p. 269). Other reforms, such as the inclusion in the curriculum of mathematics or other non-Islamic subjects, were influenced by the colonial educational system.

Modern-style Islamic organisations, such as Muhammadiyah, were key in the transition to modern school structure and changes in curriculum (cf. Steenbrink, 1986, pp. 58–64). These organisations provided theological cover for the decision to change format or include secular subjects, and they also provided educational networks that produced teachers who could instruct in this new style. This was not limited to the so-called theological reformists, however; innovations were also underway among Indonesia's theological traditionalists (Steenbrink, 1986, pp. 70–71; Pengurus Besar Al Djamijatul Washlijah, 1955; Nu'man, 1999, chapter 6).

Islamic schools added secular subjects for many reasons. One was to benefit the students already studying there. Another was to attract attention from potential new students. The Alchairaat school in Palu, Central Sulawesi, played to both sides of this. The founder, Sayyid Idrus Al-Jufri, added a football club to draw in more students, and also allowed a local Christian man to teach mathematics and bookkeeping to make the graduates more successful. (Al-Jufri figured that the scope for Christian subversion of maths into a platform for the conversion of Muslim children was limited [Bachmid, 2007, p. 37].)

There was great disruption in Islamic education, as with all education, between 1942 and 1950, the period that encompassed the Japanese occupation of Indonesia during World War II (when most schools were shut down) and the Indonesian revolution for independence from the Dutch. During the revolution, Islamic schools and Islamic students contributed to the armed struggle (Fogg, 2016). After independence, however, the same trend of reformation, modernisation, and the addition of non-religious subjects intensified. In the context of independence, the trend was pushed forward by a new bureaucratic power: the Ministry of Religion.

In the 1950s, if a religious teacher wanted a Ministry of Religion subsidy for his school, the school had to follow the Ministry's curricular guidelines (which also required specified amounts of time for non-religious subjects)[8]. In 1952, the Ministry of Religion certified a religious education curriculum, the result of work by a committee led by K.H. Imam Zarkasyi from the famous 'modern' *pesantren* at Gontor, Ponorogo, East Java (Mustafa and Aly, 1998, p. 125; Steenbrink, 1986, p. 169). This curriculum was certainly implemented in the new system of *madrasas* established directly under the Ministry of Religion in the 1950s, to mirror the secular state schools (Steenbrink, 1986, p. 97).

The overall direction of Islamic schools in this period of reform – both before and after the declaration of Indonesian independence – was to draw closer to the state school system in form, and to draw closer to the Indonesian national project in many aspects of content. Before independence, Islamic schools were hotbeds of nationalist activity. After independence, Islamic schools were supportive of the state's goal to create productive, pious citizens. This happened largely on the initiative of the schools themselves, although not everyone in the state was satisfied. The general instinct of the Indonesian state under President Soekarno (1945–67) was still to push towards a modernising, secular educational system.

Although President Soekarno proposed (twice) that religious schools should be merged with the state educational system, the parliament rejected this plan in both 1960 and 1963 (Steenbrink, 1986, p. 99). By the end of his presidency, Soekarno had relented; he gave a seminar in July 1965 in which he extolled the Islamic educational system as vital for the country, in part a recognition of how Islamic schools had embraced general education and started to modernise themselves (Departemen Agama Republik Indonesia, 1965, pp. 114ff.). In this era, however, the Islamic system was still seen as separate, and it would take reforms in the state schools sector to bring real convergence.

State schools add religious subjects

The changes in Indonesian state schools to add religious subjects were less radical and also more gradual[9]. The state educational system in Indonesia at the moment of independence was merely the remnants of the Dutch colonial educational system (Supomo, 1955), so the outlook initially was fundamentally secular. The independent Indonesian government, however, incorporated religion as a key feature of the nation, placing *Ke-Tuhanan Yang Maha Esa* (loosely, 'Belief in One Almighty God') as the first principle of the national ideology Pancasila, or 'Five Principles' (Hidayah, 2010). This theistic national ideology then became the 'basis of education and instruction' for national schools from 1950 forward (Mustafa and Aly, 1998, p. 115).

While Islamic schools embraced the goal of creating pious Indonesian citizens of their own will, state schools were built to serve this purpose exclusively. The Indonesian ambassador to the United Kingdom in the 1950s explained that 'the aim of [Indonesia's] educational system is to imbue our students with a feeling of responsibility towards the state and to help them become mature and useful citizens'; he also spoke of introducing students to Indonesia's 'cultural heritage which is, in itself, essentially religious' (Supomo, 1955). As the theistic implications of the foundations of the Indonesian state became clear, the place for religion in state schools became more and more concrete.

As early as 1945, the foundation of the independent Indonesian state, there were already legislative moves in the direction of including religious education in the national curriculum (Steenbrink, 1986, p. 91). These became material with the 1950 education law, where Article XII mandated the inclusion of religious instruction in state schools, but added a caveat: 'parents will decide whether their children should participate in this instruction' (Mustafa and Aly, 1998, p. 119). Initially, students were not incentivised to excel in religious subjects, because failing in this class could not prevent them from advancing grades (Steenbrink, 1986, p. 91). Not all schools were even able to offer religious instruction: the Ministry only provided a teacher if a minimum of ten students of a particular religion needed instruction (Mustafa and Aly, 1998, p. 125). In practice, many state schools above this quota also went without religious teachers, even into the 1970s (Steenbrink, 1986, p. 94). At the same time, strong demand for religious education – especially in particularly Islamic areas – moved the Minister of Education and the Minister of Religion to issue a joint decree in 1951 that allowed regions to begin religious instruction before Grade IV (the default year under the 1950 law) and to allow it to exceed the mere two-hours-per-week national guideline (*Peraturan Bersama*, article 2).

One of the manifestations of the increasing centrality of religious education in state schools was in the diminishing possibility to exempt children from such education. Under the 1951 joint regulation, state schools had to seek approval from parents before providing religious instruction. In 1960, the national parliament reversed the burden for permission regarding religious education, requiring parents to object before students would be excused. Both of these are likely to have been hard to implement on the ground. In 1966, amid regime change and widespread fears of atheistic Communism, religious education became mandatory for all students from elementary school through university (Mustafa and Aly, 1998, p. 125).

The role of religion in the state educational sector was important in the immediate wake of independence because state schools were rapidly expanding their reach. At the moment of independence, very few schools were available, and even with running separate morning and evening classes the buildings and personnel could not keep pace with the populace's demand for education. Through the 1950s the state education system opened more schools, trained more teachers, and took in a higher and higher proportion of the country's children, making state schools rather than Islamic schools the default choice of many Islamic communities. As basic religious instruction reached the ever-expanding numbers of students attending state-backed elementary and later secondary schools, this surely would have been the first Islamic training for children in many non-pious families. Additionally, pious Islamic families could feel more comfortable sending their children to state schools, knowing that some moral instruction was included[10]. This allowed for greater institutional overlap and integration of previously separate communities.

The Suharto era: Convergence

The stakes of teaching religion in state schools, and of integrating religious schools into the national system, rose markedly after the alleged attempt at a Communist coup in 1965 and the immediate army counter-coup, which placed the strongman Suharto in charge of Indonesia for the next three decades. Under Suharto's presidency (1967–98), Islamic education and state education began to converge. This process was in fact part of a wider trend in Suharto's Indonesia, in which Islamic institutions were pulled more tightly under the control of the state – for example by having to take the national ideology Pancasila as their sole foundation – and simultaneously in society Islamic orthodoxy was overtaking syncretism, resulting in a general Islamisation of society (Ricklefs, 2012, chapters 5 and 6). The Islamisation of society was facilitated by the Suharto regime's use of religion as a bulwark and ally against the perceived existential threat of atheistic Communism, leading to an emphasis on religious belief as a crucial part of state-sponsored

Indonesian identity. As a consequence, the Ministry of Religion gained a freer hand, and Islamic social groups who had participated in attacking suspected Communists were appreciated for supporting the Government (Fealy and McGregor, 2010).

The renewed state support for religious life led to the extension of Islamic teachers' colleges into most provincial capitals and Islamic state elementary schools (*madrasah ibtida'iyah*) into most district capitals by 1971 (Steenbrink, 1986, p. 122). There was also a slightly heightened enforcement of religious education in state schools, preventing children from opting out of this lesson (Mustafa and Aly, 1998, p. 125). Still, the convergence of Islamic and state education did not happen overnight.

The real turning point in the relationship between Islamic and state education came after ten years of consolidation of the Suharto regime, in 1975. Some minor bureaucratic developments happened at that time, including the formalisation of the Directorate of Islamic Education in the Ministry of Religion (Direktorat Jenderal Pendidikan Islam, 2015). More important, though, was the new legal instrument of the Joint Letter of Three Ministers (representing the Religion, Education, and Home Affairs ministries), ostensibly with the purpose of 'Raising the Standards of Madrasas'. This new regulation encouraged Islamic schools to teach a curriculum that was 30 per cent religious subjects and 70 per cent general subjects, through the incentives of some available funding but, more importantly, the ability of their graduates to study at state universities (R. Hefner, 2009, p. 65). This was the first key concession that would lead to the transferability of credentials between the two systems, such that many students from this era forward went from Islamic education to state education or *vice versa*.

By the 1980s, the vast majority of religious schools (especially those in the formalised *madrasa* mode, as opposed to the residential and personalised *pesantren* format) were following Ministry of Religion curriculum, or at the very least following the Ministry of Religion guidelines for Islamic schools to teach 30 per cent religious subjects and 70 per cent general subjects. Those that diverged from this standard (such as the great Nahdlatul Ulama *pesantren* at Lirboyo) were intended to be exceptional, producing exclusively religious scholars rather than mass-educating students (Mastuhu, 1994, p. 142; R. Hefner, 2009, p. 67). These schools with a less integrated curriculum, called *diniyyah*, remain outside of the general trend of integration, and they provide an important caveat to the general story of convergence (R. Hefner, 2009, pp. 66–69; van Bruinessen, 2008, p. 222).

The Law no. 2 of 1989 on the National Education System was the next major step in ending the split between the Islamic and state educational systems (Undang-undang nomor 2 tahun 1989 tentang Sistem Pendidikan Nasional, 1989). The law drew exact parallels between levels in the two systems (although it did not yet equalise them). It also made religious education one of only three subjects (the other two were Pancasila and citizenship education) that had to be taught at all levels in all tracks, even at state and non-religious private schools. This was a major increase in prestige for religious education in state schools (especially the expansion into higher education). It may only have been possible because Suharto had already defanged Islam by having all Islamic organisations accept Pancasila, or it may have been that this was pushed onto the Suharto regime by the religious revival that was under way within society at the time.

In addition to the legal convergence of these two systems, they were also drawing closer in ideology. From the 1980s, non-governmental organisations, both foreign and domestic, encouraged traditional Islamic schools to engage in the project of development (the favourite buzzword of the Suharto state) and prompted engagement on issues of human rights, women's rights, majority-minority relations, and other international discourses (van Bruinessen, 2008, pp. 228–229; Kull, 2012, p. 402). By the 1990s, the Islamisation of society intensified, leading to the creation of new after-school institutions that were intended to teach children at state schools more intensively about reciting and studying the Qur'an (Anonymous, 1994). This meant that by the time the Suharto regime fell in 1998, the Islamic education system was producing increasing numbers of graduates who were fully prepared to engage in the trappings of the Indonesian state and the globalising world, while increasing numbers of state school graduates were intensely pious in their religious belief and practice.

Islamic and state education today

Today, the Islamic and state educational systems are fully equalised in official status and commingled in Indonesian society. This is a result both of the Law No. 20 of 2003 on the National Educational System and the broader integration of the Islamic community into the national project and state life.

Law No. 20 of 2003 goes further than any previous legislation in equalising the two systems, and it seems to settle the issue for the foreseeable future by recognising both state and Islamic education as equivalent and equally important contributions to the Indonesian national educational system (Undang-undang nomor 20 tahun 2003 tentang sistem pendidikan nasional, 2003). As with previous educational laws, religious education is one of only three subjects that must be taught at all levels (the others now are citizenship and language), and the law emphasises repeatedly (at seven points throughout the document) that one of the overall goals of education – in line with the theism of Pancasila – is to instill *iman dan takwa* (faith and piety) among students.

Subsequent regulations have further extended the state's regulation of the Islamic education sector, while also specifying the nature of religious education in state schools. One major step was the Minister of Religion Regulation No. 13 of 2014 on Islamic Religious Education (Peraturan Menteri Agama nomor 13 tahun 2014 tentang pendidikan keagamaan Islam, 2014). This regulation was notable for its efforts to incorporate not just formal Islamic education (schools with full-time students), but also informal and non-formal education that had previously been outside the concern of the state.

The Islamic sector has remained fairly constant as a percentage of students in the country. Steenbrink (1986, p. 102 n.180) estimated in 1986 that roughly 10–15 per cent of the students in the country were in traditional Islamic schools. The figures are only slightly higher today. According to the Ministry of Religion's handbook on Islamic education for the academic year 2013–2014, 15 per cent of the overall number of students in the country were in the Islamic educational system. This is highest at the primary education level, where a full 20 per cent of students are in Islamic schools, dipping down sharply to six per cent for secondary education (before rising again to 17 per cent for tertiary education) (Direktorat Jenderal Pendidikan Islam, 2015)[11]. These students are spread across the relatively small number of state-run *madrasas* (3,882 in total) and the much larger number of privately-owned *madrasas* (43,339), *pesantren* (27,290), and *diniyah* schools (73,834). There are additionally a great many institutions that provide Qur'anic or Islamic tutoring for students outside of their normal (usually state) schooling.

In some ways, though, the way these systems have become interdigitated goes beyond the above statistics. The pinnacle of the integration of state and Islamic education can be found in Aceh, the province on the northern tip of Sumatra that received special autonomy from 2005 to implement more religious governance. This accommodation has allowed the province to build a 'National plus Islamic Educational System', enforcing religious content at a high level in all school systems run by the state (Srimulyani and Buang, 2014). Although other provinces may not be so extreme in remodelling their curriculum, Islamic knowledge has been enforced in other ways, for example by requiring students to demonstrate specific standards of Qur'an literacy to continue in state schools (Crouch, 2009). This shows the thorough integration of Islamic knowledge, and thus the centrality of Islamic education, in the state educational sector.

On the other end, graduates of the Islamic educational system are thoroughly socialised into good Indonesian citizenship. A survey of 1000 Islamic school students (*santri*) in East Java in 2012 found that '93.6% of religious student in East Java [a province with a particularly large Islamic educational sector] supported Pancasila as the national ideology' instead of Islam (Ruslan, 2012, p. 183). The Government has also increasingly embraced students in Islamic schools as an important constituency. President Joko Widodo (2014–present) inaugurated 'Santri [Islamic Students] Day' in October 2015 in appreciation of the contributions of Islamic students during Indonesia's revolution for independence and contributions before and after (Keputusan Presiden nomor 22 tahun 2015, 2015).

For all the points of integration, however, there are still a few areas in which the Islamic and state educational systems are not yet converging. One continuing area of difference is in separation of the sexes: Islamic schools are significantly more likely to educate boys and girls separately, very often in entirely separate institutions. In part because of gender segregation, female participation in Islamic education is very high. Families may choose to send their daughters to Islamic schools even when their sons attend state schools, because they see Islamic schools as a good way to protect their daughter's morals and prevent perceived negative side-effects of 'free socialising' between the sexes (C.-M. Hefner, 2016). At the same time, many women (and male feminists) agree that female Islamic institutions are affirming and encouraging environments for young Muslim women (Kull, 2012, p. 403).

Another point of divergence is in the ongoing vibrancy of special Islamic schools with permission to exceed the 30 per cent maximum of Islamic subjects as part of the curriculum, called *diniyyah* schools. These can be particularly influential because they graduate the individuals who will become the teachers and leaders in other Islamic institutions. These types of schools were declining in numbers in the 1970s and 1980s, but seem to be rising in popularity again since the 1990s, bucking the trend of greater integration (R. Hefner, 2009, pp. 68–69). Today, the Ministry of Religion's statistics suggest these schools make up almost half of all Islamic educational institutions in Indonesia today, but although they are numerous they are generally smaller in size, making up much less than half of the students in this sector (Direktorat Jenderal Pendidikan Islam, 2015).

Finally, Islamic schools cannot seem to close the achievement gap with state schools in terms of student performance on national exams; the failure rates at Islamic secondary schools are as much as two-and-a-half times the rates at state schools. Azra, Arianty and Hefner (2010, pp. 181–182) point to the poorer constituencies of Islamic schools as a key part of the challenge, but it remains to be seen how the Islamic schools might overcome this and other obstacles to raise their performance.

Conclusion

Thinking about Indonesian religious education in a regional context, it is both similar to and different from its neighbours. The Islamic educational institutions across Southeast Asia developed from similar roots, in local institutions that taught classical religious texts (Ahmad Fauzi Abdul Hamid, 2015, p.18). In modern times, however, the relationship between Islamic schools and state schools is varied. Malaysia also saw a split system between Islamic and colonial education develop around the turn of the twentieth century (Ahmad Fauzi Abdul Hamid, 2010, p. 18), but Islamic instruction was mandated in state schools from the early independence period (Ahmad Fauzi Abdul Hamid, 2010, p. 27), similarly to in Indonesia. In Malaysia more than Indonesia, however, increasing Islamic content at state schools seems to have made non-state-run Islamic schools less successful. In the last two decades, the drive towards integration of schools in the state system may reflect not only a bureaucratic instinct for centralisation but also political considerations, with the majority of independent Islamic schools loosely affiliated to an opposition Islamic party (Ahmad Fauzi Abdul Hamid, 2010, pp. 4, 45–47; Noor, 2008). While Islamic education has become increasingly the province of the Malaysian state, the greater challenge in that country has been integration between schools of different languages and schools catering to different ethnic minorities, rather than between Islamic education and state education. Thus, Islamic education in Indonesia is less controlled by the state, even as the integration of Islamic and state systems has advanced in both countries.

A different contrast can be made in the minority-Muslim countries of Thailand and the Philippines. Among Muslim Thais and Filipinos, Islamic schools have played a key role in preserving local Islamic identity – rejecting integration with the state educational system. In Thailand, although the state mandates two hours per week of Islamic instruction in state schools (similar to Indonesia's provision of religious instruction) (Liow, 2009, p. 144), Muslims in the southern provinces remain deeply suspicious of the state. The Thai state, in turn, remains deeply suspicious of Islamic schools, which are perceived as a hotbed of potential anti-state or even terrorist activity, and the government has attempted with limited success to draw these schools into tighter state control (Liow, 2009; McCargo, 2004, p. 6). In the southern Philippines, similar mutual suspicions between the Muslim minority and the Government have meant that an even lower proportion of schools are registered with the state, and integration of the Islamic and state systems is minimal (McKenna and Abdula, 2009, p. 213). The situation there looks much like Indonesia in the 1930s, when many students would attend state schools during the week and Islamic schools on nights or weekends (McKenna and Abdula, 2009, p. 223). Seen in contrast with these neighbours, Islamic education in Indonesia is more deeply infused with state values and more thoroughly connected to the secular education system – but this situation is indeed the result of a century of evolution.

Overall, the past century has seen a tremendous transformation of education in Indonesia from a total bifurcation between Islamic and state education to a thoroughly integrated, parallel, and often overlapping system of national education that draws in both secular and religious subjects. In keeping with the theories of Bourdieu (2011) on education and social reproduction, this has positive implications for the integration and unity of Indonesian society. Whereas the twentieth century was marked by partition along lines of religious piety (the famous *aliran* divisions), the convergence of Islamic and state education has the potential to build a twenty-first century in which the splits are not so clean. The fuller spectrum of experiences when it comes to religious socialisation through education are likely to mean the erasure of the *aliran* orientations.

Notes

1 This argument was pioneered by Karel Steenbrink (1986). However, many of the critical developments in this process occurred after his book was published,

including the 1989 education law, the 2003 education law, and the 2014 regulations on Islamic education. Furthermore, Steenbrink and others do not consider the developments on the side of state schools nor the broader consequences for social integration.
2 A key level for the development of Islamic education and the movement of students from one system to another has been Islamic higher education (see Jabali and Jamhari, 2003). Unfortunately, due to constraints of space, Islamic higher education will not be covered in this chapter.
3 The system that I refer to throughout this paper as 'Islamic education' could just as easily be called 'traditional education', as many features of its content and form are indicative of its deeply embedded cultural roots in particular ethnic communities in the archipelago and are certainly not imported wholesale from the Arab heartlands of Islam. In the twentieth century, however, it has both become more orthodox and more commonly associated with the religion, so Islamic education has become the accepted term in the literature.
4 Despite the unfounded claims of centuries of Islamic educational institutions along the lines of the *pesantren* in Southeast Asia (e.g. Ahmad Fauzi Abdul Hamid, 2015), this should be understood as traditional, but not necessarily classical or ancient in its institutional life. Ricklefs has found no records pointing to the existence of *pesantren* 'before the 18th century and it is only in the 19th century that they became a major phenomenon' (Ricklefs, 2012, p. 14).
5 The positive effect on education was not uniform, though; in West Sumatra it resulted in the stagnation of existing schooling while other regions caught up (Graves, 2010, pp. 225–226).
6 This was part of explicit competition between Christian and Muslim institutions more broadly, with the Christians getting colonial support (Ko, 2016).
7 This is not to say that women did not engage in public rituals of sharing ideas, even through reading and writing; see Kratz, 1977.
8 For more on the expansion of religious education in this time period with the support of the Ministry of Education, see Fogg, 2012, pp. 231–236.
9 For more information on the initial reforms to introduce religion into state schools in the 1950s, see Fogg, 2012, pp. 236–41.
10 Some of my thinking on the importance of this institutional convergence was inspired by an oral history with H. Sjarifuddin, Banjarmasin, 21 September 2010. Sjarifuddin was a state school teacher in the 1950s, but of a pious Muslim background.
11 I thank Adora E. Jones for crunching the numbers in the report.

References

Abdullah, T. 1971. *Schools and politics: The Kaum Muda movement in West Sumatra (1927–1933)*. Ithaca, NY: Cornell Modern Indonesia Project.
Ahmad Fauzi Abdul Hamid. 2010. *Islamic education in Malaysia*. Singapore: S. Rajaratnam School of International Studies.
Ahmad Fauzi Abdul Hamid. 2015. Globalization of Islamic education in Southeast Asia. In: Miichi, K. and Farouk, O. ed(s). *Southeast Asian Muslims in the era of globalization*. Basingstoke: Palgrave Macmillan.
Anderson, B. R. 1972. *Java in a time of revolution: Occupation and resistance, 1944–46*. Singapore: Equinox Press.
Anonymous. 1994. 'Teaching children to read the Qur'an'. *Studia Islamika*, 1(1), p. 132.
Azra, A., Arianty, D. and Hefner, R.W. 2010. Pesantren and madrasa: Muslim schools and national ideals in Indonesia. In: Zaman, M. Q. and Hefner, R. W. ed(s).

Schooling Islam: The culture and politics of modern Muslim education. Princeton, NJ: Princeton University Press. pp. 172–198.

Bachmid, A. 2007. *Sang bintang dari timur: Sayyid Idrus al-Jufri, sosok ulama dan sastrawan.* Jakarta: Studia Press.

Bourdieu, P. 2011. Forms of capital. In: Szeman, I. and Kaposy, T. ed. 2011. *Cultural theory: An anthology.* Oxford: Wiley-Blackwell. pp. 81–93

Crouch, M. 2009. 'Religious regulations in Indonesia: Failing vulnerable groups?'. *Review of Indonesian and Malaysian Affairs,* 43(2).

Daniels, T. 2009. *Islamic spectrum in Java.* Burlington: Ashgate.

Departemen Agama Republik Indonesia. 1965. *Peranan Departemen Agama dalam revolusi dan pembangunan bangsa.* Jakarta: Departemen Agama R.I.

Direktorat Jenderal Pendidikan Islam. 2015. *Buku statistik pendidikan Islam tahun pelajaran 2013–2014.* Jakarta: Kementerian Agama Republik Indonesia. Available at: http://pendis.kemenag.go.id/ebook/saku20132014/. Accessed 6 April 2016.

Fealy, G. and McGregor, K. 2010. 'Nahdlatul Ulama and the killings of 1965–1966: Religion, politics, and remembrance'. *Indonesia,* 89, 37–60.

Federspiel, H. M. 2001. *Islam and ideology in the emerging Indonesian state: The Persatuan Islam (PERSIS), 1923 to 1957.* Leiden: Brill.

Fogg, K.W. 2012. *The fate of Muslim nationalism in independent Indonesia.* Ph.D thesis. Yale University.

Fogg, K.W. 2016. 'Decolonization and religion: Islamic arguments for Indonesian independence'. *Leidschrift,* 31(3), pp. 109–124.

Geertz, C. 1960. *The religion of Java.* Glencoe: The Free Press.

Graves, E. E. 2010. *The Minangkabau response to Dutch colonial rule in the nineteenth century.* Singapore: Equinox Press.

Hadler, J. 2008. *Muslims and matriarchs: Cultural resilience in Indonesia through jihad and colonialism.* Ithaca, NY: Cornell University Press.

Hefner, C.-M. 2016. *Achieving Islam: Women, piety, and moral education in Indonesian Muslim boarding schools.* Ph.D thesis. Emory University.

Hefner, R. 2000. *Civil Islam: Muslims and democratization in Indonesia.* Princeton, NJ: Princeton University Press.

Hefner, R. 2009. Islamic schools, social movements, and democracy in Indonesia. In: Hefner, R. ed. *Making modern Muslims: The politics of Islamic education in Southeast Asia.* Honolulu: University of Hawai'i Press. pp. 55–105.

Hidayah, S. 2010. Translating 'Ketuhanan Yang Maha Esa': An amenable religious ideology. In: Dhont, F., Hoadley, M. and Conners, T. (ed.). *Pancasila's contemporary appeal: Re-legitimizing Indonesia's founding ethos.* Yogyakarta: Sanata Dharma University Press. pp. 239–254.

Jabali, F. and Jamhari. 2003. *IAIN & modernisasi Islam di Indonesia.* Jakarta: UIN Jakarta Press.

Keputusan Presiden nomor 22 tahun 2015. 2015. Available at: www.kemenkopmk.go.id/sites/default/files/produkhukum/Kepres.%20No.%2022%20Tentang%20Hari%20Santri.pdf. Accessed 6 April 2016.

Ko, K. 2016. *Modern bodies, modern souls: Religion, medicine, and the public imagination in late colonial Indonesia.* Ph.D thesis. Yale University.

Kratz, E. U. 1977. 'Running a lending library in Palembang in 1886 AD'. *Indonesia Circle: School of Oriental and African Studies Newsletter,* 5(14), pp. 3–12.

Kull, A. 2012. 'Gender awareness in Islamic education: The pioneering case of Indonesia in a comparison with Pakistan'. *Studia Islamika,* 19(3), pp. 397–435.

Latif, Y. 2008. *Indonesian Muslim intelligentsia and power*. Singapore: ISEAS.
Liddle, R. W. and Mujani, S. 2007. 'Leadership, party, and religion: Explaining voting behavior in Indonesia'. *Comparative Political Studies*, 40(7), pp. 832–857.
Liow, J. C. 2009. Islamic education in Southern Thailand: Negotiating Islam, identity, and modernity. In: Hefner, R. ed. *Making Modern Muslims: The politics of Islamic education in Southeast Asia*. Honolulu: University of Hawai'i Press, 141–171.
Mastuhu. 1994. *Dinamika sistem pendidikan pesantren: Suatu kajian tentang unsur dan nilai sistem pendidikan pesantren*. Jakarta: INIS.
McCargo, D. 2004. *Southern Thai politics: A preliminary overview*. POLIS Working Paper, no. 3, School of Politics and International Studies, Leeds University.
McKenna, T. M. and Abdula, E. A. 2009. Islamic education in the Philippines: Political separatism and religious pragmatism. In: Hefner, R. ed. *Making Modern Muslims: The politics of Islamic education in Southeast Asia*. Honolulu: University of Hawai'i Press, pp. 205–236.
Mustafa, H. A. and Aly, A. 1998. *Sejarah pendidikan Islam di Indonesia (SPII) untuk Fakultas Tarbiyah, komponen MMK*. Bandung: Pustaka Setia.
Noor, F. A. 2008. From pondok to parliament: The role played by the religious schools of Malaysia in the development of the Pan-Malaysian Islamic Party (PAS). In: Noor, F. A., Sikand, Y. and van Bruinessen, M. eds. 2008. *The madrasa in Asia: Political activism and transnational linkages*. Amsterdam: Amsterdam University Press.
Nu'man, A. H. 1999. *Maulanasysyaikh TGKH. Muhammad Zainuddin Abdul Madjid: Riwayat hidup dan perjuangannya*. Pancor, Lombok: Pengurus Besar Nahdlatul Wathan.
Pengurus Besar Al Djamijatul Washlijah. 1955. *Al Djamijatul Washlijah ¼ abad*. Medan: Pengurus Besar Al Djamijatul Washlijah.
Peraturan Bersama Menteri Agama dengan Menteri Pendidikan, Pengajaran dan Kebudayaan no. No: K/I/9180 tanggal 16 Djuli 1951 (Agama). [archival material] Koleksi RA7. 164. Jakarta: Arsip Nasional Republik Indonesia.
Peraturan Menteri Agama nomor 13 tahun 2014 tentang pendidikan keagamaan Islam. 2014. Available at: http://kemenag.go.id/file/file/ProdukHukum/lghv1404288771.pdf. Accessed 6 April 2016.
Rasyad, A., Salim, L. and Saleh, H. ed(s). 1991. *Hajjah Rahmah El Yunusiyyah dan Zainuddin Labay El Yunusy: Dua bersaudara tokoh pembaharuan sistem pendidikan di Indonesia – riwayat hidup, cita-cita, dan perjuangannya*. Jakarta: Pengurus Perguruan Diniyyah Puteri Padang Panjang.
Reid, A. 2014. *The blood of the people: Revolution and the end of traditional rule in Northern Sumatra*. 2nd ed. Singapore: NUS Press.
Ricklefs, M. C. 2007. *Polarizing Javanese society: Islamic and other visions (c. 1830–1930)*. Honolulu: University of Hawai'i Press.
Ricklefs, M. C. 2008. *A history of modern Indonesia, since c. 1200*. 4th ed. Stanford, CA: Stanford University Press.
Ricklefs, M. C. 2012. *Islamisation and its opponents in Java: A political, social, cultural and religious history, c. 1930 to the present*. Singapore: NUS Press.
Ruslan, H. 2012. Wow, 70,6 persen santri tolak syariat Islam ganti Pancasila. *Republika* [online]. 12 February. Available at: www.republika.co.id/berita/nasional/politik/12/02/12/lz98f7-wow-706-persen-santri-tolak-syariat-islam-ganti-pancasila. Accessed 13 February 2012.

Srimulyani, E. and Buang, S. 2014. Pendidikan Islami (Islamic education): Reformulating a new curriculum for Muslim schools in Aceh, Indonesia. In: Buang, S. and Chew, P. G. ed(s). *Muslim education in the 21st century: Asian perspectives.* New York: Routledge. pp. 90–108.

Steenbrink, K. 1986. *Pesantren, madrasah, sekolah: Pendidikan Islam dalam kurun moderen.* Jakarta: LP3ES.

Supomo. 1955. *Education in Indonesia: Address given by His Excellency the Indonesian Ambassador at a meeting organised by the Oxford Committee of the World University Service.* [typescript] Oxford: Bodleian Library.

Ufen, A. 2008. 'From aliran to dealignment: Political parties in post-Suharto Indonesia'. *South East Asia Research*, 16(1), pp. 5–41.

Undang-undang nomor 2 tahun 1989 tentang Sistem Pendidikan Nasional. 1989. Available at: http://luk.staff.ugm.ac.id/atur/UU2-1989Sisdiknas.pdf. Accessed 6 April 2016.

Undang-undang nomor 20 tahun 2003 tentang Sistem Pendidikan Nasional. 2003. Available at: http://kemenag.go.id/file/dokumen/UU2003.pdf. Accessed 6 April 2016.

Van Bruinessen, M. 2008. Traditionalist and Islamist pesantrens in contemporary Indonesia. In: Noor, F., Sikand, Y. and van Bruinessen, M. ed(s). 2008. *The madrasa in Asia: Political activism and transnational linkages.* Amsterdam: Amsterdam University Press, 2008. pp. 217–246.

Wildan, M. 2013. Mapping radical Islam: A study of the proliferation of radical Islam in Solo, Central Java. In: van Bruinessen, M. ed. 2013. *Contemporary developments in Indonesian Islam: Explaining the 'conservative turn.'* Singapore: ISEAS. pp. 190–223.

Woodward, M. R. 1989. *Islam in Java: Normative piety and mysticism in the Sultanate of Yogyakarta.* Tucson: University of Arizona Press.

12 American Education in the Philippines and Filipino Values

Jeremiah A. Lasquety-Reyes

KATHOLIEKE UNIVERSITEIT LEUVEN

The history of American education in the Philippines

After the American victory in the Spanish-American war of 1898, the Treaty of Paris was signed which allowed the United States to obtain the Philippines for 20 million dollars (Agoncillo, 1990, p. 212). Prior to that, the revolutionary Philippine government of Emilio Aguinaldo had also been engaged in a war with the Spanish forces. After the turnover of the Philippines, the Spanish were replaced by the Americans, and the three-year period from 1898–1902 marked the Filipino-American war (Agoncillo, 1990, pp. 217–231). One of the first and most urgent projects of the Americans, in the midst of hostilities, was to establish a public school system (Agoncillo, 1990, pp. 371–372). This was intended as a means of pacification and for sowing the seeds for eventual Philippine self-government and independence. American soldiers became the new system's first teachers, despite the lack of books and materials. 'In many cases a school was the first thing established by the army in a town, even preceding the rudiments of municipal government' (Gates, 1973, p. 87). This strategy, fully approved and endorsed by General Elwell Otis, was highly effective and even welcomed by the general populace. It gave a humane face to the new American colonisers.

This rudimentary education by soldiers was soon replaced after the arrival of the first American educationalists, most notably the largest contingent of six hundred teachers, called the *Thomasites*, who arrived on the transport ship *SS Thomas* in August 1901 (Agoncillo, 1990, p. 372). Their arrival was in fulfilment of Act No. 74 of the Philippine Commission, which among other things, also established a Department of Public Instruction, made English the primary medium of instruction, and founded the Philippine Normal School in order to train the first generation of Filipino teachers (Estioko, 1994, pp. 187–190). Given the limited resources and the challenge of teaching thousands of children who were never schooled, a three-year programme was devised containing 'three years of English, two years of elementary arithmetic and one year of geography' (Barrows, 1907, p. 75). An intermediate curriculum was soon introduced in 1904, and from 1907 to 1940 a basic seven-year elementary curriculum was in place. (UNESCO-Philippine Educational Foundation, 1953). As early as 1903 the Americans also established a *pensionado* (scholarship) programme which brought promising Filipino students from different regions to study in the USA, and have them come back to work in the Philippine civil service after graduation, a precursor of the Fulbright programme which was later established in 1948 (Calata, 2002, pp. 91–93). Many Filipino students were given educational opportunities that were never possible for them during the Spanish period, when only the wealthiest class was able to send their sons to a university, much less study abroad.

Act No. 74 emphasised the separation between Church and State, and thereby no longer allowed public education to serve as a venue for religious instruction. Nevertheless, it allowed the continued existence of private schools, of which there were around 1,329 in 1903 (325 sectarian and 1,004 non-sectarian) (UNESCO-Philippine Educational Foundation, 1953, p. 105)[1]. In the course of several decades numerous bills were required to control and supervise the quality of these private schools, which were generally inferior to their public counterparts. Protests were also raised from Catholics, not only in the Philippines but also in the USA, concerning the secular and Protestant schooling given to Catholic children in the Philippines, which tended to undermine their faith (Raftery, 1998)[2]. On a positive note, older Catholic universities such as the University of Santo Tomas, founded in 1611 by the Dominicans, and the Ateneo De Manila, founded in 1859 by the Jesuits, were forced to improve their quality of education to keep pace with the newer secular and Protestant institutions.

One of the most important figures during the formative years of American education in the Philippines was undoubtedly David Prescott Barrows, superintendent of education for the whole Philippines from 1903 until his resignation in 1909 (Clymer, 1976, pp. 500, 517). For Barrows the goal of education was nothing less than complete social transformation, one which would prepare the country for democratic government. One of his aims was to eradicate what he considered the main problem of Philippine society, *caciquismo*, a political system where peasants were indebted their whole lives to local bosses (Barrows, 1907, p. 73; Clymer, 1976, pp. 503–504). Literacy was crucial for the liberation of peasants and the formation of a strong middle class. Barrows, who obtained his PhD from the University of Chicago and wrote a dissertation about the Cahuilla Indians of California, was also perfectly placed to reapply the educational strategies previously used on the American Indians (Paulet, 2007, p. 189). Education was to be forced upon the Filipinos, as it had been forced upon the Indians, for their own benefit[3].

Just as with the Indian policy, English was considered necessary for teaching the concepts of liberty and democratic government (Paulet, 2007, p. 200). As Barrows also explained, the general teaching of English was a practical decision, since there was no single common language spoken by the native inhabitants that could be used, and Spanish was limited to only a small and wealthy minority (Barrows, 1907, p. 74). In any case it was much easier for American teachers to teach a language they already knew, rather than take pains to learn a foreign one. Filipino schoolchildren were exposed to English poems and literature, some of the most popular being Longfellow's poems *Evangeline* and *The Song of Hiawatha* (Martin, 2004, p. 131)[4]. The exclusive use of English as the medium of instruction in public schools was enforced until 1940 (Martin, 2004, p. 129). By that time the Philippine government had already chosen Tagalog as a base for a national language[5], but this and subsequent developments did not detract from the privileged place of English in education.

Filipino historian Renato Constantino, writing several decades later, complained about the cultural shift which was produced by English education, and how it was used to merely fashion Filipinos into the split-image of their American colonisers.

> 'The first and perhaps the master stroke in the plan to use education as an instrument of colonial policy was the decision to use English as the medium of instruction. English became the wedge that separated the Filipinos from their past and later was to separate educated Filipinos from the masses of their countrymen. English introduced the Filipinos to a strange, new world. With American textbooks, Filipinos started learning not only a new language but also a new way of life, alien to their traditions and yet a caricature of their model.'
>
> (Constantino, 1970, p. 24)

Of course, it would be useful to distinguish between several components of education: 1) English language and literacy, 2) the public education system, and 3) the content of the education as contained, for example, in various textbooks. Though the last would leave much to be desired in terms of cultural sensitivity (with which no colonising power was concerned during those times), the first two cannot easily be dismissed as negative. English literacy provided access to a vast store of Western knowledge which would not otherwise be accessible to Filipinos (there was, on the other hand, very little native literature to read)[6]. Rates of literacy in English in the Philippines soared from five to eight per cent prior to the arrival of the Americans to 49.2 per cent in 1918 and 65 per cent in 1935 (Agoncillo, 1990, pp. 372–373). The public education system was also wider and more comprehensive in scope than anything that the Spanish Government – or, had it succeeded, Aguinaldo's revolutionary government – could possibly match.

> 'In the school year 1903–1904 there were 2,286 elementary schools with an enrolment of 279,414 pupils. After the lapse of approximately thirty-seven years, or immediately before the outbreak of the Pacific War in 1941, the number of elementary schools rose to 12,249 with an enrolment of 1,922,738 pupils. In other words, the elementary schools increased by

435.83 per cent; and the enrolment by 588.13 per cent. In April, 1950, the number of elementary schools soared to 20,768 or an increase of 808.48 per cent; and the enrolment to 3,960,375, or an increase of 1,317.38 per cent.'

(UNESCO-Philippine Educational Foundation, 1953, p. 86)

Besides elementary schools, the Americans also founded the University of the Philippines (UP) in 1908 with departments of medicine, agriculture, engineering, liberal arts, education, and law, among others (UNESCO-Philippine Educational Foundation, 1953, pp. 126–127). The UP would eventually become the premier higher learning institution in the country, offering reduced tuition fees to less privileged students based on merit. It remained the top university in the country into the twenty-first century. Of special note was the Department of Anthropology founded at the UP in 1914 by Henry Otley Beyer, who chaired it until his retirement in 1954 (Zamora, 1976, p. 314). It was the first anthropology department in Southeast Asia, pioneering important academic research projects on the peoples of the Philippines, especially those which were unconquered during the Spanish period, such as the mountain tribes in the Cordillera region. Such knowledge was especially useful for the US administration of the islands. Special contributions in anthropology also came from the University of Chicago. Fred Eggan, a professor of anthropology and director of the Philippine Studies Program at the University of Chicago from 1953–1977, trained several anthropologists who would leave a lasting mark on Philippine studies, most famously, the American Frank Lynch and the Filipino F. Landa Jocano (Zamora, 1976, p. 320). These two would leave a legacy in the field on 'Filipino values', as I will show below. Fred Eggan was also the director for the 1956 *Area Handbook of the Philippines*, a comprehensive survey of the various cultural and geographical features of the country and which already contained, in germ, discussions of several Filipino values (Philippine Studies Program, University of Chicago, 1956).

Another noteworthy accomplishment of American scholarship was the massive amount of translation work carried out by James Robertson and Helena Blair on historical Spanish documents, resulting in the 55-volume *The Philippine Islands: 1493–1898*. The initial reception of this work was rather lukewarm, and as Cano argues, the selection of historical documents was manipulated towards vilifying the previous Spanish Government and vindicating American colonisation, mainly through the influence of James LeRoy, secretary and political adviser to William Howard Taft (Cano, 2008, p. 9). However, since it was the most comprehensive collection of historical documents on the Philippines in English, it eventually became absolutely indispensable for researchers who did not know Spanish (Cano, 2008, p. 35). It was certainly successful, as LeRoy hoped it would be, in furthering a negative image of Spain and justifying American colonisation. In a way LeRoy, through his editorship of *The Philippine Islands* and authorship of other books, was merely repeating the negative propaganda mustered against Spain by the Protestant reformation and European enlightenment centuries before, except that he used this to further American ends (Cano, 2013). His stance was echoed in various levels of American education and scholarship This was unfortunate, since as Nick Joaquin points out, the Spanish also made many positive contributions to the Philippines in the course of their three-hundred year rule, and an ignorance of the Spanish heritage can only prevent one from fully understanding Filipino culture and society (Joaquin, 2004).

American education did manage to prepare the Philippines for democratic government, and by the time the Philippines received its independence, on 4 July 1946[7], the nationwide educational institutions were firmly set in place. However, it was perhaps a bit too optimistic on the part of the Americans to think that a span of fifty years would be enough to eradicate deeply entrenched, centuries-old social traditions and replace them with a mirror copy of American culture. The tribal and kinship orientation prevalent in Southeast Asia, and the Spanish Catholic inheritance, continued to persist and modify the reception of American ideas, causing a fair amount of cultural confusion. Nevertheless, the effective and wide-scale implementation of public education ensured that Americans would, in so short a span of time, leave a mark as strong as or even stronger than the three hundred years of Spanish rule. As Mojares says, 'It was in the American "gaze" that much of what subjectively constitutes *nation* for Filipinos was formed' (Mojares, 2006, p. 12). After the Philippines gained independence from the USA in 1946, scholars and nationalists struggled to find that core of Philippine identity that was distinct from colonial influence. One of the most promising proposals was, ironically, made possible only through American scholarship: Filipino values.

Filipino values

Scholarly interest in Filipino values can be traced to Frank Lynch's groundbreaking article 'Social Acceptance' (Lynch, 1961). Lynch, as was said above, was a student of Fred Eggan at the University of Chicago. He was also a Jesuit and taught at the Ateneo De Manila University, where he founded the Institute of Philippine Culture in 1960. The article 'Social Acceptance' was the first article of the book *Four Readings on Philippine Values* (1961), which went through four editions, the last one in 1973. This work made Lynch a leading scholar in the Philippines virtually overnight, and was pivotal in establishing the field of research on Filipino values.

Even though others before Lynch had made attempts to articulate the unique facets of Filipino culture and society, it was the way in which Lynch and his colleagues utilised anthropology and psychology that made a difference. Their attempt seemed more objective in that it was not driven purely by sentiments of nationalism, but was also grounded on empirical research. In particular, Lynch employed the Values Orientation Theory of Clyde Kluckhohn, a famous American anthropologist of the 1950s. Kluckhohn defined value as 'a conception, explicit or implicit, distinctive of an individual or characteristic of a group, of the desirable which influences the selection from available modes, means and ends of action' (Kluckhohn, 1951, p. 395). F. Landa Jocano, who was also a student of Eggan at the University of Chicago, and who became the most famous Filipino anthropologist of the twentieth century, accepted Kluckhohn's definition as the 'classic and universally accepted definition of value' (Jocano, 1997, p. 17). This definition and framework would be taken for granted by the next generation of Filipino scholars. According to Lynch, the main value of Filipino culture is something he called 'smooth interpersonal relations' (SIR)[8]:

'SIR may be defined as a facility at getting along with others in such a way as to avoid outward signs of conflict: glum or sour looks, harsh words, open disagreement, or physical violence. It connotes the smile, the friendly lift of the eyebrow, the pat on the back, the squeeze of the arm, the word of praise or friendly concern. It means being agreeable, even under difficult circumstances, and of keeping quiet or out of sight when discretion passes the word. It means a sensitivity to what other people feel at any given moment, and a willingness and ability to change tack (if not direction) to catch the lightest favoring breeze.'

(Lynch, 1962, p. 89)

Numerous criticisms against SIR were made immediately. One criticism was that it gave the impression that Filipino culture was shallow, or at worst, hypocritical. Preventing outwards signs of conflict despite inner tensions seemed to encourage a kind of deception. This criticism was complicated by the fact that Lynch's analysis was indeed *partly* right. It is true that Filipinos generally value smooth interpersonal relations, but the question is, was there not more to it than outward appearance? It also did not help that Lynch was an American educating Filipinos about their own social behaviour. Some Filipino scholars believed that to get to the heart of the matter required Filipino scholars talking about Filipino values with Filipino words and concepts. The most formidable challenge to the school of Lynch in Ateneo de Manila came from the *Sikolohiyang Pilipino* (Filipino psychology) movement founded by Virgilio Enriquez at the UP in the 1970s. Virgilio Enriquez was also American-trained, finishing his PhD in Psychology at Northwestern University. However, the Filipino psychology movement that he founded also represented a response to the dominant Western psychologies of the time (Freud, Skinner, etc.) which, according to Enriquez, were not suitable for explaining Filipino values. In many ways the Filipino psychology movement shows how American education provided the opportunity for Filipino scholars to absorb and then rebel against the Western academic tradition. In contrast to SIR, Enriquez proposed the Filipino concept of *kapwa* as the 'core value' of Filipinos:

'In the Philippine value system, *kapwa* is at the very foundation of human values. This core value then determines not only the person's personality but more so his personhood or *pagkatao* [humanity].'

(Enriquez, 1992, p. 76)

He proceeded to describe *kapwa* in this way:

'When asked for the closest English equivalent of *kapwa*, one word that comes to mind is the English word "others". However, the Filipino word *kapwa* is very different from the English word "others". In Filipino, *kapwa* is the unity of the "self" and "others". The English "others" is actually used in opposition to the "self", and implies the recognition of the self as a separate identity. In contrast, *kapwa* is a recognition of shared identity, an inner self shared with others.'

(Enriquez, 1992, p. 52)

According to Enriquez, it is through this core value of *kapwa* that we are able to understand Filipino social behaviour as well as the other Filipino values. *Kapwa* should serve as the starting point. One advantage was that *kapwa* was conceptually 'deeper' than SIR. It signified not just a harmony of appearances but a genuine harmony of selves. In fact, the appeals to phrases such as a 'shared identity' or a 'unity of self and others' almost lent it a semi-mystical property, as is evident in the work of Enriquez's student Katrin de Guia.

'The core of Filipino personhood is *kapwa*. This notion of a "shared Self" extends the I to include the Other. It bridges the deepest individual recess of a person with anyone outside him or herself, even total strangers.'

(De Guia, 2005, p. 28)

In general, Filipino scholars were more sympathetic to the concept of *kapwa* than towards SIR. It summarised the collective nature of Filipino social behaviour, with its strong family ties and kinship-like relationships, using a Filipino word. With this, the Filipino psychology movement also espoused an 'indigenous psychology', one which was more in tune with the thoroughly interpersonal aspect of Filipino culture, and which encouraged unconventional (by Western standards) techniques of research[9].

The syncretism of the Southeast Asian tribal tradition and the Spanish tradition for more than three hundred years prior to the arrival of the Americans is what can reasonably be identified as the source for *kapwa* and other Filipino values. One must remember that the USA possessed all the benefits of European intellectual history, from the Protestant Reformation to the Enlightenment. The Philippines, meanwhile, knew none of these historical developments, being situated half a world away, and insulated by a medieval Spanish world view. The importance of tribal and kinship relationships was paramount for the first tradition, and only enhanced by the conservative and religious family values from Spain (Morais, 1979, pp. 46–47). As Guthrie observes:

> 'If there is one aspect of Philippine life that impresses a Western observer, it is the role of the family in the life of the individual. Filipinos inculcate a strong sense of family loyalty which spreads beyond the nuclear family of parents and children. Family obligations extend to cousins several times removed, to in-laws, and to others who are at a marriage or baptism.'
>
> (Guthrie, 1968, p. 55)

This family life is what provides the pattern and prototype for Filipino social life (Guthrie, 1966, p. 194). Just as the preservation of smooth relationships inside a family is of particular importance for the happiness and well-being of its members, so the same smooth relationships are sought outside the family (which is why Lynch's SIR was partly right). As Mercado, a pioneering Filipino philosopher, says, 'the Filipino spirit of harmony is also at work in his relations with his fellowmen. The Filipino harmonises his individuality with others.' (Mercado, 1972, p. 233.) This 'spirit of harmony' was challenged by a different perspective on the relation between the individual, family, and society, promoted by American culture and education. Defenders of *kapwa* pointed to this American brand of individualism as something directly inimical to the preservation of Filipino values, as will be discussed below.

It is clear, however, that the very pursuit and investigation of Filipino values was made possible through the foundations laid by American education itself, which introduced and fostered the growth of such disciplines as anthropology, psychology, and other social sciences. The theories and empirical research provided by these disciplines gave more credence to Filipino values beyond the speculations of previous Filipino scholars. Even as the study of values waned in American academic circles, the local research on Filipino values remained (Racelis, 2004, p. xxiii). Active research on Filipino values reached its peak during the years following the 1986 EDSA 'People Power' Revolution.[10] Senate Resolution No. 10 was sponsored by Senator Leticia Shahani in 1987 with a direct appeal to these scholarly disciplines. It resolved to:

> '[...] immediately conduct a joint inquiry into the strengths and weaknesses of the character of the Filipino with a view to finding solutions to the ills plaguing our society and strengthening the moral fiber of the nation [...] to invite resource persons from the appropriate departments of the Executive Branch of government and recognised experts in the fields of psychiatry, psychology, sociology and other social sciences, who may be of assistance in identifying such strengths and weaknesses and in the formulation of measures to solve the social ills and strengthen the nation's moral fiber.'
>
> (Shahani, 1993, pp. 6–7)

The result was a report called the 'Moral Recovery Program', headed by psychologist Patricia Licuanan, which listed the general strengths of Filipino culture such as *pakikipagkapwa-tao* (treating others as *kapwa*) and family orientation, and weaknesses such as extreme personalism[11] and colonial mentality (Licuanan, 1994). Under President Corazon Aquino the Department of Education, Culture and Sports made values education one of its priorities, culminating in its Values Education Framework in 1988 (Palispis, 1995, pp. 10–23). The teaching of values continues until now, even after the Philippines' recent shift (in 2012) to a K-12 education programme (Department of Education, 2013). Yet as the name of the initial report by Licuanan suggests, there was the desire to 'recover' something believed to be damaged or lost.

Filipino values versus individualism

Even as American education prepared the ground for the discovery of Filipino values, the content of this education, and of American culture in general, contained elements which directly undermined such values. Filipino scholars are almost unanimous in their criticism of the 'individualism' promoted by American culture. I suggest that a distinction must be made between moderate individualism that is simply a concern for the welfare and fulfilment of the individual, and an excessive individualism that promotes freedom and self-assertion as a fundamentally *higher* priority than the welfare and good of the community. The first one, which may involve a defence of basic rights of the individual (such as a person's right to vote, right to education, right to choose whom to marry, and so on), is positive in how it can simultaneously benefit both the individual and the community at large. Such a moderate individualism promotes rights and practices that are fully compatible with *kapwa*.

The latter, more extreme form of individualism 'sees in the individual the supreme and fundamental good, to which all interests of the community or the society have to be subordinated' (Wojtyla, 1979, p. 273). Taylor, who traces and catalogues the various strains of individualism, labels this an 'individualism of self-fulfilment'. I prefer to call it an 'exclusive individualism' in the sense that it can virtually 'exclude' anything or anyone outside the self in the consideration of what constitutes the good life.

> '[The] principle is something like this: everyone has a right to develop their own form of life, grounded on their own sense of what is really important or of value. People are called upon to be true to themselves and to seek their own self-fulfillment. What this consists of, each must, in the last instance, determine for him- or herself. No one else can or should try to dictate its content.
>
> This is a familiar enough position today. It reflects what we could call the individualism of self-fulfilment, which is widespread in our times and

has grown particularly strong in Western societies since the 1960s [...] This individualism involved a centring on the self and a concomitant shutting out, or even unawareness, of the greater issues or concerns that transcend the self, be they religious, political, historical. As a consequence, life is narrowed and flattened.'

(Taylor, 1991, p. 14)

The concern of Filipino scholars seems to be not so much individualism *per se*, but this exclusive individualism which clashes with the familial, relational, and collectivist emphasis of *kapwa*. 'The new values of individualism are coming up, but are clashing with old family-oriented values' (Bulatao, 1992, p. 197). Of course, the distinction between the two kinds of individualism is a complex affair, since the same sources and justifications for moderate individualism may easily be used to promote exclusive individualism. There is not a thick line between the two but a blurred boundary. American education was one of the main conduits for both kinds of individualism, but one could equally point to the US media, and to the influence of Hollywood[12]. Jocano also mentions the professional workplace, patterned as it is on Western models (Jocano, 1997, p. 63). Of course, individualism in general had the air of progress and modernity which the older values did not, and this made them more attractive to the younger generations.

'The Western world today [...] takes for granted that individualism is a higher stage of development than tribalism or any model that emphasizes the group at the expense of the individual. We in Asia, as a result probably of centuries of the industrial and technological superiority of the West and of a resulting imperialistic-colonialistic mentality, find ourselves, when educated by the West, in the dilemma of having to accept Western individualistic ideals, ethics, and life goals, while at the same time remaining an integral part of our primary groups with our roots deeply intertwined.'

(Bulatao, 1992, p. 92)

Miranda, a Filipino theologian, says practically the same thing:

'The Western tradition found value in individuality, but also discovered its distortion in the extreme. That is why there is a nostalgia, if not a need to recover the value of community. Even if our own Philippine tradition might need a bit more individualization, we have not yet fully given the values of relatedness their due. That relatedness is the relationship of *pakikipagkapwa-tao* [relating to others as *kapwa*].'

(Miranda, 2003, p. 103)

Such individualism, De Guia laments, stunted the expansion and appreciation of *kapwa*. Whereas the idea of *kapwa* was meant to naturally expand and assimilate other people as part of a greater tribe or family, where sacrifices are regularly made for each other and the common welfare, exclusive individualism constricts to make one's circle of concern narrower and narrower. 'Rather than the shared Self, it's the expanded Ego [...] The all-inclusive *kapwa*, now, extends only to immediate kin and friends' (De Guia, 2005, p. 367). She also attributes this in large part to the 'intellectual training' received by the Filipinos from the West (De Guia, 2005, p. 365).

It is clear that Filipino scholars point to individualism as the main culprit in the disintegration of older Filipino values. I argue that the solution is not a complete reversion to a time prior to American education, which is obviously impossible, but rather a more thoroughgoing understanding of these so-called Filipino values, and a conscientious attempt to synthesise the multiple traditions (Southeast Asian, Spanish, and American) present in Filipino culture. A challenging project, to be sure, but one that can be done with the resources at hand. For example, despite the decades of research on Filipino values, it has hardly been questioned whether or not the values framework used by Lynch and adopted by Enriquez is actually the best intellectual framework to use in the first place. I have argued elsewhere for a shift from 'values' to 'virtue ethics' as a much more enlightening framework for understanding *kapwa* and a host of other Filipino ethical concepts (Reyes, 2015). The fact that the values framework comes from American anthropology makes it an arbitrary choice that can reasonably be replaced with any other, especially if another framework is more capable at explanation. It is not necessary to talk of Filipino ethical concepts as 'values', even if that is how they were first designated.

Also, there are elements from the American tradition that have already left an indelible and positive mark on Filipino society, such as the concept of 'democracy'. It remains for Filipino scholars, who have taken a long time to even come to grips with American democracy itself, to re-conceptualise what democracy would mean when the older Filipino values are properly recognised and integrated. Again, it is a matter of taking into account the unique intellectual history of the Philippines, which is very different from that of the USA. The infamous charge that the Philippines has a 'damaged culture' (Fallows, 1987) because it failed to become a copy of the USA after half a century of tutorship, evinces an uninformed assessment of how older traditions can live on and influence modern institutions in spite of massive programmes of public education.

Conversely, there are facets of *kapwa*-mentality which need to be adapted to the modern world, or would otherwise become detrimental to modern professionalism. Take for instance the value of *utang-na-loób* or debt-of-will, which builds personal relationships through an ever increasing cycle of mutual help and favours. Such a value, which was beneficial for the survival of tribal societies and close-knit groups, has been the cause of many cases of corruption and bribery in Philippine government (Holnsteiner, 1973, p. 79; Simbulan, 2005, p. 184). The respect for this value as a genuine Filipino practice, which in certain contexts remains laudable, must be reconciled with the need for formal and impersonal justice in democratic government. The key is a synthesis and reconciliation between the old and the new.

> 'We must be realistic. The Filipino himself is capable of thinking [in] new ways; it is necessary for him to establish contact with other cultures; the advance of science and technology is irreversible. We should rather reassess our traditional family values instead of clinging to them romantically. There are values to be shed off, to be reoriented, to regain, and to acquire. The secret of education for liberation is openness to the *new*.'
> (Estioko, 1994, p. 223)

What is promising is that Filipino scholars already have the ideas and capacities to effect this 'reorientation', it is only a matter of initiative and commitment on their part to do it.

Conclusion

American education in the Philippines had its advantages and disadvantages. Some of the advantages include: 1) the introduction of English, which opened up a vast deposit of Western knowledge; 2) a highly effective public education system which was successfully implemented nationwide; and 3) the introduction of modern academic disciplines – most notably, in the case of Filipino values, the disciplines of anthropology, psychology and other social sciences. The disadvantages include: 1) the negative propaganda against the previous Spanish tradition, concealing the fact that Spain also had its positive contributions, and 2) the emphasis on an individualism that contradicts older Filipino values. Agoncillo, one of the foremost Filipino historians, also expresses a similar nuanced view of American colonisation:

> 'Universal education was stressed; public health and welfare was carried to the remote barrios; commerce, industry, and trade were given impetus; basic individual freedoms were respected; means of communication and transportation were greatly improved; and political consciousness was developed through the introduction of American political institutions and practices. Side by side with these positive results of the American occupation were the negative results: the general economic dependence on the United States, the partial loss of the racial heritage, the continuance of the colonial mentality, and *a distorted sense of values* [...]'
> (Agoncillo, 1990, p. 371, emphasis added)

This distorted sense of values – distorted primarily due to individualism – can, however, be offset through a diligent and responsible rethinking of Western knowledge, and its reconciliation with Filipino culture. The very fact that American education already provided the scholarly resources for Filipino scholars to both articulate Filipino values and criticise the individualism of the West shows promise for the task of synthesis. It is reasonable to hope that a future generation of Filipino scholars will be successful in making Filipino values adapt to a modern world.

Notes

1 For a list of both public and private schools founded during the early part of the American period, see Estioko (1994, p. 191–197).
2 Bulatao (1992, p. 15) describes the bias against Catholics during the period of American education: 'With the coming of American secularism, the Filipino intellectuals found an outlet for their long-burning rancor against the Catholic Church. The American formula, "Separation of Church and State", became the rallying cry, but the spirit behind the cry was not the reconciliative spirit of the American founding fathers but the angry, long-frustrated 'Ecrasez l'Infâme' of the French Revolution. Not only was there a wall between Church and State but an intense enmity. No wonder then that public school supervisors tended to be Protestants. No wonder that till the Second World War, a practicing Catholic had a hard time becoming president of the University of the Philippines. No wonder that till long after the Second World War, the secretary of education in this overwhelmingly 'Catholic' country had to be a Mason.'
3 'Major philanthropists, long involved in U.S. Indian policy, believed that American Indian education was a good guide for actions in the Philippines and that, in both instances, it was the duty of the United States to educate the people no matter what the people themselves might want' (Paulet 2007, p. 182).
4 'Throughout four decades of American public education, Filipino students were exposed to a canon of literature which included works of Henry Wadsworth Longfellow, Washington Irving, Ralph Waldo Emerson, as well as those of Shakespeare, George Elliott, Matthew Arnold, and the romantic poets' (Martin, 2004, p. 130).
5 Executive Order No. 134, 'Proclaiming the National Language of the Philippines Based on the 'Tagalog' Language,' proclaimed by President Manuel Quezon on December 30, 1937.
6 Constantino (1970, p. 23) was forced to concede as much: 'This does not mean, however, that nothing that was taught was of any value. We became literate in English to a certain extent. We were able to produce more men and women who could read and write. We became more conversant with the outside world, especially the American world.'
7 This date was recognized as the official date of Philippine independence until 1964, when President Diosdado Macapagal, urged by historians and nationalists, signed Republic Act No. 4166, which changed Independence Day to 12 July 1898 in recognition of the earlier declaration of independence from Spain by General Emilio Aguinaldo.
8 SIR was connected to other Filipino values such as *utang-na-loób* (debt of will) and *hiya* (shame). For a brief summary of such Filipino concepts, reinterpreted through the framework of virtue ethics, see Reyes (2015). For a more focused discussion on each concept see Kaut (1961) and Holnsteiner (1973) for *utang-na-loób*, and Bulatao (1964) and Lasquety-Reyes (2016) for *hiya*.
9 For a comprehensive history of the Filipino psychology movement, see Pe-Pua (2000).
10 EDSA stands for Epifanio de los Santos Avenue, the main road on which the gatherings took place. The revolution led to the departure of dictator Ferdinand Marcos, who was President of the Philippines from 1965 to 1986. Marcos ruled

under martial law from 1972 until 1981 and his regime was known for excess, corruption, and violence.
11 By which Licuanan means the readiness to take things personally even in professional contexts, such as criticism of one's work. It also means the tendency to prioritize personal and family relationships within these contexts, such as choosing to hire a friend or family member over more qualified individuals. In the case of government positions, this can easily lead to graft and corruption.
12 'There is another aspect of American influence which begun to be felt even in earlier times but which constitutes a particular problem today. American popular culture promotes its values, particularly rugged individualism, patriotic unilateralism, crass materialism, sexual hedonism and others, through films, TV programs, video and pop music and other media forms' (Miranda, 2003, p. 195).

References

Agoncillo, T. 1990. *History of the Filipino People*, 8th ed., Quezon City: Garotech.
Barrows, D. P. 1907. 'Education and Social Progress in the Philippines', *The Annals of the American Academy of Political and Social Science*, 30, American Colonial Policy and Administration, pp. 69–82.
Bulatao, J. 1964. 'Hiya', *Philippine Studies*, 12(3), pp. 424–438.
Bulatao, J. 1992. *Phenomena and their Interpretation: Landmark Essays 1957–1989*, Manila: Ateneo de Manila.
Calata, A. A. 2002. 'The Role of Education in Americanizing Filipinos'. In: McFerson, H. M. ed. *Mixed Blessing: The Impact of the American Colonial Experience on Politics and Society in the Philippines*, Westport, CT: Greenwood Press, pp. 89–98.
Cano, G. 2008. 'Blair and Robertson's The Philippine Islands, 1493–1898: Scholarship or Imperialist Propaganda?', *Philippine Studies*, 56(1), pp. 3–46.
Cano, G. 2013. 'LeRoy's The Americans in the Philippines and the History of Spanish Rule in the Philippines', *Philippine Studies: Historical and Ethnographic Viewpoints*, 61(1), pp. 3–44.
Clymer, K. J. 1976. 'Humanitarian Imperialism: David Prescott Barrows and the White Man's Burden in the Philippines', *Pacific Historical Review*, 45(4), pp. 495–517.
Constantino, R. 1970. 'The Mis-Education of the Filipino', *Journal of Contemporary Asia*, 1(1), 20–36.
De Guia, K. 2005. *Kapwa: The Self in the Other*, Pasig City: Anvil Publishing.
Department of Education. 2013. *K to 12 Gabay Pangkurikulum: Edukasyon sa Pagpapakatao*, Pasig: Kagawaran ng Edukasyon.
Enriquez, V. 1992. *From Colonial to Liberation Psychology*, Quezon City: The University of the Philippines.
Estioko, L. R. 1994. *History of Education: A Filipino Perspective*, Manila: Logos Publications, Inc.
Fallows, J. 1987. 'A Damaged Culture: A New Philippines?'. *The Atlantic Monthly*.
Gates, J. M. 1973. *Schoolbooks and Krags: The United States Army in the Philippines, 1898–1902*, Westport, CT: Greenwood Press Inc.
Guthrie, G. 1968. 'The Philippine Temperament'. In: Guthrie, G. ed. *Six Perspectives on the Philippines*, Manila: Bookmark.
Guthrie, P. J. G. 1966. *Child Rearing and Personality Development in the Philippines*, Pennsylvania: Pennsylvania State University.

Hardacker, E. 2011. *Constructing a 'Good' Colonial Society: Representations of Philippine Colonial Education at the 1887 Philippine Exposition in Madrid and the 1904 St. Louis World's Fair*, unpublished MA thesis. Loyola University Chicago.

Holnsteiner, M. 1973. 'Reciprocity in the Lowland Philippines'. In: Lynch, F. and de Guzman, A. ed. *Four Readings on Philippine Values*, Quezon City: Ateneo de Manila.

Joaquin, N. 2004. *Culture and History*, Pasig City: Anvil Publishing, Inc.

Jocano, F. L. 1997. *Filipino Value System: A Cultural Definition*, Quezon City: Punlad Research House.

Kaut, C. 1961. 'Utang Na Loob: A System of Contractual Obligation among Tagalogs', *Southwestern Journal of Anthropology*, 17(3), pp. 256–272.

Kluckhohn, C. 1951. 'Values and Value-Orientations in the Theory of Action'. In: Shils, E. A. and Parsons, T. ed. *Towards a General Theory of Action*, Cambridge, MA: Harvard University Press, pp. 388–433.

Lasquety-Reyes, J. 2016. 'In Defense of Hiya as a Filipino Virtue', *Asian Philosophy*, 26(1), pp. 66–78.

Licuanan, P. 1994. 'A Moral Recovery Program: Building a People-Building a Nation'. In: Dy, M. ed. *Values in Philippine Culture and Education*, Washington, DC: The Council for Research in Values and Philosophy.

Lynch, F. 1961. 'Social Acceptance'. In: Lynch, F. and de Guzman, A. ed. *Four Readings on Philippine Values*, Quezon City: Ateneo de Manila, pp. 1–21.

Lynch, F. 1962. 'Philippine Values II: Social Acceptance', *Philippine Studies*, 10(1), pp. 82–99.

Lynch, F. [1961] 1973. *Four Readings on Philippine Values*, 4th ed., Quezon City: Ateneo de Manila.

Martin, I. P. 2004. 'Longfellow's legacy: education and the shaping of Philippine writing', *World Englishes*, 23(1), pp. 129–139.

Mercado, L. 1972. 'Filipino Thought', *Philippine Studies*, 20(2), pp. 207–272.

Miranda, D. 2003. *Kaloob ni Kristo: A Filipino Christian Account of Conscience*, Manila: Logos.

Mojares, R. 2006. 'The Formation of Filipino Nationality Under U.S. Colonial Rule', *Philippine Quarterly of Culture and Society*, 34(1), pp. 11–32.

Morais, R. 1979. 'Some Notes on the Historical Roots of Contemporary Interpersonal Relationships in the Christian Philippines', *Philippine Journal of Psychology*, 12(2), pp. 45–49.

Palispis, E. 1995. *Introduction to Values Education*, Quezon City: Rex Book Store.

Paulet, A. 2007. 'To Change the World: The Use of American Indian Education in the Philippines', *History of Education Quarterly*, 47(2), pp. 173–202.

Pe-Pua, R. and Protacio-Marcelino, E. A. 2000. 'Sikolohiyang Pilipino (Filipino Psychology): A Legacy of Virgilio G. Enriquez', *Asian Journal of Social Psychology*, 3(3), pp. 49–71.

Philippine Studies Program, University of Chicago. 1956. *Area Handbook on the Philippines*. Chicago: Human Relations Area Files.

Racelis, M. 2004. 'Frank Lynch, S. J., Ph.D.: 1921–1978'. In: Makil, P. Q. and Yengoyan, A. A. ed(s). *Philippine Society and the Individual: Selected Essays of Frank Lynch*, Revised ed., Quezon City: Institute of Philippine Culture.

Raftery, J. 1998. 'Textbook Wars: Governor-General James Francis Smith and the Protestant-Catholic Conflict in Public Education in the Philippines, 1904–1907', *History of Education Quarterly*, 38(2), pp. 143–164.

Reyes, J. 2015. 'Loób and Kapwa: An Introduction to a Filipino Virtue Ethics', *Asian Philosophy*, 25(2), pp. 148–171.

Shahani, L. 1993. 'Senate Resolution No. 10' In: *Filipino Values and National Development*. Manila: Kabisig People's Movement.

Simbulan, D. 2005. *The Modern Principalia: The Historical Evolution of the Philippine Ruling Oligarchy*, Quezon City: The University of the Philippines.

Taylor, C. 1991. *The Ethics of Authenticity*, Cambridge and London: Harvard University Press.

UNESCO-Philippine Educational Foundation. 1953. *Fifty Years of Education for Freedom: 1901–1951*, Manila: National Printing Company, Inc.

Wojtyla, K. 1979. *The Acting Person*, translated by Potocki, A. Dordrecht: D. Reidel

Zamora, M. D. 1976. 'Cultural Anthropology in the Philippines 1900–1983: Perspectives, Problems, and Prospects'. In: Banks, D. J. ed. *Changing Identities in Modern Southeast Asia*, The Hague: Mouton Publishers, pp. 311–340.

Index

Note: Page numbers in *italics* and **bold** denote references to Figures and Tables, respectively.

Abdul Rahman Talib 148–149
Adaptation of Expressions law 24–25
adult education, Thailand: curricula 56; formation of 55–56; objective of 54; problems facing 58–59; teaching methods 58; textbooks for 58–59
adult textbooks: analysing 58–60; Buddhism and 65–66; historical narratives 63–64; maps and annexed areas in 62–63; national values 64–65; nation-state-based assimilation in 60–65; phrasebook-type 59; race and culture in 60–62; reigns of kings in 63–64; *see also* textbooks
agricultural education 92
American missionaries 34, 37, 91–92
Annan Simtrakan 95
Áo Tim school 109
apprenticeships 87, 125
Aquino, Corazon 202
aristocratic elite women: bifurcation of 49; decline of 49–50; education for 41–42; in modernisation of female education 45–47; Sunanthalai Girls' School 47–48
arts and crafts: decline of 87–88; vocational education and 88–89
Arts and Crafts Fair 93
Asian Institute of Technology (AIT) 98
Association of Southeast Asian Nations (ASEAN) 74
Association of Thai Women 50

Bangkok Christian College 84
Baptist Mission Press 36

Barend jan Terwiel 84
Barnabite missionaries 33–34
Barrows, David Prescott 195
Ba Than 20–21
Ba Trieu Au 118
Ba Trung Trac 118
Beau, Paul 108
Beyer, Henry Otley 197
Blackburn, Kevin 172
Blair, Helena 197
Bó Ba Shin 21–22
Border Patrol Polic Unit (BPP) 72
Bradley, Emilie Royce 43
British Education Act of 1902 99n1
British Malaya: contradictory education principles of 140–142; educating girls 145–146; educational policy 148–149; educational system under 140; Education Ordinance of 1957 148; Education Ordinance of 1961 149; ethnic categories 148; ethnic Chinese in 144–145; Indians 143–144; Koranic education 143; language of schooling 141; Malays 143; perpetuation of income inequalities through education 148–149; plantation schools 143–144; Razak Committee 155; secondary education enrolment 146–148; Tamil-language schools 143–144; *see also* Malaysian education
Buddhism, absence in adult textbooks 65–66
Bui-van-Thu 132
Burma: British role 17–19; under British rule 36; education system in 36–37; identity in 14; Pagan Dynasty 15

Burma Baptist Convention 36
Burmanisation 16, 20
Burmese Socialist Programme Party (BSPP) curriculum 22–24
Burmese women 39

Campbell, John Gordon Drummond 87
Catholic missionaries 34, 35–36
Chanthaphimpha, Roem 50–51
Cheng Yen 74
Chinese migrant communities 85
Chinese Nationalist Army (Kuomintang-KMT) 70 see also Kuomintang Chinese communities
Chinese shoemaking 90–91
Chongchitthanom, Princess 47, 50
Choonhawan, Chatchai 74
Christian missionaries 143
Chulalongkorn (Rama V), King of Siam 42, 84; death of 49; inner court of 40, 51; modernisation of female education 45–46
clerical education 91–92
Cold War 70, 97–98
Cole, Edna 44–45
colonial control 4
colonialism, portrayed in textbooks 162, 168 see also textbooks
colonial rule 83–84
colonial technical training 123–125
Communist Party of Thailand (CPT) 71
Company of Indigenous Artillery 125
Confucianism 70, 76–80, 103, 111–112
Confucius Institutes 76
Constantino, Renato 196
Council for the Improvement of Indigenous Education 108
curriculum: adult education 56; Burmese Socialist Programme Party 22–24; centralisation of 172; China's influence on 145; commerce-related subjects 89; de-emphasising national history 161; at Franco-Annamite schools for girls 110–112; history curricula 14, 158–160, 166, 169, 171; morals 111; Myanmar 12–13; promoting inter-ethnic unity 23; religious education 182; revision process 12–13, 22–23; Taiwanese-based Chinese 73–74; for technical schools 128; for vocational education 89; for women's education 104–105
Curriculum Development Institute of Singapore (CDIS) 164–165
Curriculum Planning and Development Division (CPDD) 166–167
Curriculum Planning Division (CPD) 166, 167

Dam Phurong 112
Damrong, Prince 42, 46, 86
Damrong Ratchanuphap 84
Dao Duy Anh 132
democracy 204
Deng Xiaoping 76
differentiated social education 178
Directorate of Islamic Education in Ministry of Education 185
divided education system 178
Doan Thi Diem 41
Dong Khanh School 109
Doumer, Paul 123
Dumoutier, Gustave 106
Duong Van Mai Elliot 109
Dutch colonial schools 180

Ecole Pratique de Mécaniciens Asiatiques (Technical School for Asian Mechanics-EPMA) 124
Ecole Pratique d'Industrie (Technical Industrial School-EPI) 123–126
Ecoles Pratiques see technical schools
economic growth: education and 5–6; sustained 4
education: for aristocratic women 42; clerical education 91–92; for common women 43; Confucianism 76–78; economic growth and 5–6; in French Indochina 105–106; hygiene programme 110–111; income equalities through 148–149; monastery-based 41–42; reforming 108–110; sixth principle of 54; Western-influenced reforms 46; see also adult education, Thailand, female education, male education, vocational education, women's education
education system: in Burma 36, 46; during colonial period 146–148; colonial textbooks 20; Franco-Annamite 106–110, 118–119; in Malaysia 8, 139–141, 153–154; in Philippines 196, 205; reinforcing division of labour 141; in Singapore 158; Thai 55, 58, 69; see also Indonesian state education, Islamic educational system
Eggan, Fred 197

212 *Index*

Elementary Education Act of 1870 (United Kingdom) 141
elite women *see* aristocratic elite women, female education
Enriquez, Virgilio 199–200
European imperialism 122
excessive individualism 202
exclusive individualism 202–203
exponential silences 26

Federal Republic of Germany 97
female education: aristocratic vs. commoner girls 41–43; average number of years study *147*; bifurcation of 49; in British Malaya 145–148; Classical Confucian 104; Franco-Annamite education system 106; in King Chulalongkorn's reign 40–41; male authorities in 46; modernisation of 45–47; in Siam 41–42; in Southeast Asia 41; in Thailand 39; in Vietnam 103–105; *see also* aristocratic elite women, education, male education
females: literacy rates 39; morality books for 104; traditional education in Vietnam 103–105; *see also* aristocratic elite women, female education, non-elite women
Filipino-American war 194
Filipino psychology movement 199–200
Filipino values 198–202; individualism vs. 202–205
footwear 89–90
Forster's Education Act 141
Franco-Annamite education system: creating system 106–108; curriculum 110–112; General Code of Education 110; hygiene programme 110–111
Free China Relief Association (FCRA) 73–74
French Indochina: education in 105–106; Franco-Annamite education system 106–108; registered automobiles in **131**; technical schools in 123–125; textbooks 112–113

Geertz, Clifford 178
girls *see* female education, women's education
Glass Palace Chronicle of the Kings of Burma, The (GPC) 15–17
Goh Chor Boon 158, 172–173

Gopinathan, S. 158, 172–173
Gourdon, Henri 107
Greater Meking Sub-Region (GMS) 74
Guang Huo School 71

Hakka Chinese 90
Harriet M. House School for Girls 43–44
Harvey, G. E. 18–19
history curricula 14, 158–160, 166, 169, 171
history education, role of nation-building 163–166
Hoang Van Luan 132
House, Harriet 43–44
Howard, Randolph L. 35
Hua Xing School 71

import substitution-driven vocational education 96–98
indigenous peoples: of Burma 19–21; French Indochina 106–107; health of 110–111; in Malaysia 141–142; missionaries and 6; Thai 7, 90–91; in Vietnam 106
individualism 8, 202–205
Indonesia: divided education system 178; Law no. 2 of 1989 185–186; Law no. 20 of 2003 186; Ministry of Religion 182, 185; Suharto's presidency 184–186; transforming education in 181–183; women's institutions 180
Indonesian state education 180–181; adding religious subjects 183–184; aim of 183; Law no. 20 of 2003 186
Industrial Revolution, population growth 4–5
Institute of Technology and Vocational Education 98
institutionalised vocational education 7
inter-ethnic unity 21–23
Islamic educational system 179–183, 187–188
Islamic schools, in British Malaya 143

Jessy, Joginder 160
Jiaolian School 76
Jocano, F. Landa 197, 199
Joko Widodo 187
Judson, Adoniram 34
Judson College 36

kapwa 200–201
Karen, The: geography of 30–31; history of 30–31; legend of the lost book 31–33, 37; modern schooling 33–37; national identity 34, 36; socio-economic and cultural life 33; theological training in 35
Karen National Association 36
Kenneth Mackenzie Memorial School for Boys 92, 93
King Edward VII College of Medicine 151
King Mongkut's Institute of Technology 97
Kittiyakon-Waralak, Prince 47
Kiyoko, Kono 48
Kluckhohn, Clyde 198–199
Koranic education 143
Ko Tha Byu 34
kulá 17
Kunlasatri Wang Lang School 43–45
Kuomintang Chinese communities: adapting religious beliefs from animism 72; cultural identity 78–80; ethnogenesis of 70; schooling and education in 70–78; textbooks 75
Kyansittha (Burma king): as Burman imperialist 17–19; GPC's portrayal of 16; as *myanma* king 15–17; as Myanmar patriot 24–25; as *myanma* socialist 22–24; as *myanma* unifier 20–22; in textbooks 17–19, 22–25; as universal monarch 15

Lampang Industrial Company 92
leatherwork/leatherwork production 92, 94–95
Leatherwork School 94–95
Leatherwork School Old Boys Shop 96–97
Lee Hsien Loong 166
Lee Kuan Yew 160, 164
LeRoy, James 197–198
Licuanan, Patricia 202
literacy: to liberate peasants 195; monastery-based education 41–42; reserved for aristocratic women 51; technical schools and 129–130
literacy rates 39
Li Wen Huan 71
Loo Shwe 32
Lynch, Frank 197, 198

Mahaphritharam School of Commerce 89
Maha Vajirunhis School for Training in Various Kinds of Crafts 88
Malaya and Singapore textbook 165, 169
Malays 143, 159–160
Malaysia: economic growth 139; economic link between income and educational level 154; Islamic schools 188–189; National Language Act of 1967 150; New Economic Policy 153, 155; social stratification 143; *see also* British Malaya
Malaysian education: academic university system 151; higher education development 150–152; promoting *Bahasa Melayu* as common language 149; public education spending 152–153; reforming 153; secondary education development 149–150; *see also* British Malaya
Malaysian school system, average number of years study in *147*
Malcolm, Howard 90
male education: average number of years study *147*; modernisation of 46; *see also* education, female education
missionaries: indigenous peoples and 6; in Myanmar 33–37; vocational education and 91–92
moderate individualism 202–203
modern vocational education *see* vocational education
Mongkut, King of Siam 39
moral instruction manuals 104
Moral Recovery Program 202
Mrázek, Rudolf 122
Muslims 189
Mya Galay 41
Myakan inscription 15
myanma identity 14, 15, 16–17
myanma lumyò 23–24, 26
Myanmar government, curriculum revision process 12–13, 26
Myanmar History (textbook) 21–22

Naphaphonprapha, Princess 45
National Education (NE) 158, 166
National Education Plan 94
national identity: in Burmese textbooks 12–14, 19; French Indochina 113; Karen 34; in Myanmar 20–21, 26; role

of history in 8; in Singapore 158, 160, 172; Thai 70, 78, 80
National Institute of Education (NIE) 172
National School system 20
Ne Win 36
Ngo, Willy 129
Nguyen Huru Dinh 129
Nguyen Van Chuc 132
Nguyen Van Cura 132–133
Niphakhan School 49
Niphanopphadon, Princess 42
Nithi Eoseewong 57
Noi Khomsan 92
non-elite women: access to education 51; education for 43; rise of 50–51
Nu, Ù 21
Nu juru tho quan (Women's Press) 113–114

Office of Chinese Language Council International (Hanban) 76–77
Old Boys Shop 96–97
Ong Pang Boon 158, 161
Otis, Elwell 194

Pagan Dynasty 15
Pancasila ideology 9, 183, 184–187
Phahon Phonphayuhasena 94
Phan, Nant Bwa Bwa 32–33
Phan Thi Bach Van 113
Phan, Zoya 31
Pha-op Posakritsana 43
Phayre, Arthur 18
Phibunsongkhram, Jirawat 50, 51
Phibunsongkhram, La-iad 51
Phibunsongkram, Luang 54, 55
Philippine Islands: 1493–1898, The 197–198
Philippines: Act No. 74 of Philippine Commission 194–195; American education in 194–198, 205; democracy 204; English as medium of instruction 195–196; enrolment 196–197; Filipino psychology movement 199–200; Filipino values 198–202; Islamic schools 189; *kapwa* 200–201; private schools 195
Pho Chang School 88, 98
Phranakhon Leather School 95
Phraya Phatsakorawong 46–47
Phraya Wisut Suriyasak 85
Phunphitsamai, Princess 42, 50
plantation schools 143–144

Plueang Na-nakhon 58–59
Pradit Sapkaew 96
Prajadhipok (Rama VII), King of Siam 94

Qishi Woman of Lu, The 116–117

racial essentialisation 167, 172, 173
Raffles College 151, 165–166
Rajamangala Institute of Technology 98
Rajini School 45, 48
Ramkhamhaeng, King 63
Rangoon College 36
Rathchadamnoen Leatherwork School 95
Razak Committee 155
Reforming the Thai language campaign 57
religious education, in Indonesian state education 183–184
religious education curriculum 182
Robertson, James 197
Royal Pages School 84

Saowapha, Queen Consort of Chulalongkorn 40, 46, 47–48, 51
Sarraut, Albert 110, 127
School for the Cultivation of Artisans 88
School of Arts and Crafts 88
SEATO Graduate School of Engineering 97–98
Seng Chong 90, 93
Shahani, Leticia 201
shoemaking 89–91
Siam: education in pre-modern era 41; first girls' boarding school 43–44; women's literacy rate 39; *see also* Karen, The
Singapore: Chinese immigrants in 163; Curriculum Planning and Development Division (CPDD) 166–167; Curriculum Planning Division (CPD) 166, 167; de-emphasising national history in textbooks 161; history education role in nation-building 163–166; Indian community in 159–160; as multi-racial/multi-religious community 159–160; National Education (NE) 158; national identity 158; racial essentialisation 167; racial governmentality in 171
smooth interpersonal relations (SIR) 199

Social and Economic History textbook 165, 169
Southeast Asia Treaty Organisation (SEATO) 97–98
special education 56, 85–86, 94 *see also* vocational education
Special Secondary School of Homemaking 94–95
State Peace and Development Council (SPDC) 12
Sunanthalai Girls' School 46, 47–48
Symes, Michael 33

Tamil-language schools 143–144
Tanning Organisation 96
Tat Prathipasen 50
technical education 85–86, 97, 99, 124, 127–128 *see also* vocational education
Technical Industrial School (EPI) 123–126
Technical School for Asian Mechanics (EPMA) 124
technical schools: absconders 128–130; automobiles and 130–133; *Ecole Pratique de Mécaniciens Asiatiques* (Technical School for Asian Mechanics-EPMA) 124; *Ecole Pratique d'Industrie* (Technical Industrial School-EPI) 123–126; enrolment and graduates of **126**; former students of 129–130; of French Indochina 123–125; graduation rates 125; marketplace needs and 130–132; successful former students of 131–132; supplying technological know-how 127–128
textbooks: Burma nationalist 20–22; cultural identity in 78; de-emphasising national history 161; filial piety 115; focus on race 18–19; in French Indochina 112–113; *Hanban* textbooks 77; housing discussions 165; importing from India 144; KMT-centred slant 75; at KMT schools 77–78; Kyansittha in 17–19; *Malaya and Singapore* 165, 169; moral instruction manuals 104; multiracialism presented in 159; patriotism 115–116; phrasebook-type 59; portrayal of colonialism 168; post-Separation exigencies 169; promoting inter-ethnic unity 21–22; racial characteristics matrix 164; racially-defined loyalties 169–170; reinforcing racial essentialisation 167; revisions of 26; *Social and Economic History* 165, 169; standardising curriculums 58; State Peace and Development Council 24–25; Thai nation-building 78–79; threats to social stability 170–171; *Van quoc ngur* 113–118; women's virtue 115; *see also* adult textbooks
Thai-German Technical Institute 97
Thailand: Adult Education Department 56, 59; assimilation policy of 71–72, 75; Committee for the Promotion of Thai Language Culture 57; cross-border economic activity 74–75; education model 55–56; Islamic schools 189; joining Southeast Asia Treaty Organisation 97; map of 62; National Education Act 85; national education policy 75; nationalism 55; people's identification with national belonging 62; reforming language 57–58; State Conventions 56, 64; *see also* adult education, Thailand, adult textbooks, Kuomintang Chinese communities, Thailand education
Thailand education: centralised system of 84–85; levels of 85; *see also* vocational education
Tholance, Eugène 128
Thomasites 194
tinkerers 131
traditional arts and crafts 87–88
Treaty of Paris 194
Tregonning, Kennedy 160
Trinh Van Chieu 130
Trouillot, Michel-Rolph 13
Trung Vuong School 109
Tun Abdul Razak 148
Turkish education reform 57
Tzu Chi Foundation 74

United Nations Children's fund (UNICEF) 97
University of Malaya 151–152
University of the Philippines (UP) 197

Vajiravudh (Rama VI), King of Siam 49, 88, 93
Vajirunahis, Prince 88
Values Orientation Theory 198–199
Van quoc ngur textbook 113–118
Van Thao Trinh 108

Vietnam 39, 103–105 *see also* French Indochina
village school 43
Vincent, Howell S. 92
vocational education: American missionaries and 91–92; apprenticeships and 87; concept of 85–87; creating national citizenry 98; emergence of 83–84; import substitution industrialisation strategy 96–98; leatherwork production 92; mismatch with employment opportunities 86–87; shoemaking 89–91; state-sponsored 88–89; *see also* education
Vo-van-Duc 132

Wachirayan, Prince 87
Wade, Jonathan and Deborah 34–35
Wang Lang School 43–44, 49
Watthana Academy 45, 50–51
Wilkinson, R. J. 141
Witthayaprichamat, Princess 42
women's education *see* female education
Women's Labour-Study Association 112
written word, as source of spiritual and political power 35

Yasu Tetsu 48
Yeoh, Brenda 166
Yunnanese Chinese Associations 73–74

Zarkasyi, K.H. Imam 182

Printed in the United States
By Bookmasters